Texts AND Lessons

for CONTENT-AREA WRITING

Nancy **Steineke** / Harvey "Smokey" **Daniels**

Texts AND Lessons

for CONTENT-AREA WRITING

with more than **50** Texts from

National Geographic

The New York Times • *Prevention*

The Washington Post • *Smithsonian*

Harvard Business Review

and many others

HEINEMANN
Portsmouth, NH

Heinemann
361 Hanover Street
Portsmouth, NH 03801–3912
www.heinemann.com

Offices and agents throughout the world

The authors and publisher wish to thank those who have generously given permission to reprint borrowed material:

Copyright © 2010. National Governors Association Center for Best Practices and Council of Chief State School Officers. All rights reserved.

Comprehension and Collaboration, Revised Edition, by Stephanie Harvey and Harvey "Smokey" Daniels. Copyright © 2009, 2015. Used by permission of Heinemann. All rights reserved.

continues on page x

Library of Congress Cataloging-in-Publication Data
Names: Steineke, Nancy.
Title: Texts and lessons for content-area writing : with more than 50 articles from
     National Geographic, the New York Times, Prevention Magazine, the Harvard
     Business Review, the Washington Post, and many others / Nancy Steineke, Harvey
     "Smokey" Daniels.
Description: Portsmouth, NH : Heinemann, 2016 | Includes bibliographical references.
Identifiers: LCCN 2016004637 | ISBN 9780325077673
Subjects: LCSH: Composition (Language arts)—Study and teaching—United
     States. | Language arts—Correlation with content subjects—United
     States. | English language—Composition and exercises—Study and teaching—
     United States.
Classification: LLC LB1576 .S74 2016 | DDC 372.62/3044—dc23
LC record available at http://lccn.loc.gov/2016004637

Editor: Tobey Antao
Production management: Sarah Weaver
Production coordination: Patty Adams
Typesetter: Gina Poirier Graphic Design
Cover and interior designs: Lisa Anne Fowler
Manufacturing: Steve Bernier

Printed in the United States of America on acid-free paper
20 19 18 17 16 PAH 1 2 3 4 5

CONTENTS

TO ACCESS THE ONLINE RESOURCES FOR TEXTS & LESSONS FOR CONTENT-AREA WRITING

1. Go to **http://hein.pub/textsandlessonscaw** and click the **Log In** link in the upper right. (If you do not already have an account with Heinemann, click the **Create Account** link in the upper right.)
2. Register your product by entering the code **T&LCAW**.
3. You will need to have your copy of *Texts and Lessons for Content-Area Writing* with you to complete registration.
4. Once you have registered your product it will appear in the list of **My Online Resources**.

WRITING TO LEARN CONTENT

GREETINGS, COLLEAGUES. Welcome, teachers of science, social studies, language arts, math, art, world languages, business, technology, shop, music, PE, and every other subject we teach in middle and high school.

We are Smokey Daniels and Nancy Steineke, joining you with a new resource that we hope you'll find useful. This is the third in our series of *Texts and Lessons* books, each designed to help teachers of any subject enhance their students' ability to understand—and this time, to also *write about*—texts and topics.

Before we talk (briefly) about how the book will benefit you, let us mention some things it *won't do*.

- Steal gobs of class time from your course objectives
- Require your students to do long, tedious writing exercises
- Ask kids to write about anything except content-area material
- Send you home with papers to grade
- Require you to teach spelling, grammar, or sentence diagramming
- Have you assign or orchestrate any term or research papers
- Turn you into an English teacher (unless you already are one, in which case, thanks for joining us!)

Here is what this book *will* do for you:

- Build students' writing fluency, confidence, clarity, correctness, and craft through frequent, high-quantity practice (in short: improve student writing)
- Dramatically increase student engagement
- Build and extend your students' subject-area knowledge
- Nurture a supportive, collaborative learning climate
- Spark thoughtful, lively discussion
- Help you teach thirty-five ready-to-use content-literacy lessons
- Introduce your kids to more than fifty kid-friendly "mentor texts" that demonstrate the "moves" of skillful nonfiction writers
- Generate concrete evidence of kids' thinking and writing skills
- Provide one hundred example topics for extended writing projects
- Create a safe space for respectful peer feedback on writing
- Complement the efforts of all your school colleagues as you prepare kids for high-stakes external assessments.

Is that a deal?

Since the first *T&L* book came out in 2011, we have worked with schools in twenty-three states, conducting workshops for teachers and offering demonstration lessons in middle and high school classrooms. Nancy has just retired from her longtime "day job" at Victor J. Andrew High School in suburban Chicago, and now consults full time with schools and districts around the country. Smokey continues to serve as a guest teacher in places like Texas, California, Chicago, Georgia, New York, Los Angeles, Wisconsin, Colorado, and the extraordinary Federal-Hocking schools in Appalachia. Everywhere we go, our job is to support teachers with content to teach, like you.

Feel Any Pressure?

These days, all of us who teach are being called upon not just to cover our own (often voluminous) content, but also to help kids grow as writers, readers, researchers, and lifelong learners (not to mention digital citizens and non-bullies). It seems like nothing ever gets subtracted from the agenda, only added.

There's pressure on us from our departments and principals, from our school districts, from the state and national standards, and especially from all those high-stakes tests. Maybe we are not directly responsible for a given kid's writing performance on the state test, but there is a new emphasis on team accountability. Everyone wants us "content-area" teachers to do our part to make sure that kids can write, read, understand, remember, and apply the subject matter in our own disciplines—and all across the curriculum.

If it really does take a village to raise a child, we are inescapably among the villagers. The Common Core State Standards (2010) for "Literacy in History/Social Studies, Science and Technical Subjects" require that "Beginning in grade 6, the literacy standards allow teachers of history/social studies, science, and technical subjects to use their content area expertise to help students meet the particular challenges of reading, writing, speaking, listening, and language in their respective fields." Math teachers are conscripted also: the Common Core math standards strongly encourage the use of prose writing, note taking, drawing, modeling, mapping, and other graphic representations as ways for students to achieve and communicate mathematical understanding.

As all these tasks are added to our already full plates, perhaps we might be forgiven for saying: Wait a minute! We are swamped over here! We need all the time we have to teach our science, math, history, literature, economics, health, and French. It's not like our schedules are riddled with "fallow" class periods, left free, like untilled fields. Nor are we silently hoping that some fresh mandates will come along to fill our idle hours.

Good News

But wait. This so-called mandate actually works for us. Those writing activities we are being encouraged to do with our kids? Among them are some of the most valuable and powerful teaching strategies (forget writing!) ever. We are not becoming writing teachers at all—instead, we are getting a whole new repertoire of teaching strategies that help kids *learn our subjects*. When you start doing some of these quick writing-to-learn activities—giving one, three, or five minutes to having kids do a quick write and talk about it—you see much higher engagement, more curiosity, better distributed participation, and more thoughtful ideas. Bottom line: when we use these quick writes, students retain more of our content than they do when we simply tell and present.

And here's the bonus you'll only believe once you try this stuff: these strategies add joy to our teaching. Classes feel crisper and more energetic; there is flow between writing and talking, quiet and loud, reflection and action. Kids take more responsibility, and some pressure slides off us; the shy or introverted kids, the language learners, the kids with IEPs, now get equal "airtime" with everyone else. Having chances to rehearse their thinking quietly in writing and then out loud in safe small groups, they become far more likely to speak up, even in the whole class. Kids gradually shift into new dimensions. Who thought that Ilsa would ever shine so bright? Who thought that Devin would come this far as a learner? Who thought these kids could actually work together so well?

When we use these quick writes, students retain more of our content than they do when we simply tell and present.

Standards and Realities

While the Common Core has lost some of its national consensus, it has had a great influence on our thinking about writing in states and districts. The anchor standards for writing include the following ten items, which are also the basis for many "revised" state standards.

TEXT TYPES AND PURPOSES

1. Write *arguments* to support claims in an analysis of substantive topics or texts using valid reasoning and relevant and sufficient evidence.

2. Write *informative/explanatory* texts to examine and convey complex ideas and information clearly and accurately through the effective selection, organization, and analysis of content.

3. Write *narratives* to develop real or imagined experiences or events using effective technique, well-chosen details, and well-structured event sequences.

PRODUCTION AND DISTRIBUTION OF WRITING

4. Produce clear and coherent writing in which the development, organization, and style are appropriate to task, purpose, and audience.

5. Develop and strengthen writing as needed by planning, revising, editing, rewriting, or trying a new approach.

6. Use technology, including the Internet, to produce and publish writing and to interact and collaborate with others.

RESEARCH TO BUILD AND PRESENT KNOWLEDGE

7. Conduct short as well as more sustained research projects based on focused questions, demonstrating understanding of the subject under investigation.

8. Gather relevant information from multiple print and digital sources, assess the credibility and accuracy of each source, and integrate the information while avoiding plagiarism.

9. Draw evidence from literary or informational texts to support analysis, reflection, and research.

RANGE OF WRITING

10. Write routinely over extended time frames (time for research, reflection, and revision) and shorter time frames (a single sitting or a day or two) for a range of tasks, purposes, and audiences.

The lessons in this book support *every one* of these standards. By their very design, they build the fluency, confidence, clarity, audience awareness, curiosity, and correctness that kids need to write to others—and generate stamina for longer pieces. In this content-area resource, we specialize in the "shorter time frame" writings that most directly enhance day-to-day learning in content fields. As you use these quick writes, you will be making a contribution to your school's overall efforts toward literacy, while still focusing on your own curriculum.

We feel that longer, highly polished public writings are the special province of the ELA teacher, who can use class time to enact the full process-writing model, routinely demonstrate her own work, set up writing workshops, present skill minilessons, confer one-to-one with young authors, and help kids shape pieces over days and weeks. However, for those times when it is genuinely useful to your content-area study to have students work through a longer writing assignment, we've provided some help. At the end of each lesson in Chapters 3 through 10, you'll find a list of ideas for using students' work in the lesson as the foundation for larger research and writing projects, with options for narrative, informative/explanatory, and persuasive writing. The suggestions give both a general direction for a writing assignment, no matter what content area you're in, and a fully developed example of what that kind of assignment might look like. All of these suggestions parallel specific Common Core writing standards, and, if you are so inclined, you can easily address *all* of the CCSS writing requirements by working through a few of these assignments over the course of the year. (To help you plan, in Appendix 2 we offer a chart that correlates all the lessons in this book to the CCSS for writing.)

Balance in Writing

Unfortunately, the Common Core writing standards really missed the boat on *balance* in writing tasks. If you read through the various grade-level writing standards and the student writing samples in Common Core Appendix C, you'll see a distinct emphasis on occasional long reports and essays, featuring full-process multiple-draft pieces resulting in highly polished and edited final work that is graded on complex and exacting rubrics. In other words, the Core leans toward having kids write *big pieces once in a while.*

But where are those longer formal writings supposed to come from? What foundation are they built upon? Magic? Alien ghost writers? Listen, if kids can't get lots of words on the page quickly, with confidence and stamina and awareness of how they sound to readers, they're not going to be crafting big public pieces anytime soon. Above all, students need huge helpings of writing *practice*, starting small and working their way up.

So the CCSS are backwards and wrong. Kids should be writing:

- much more often than the CCSS call for
- far more than teachers could ever read, much less grade
- about curriculum content in every class
- five, seven, or twelve times a day (a couple of minutes each)
- about science experiments, news articles, textbooks, novels, math problems, current events, and more
- about some topics they have chosen for themselves
- to put ideas and concepts into their own words constantly
- to build fluency, stamina, and strategies for engaging an audience
- to receive immediate responses from live readers (classmates, not just overloaded teachers)
- without fear of demoralizing red-ink feedback

The Core authors—mostly standardized test makers and literary scholars—didn't understand the complementary roles of writing to learn (WTL) and formal public writing. The chart below lays out the distinctions between quick writes and those longer public pieces in detail.

WRITING TO LEARN	PUBLIC WRITING
Short	Substantial
Limited sharing	Open to the public
Spontaneous	Planned
Exploratory	Authoritative
Informal	Conventional
Single-draft	Multiple-draft
Unrevised and unedited	Revised and edited
Ungraded but used in class	Designed to yield a grade

Kids need to work both sides of this dichotomy. Some of their writing practice needs to include tasks that are short in both length and time (free writing, brainstorming, note taking, modeling, listing, mapping, and exchanging short notes with classmates). Building on this experience (and upon their reading, and what they are learning in English classes), kids can move up to longer, more staged and polished pieces like essays, reports, term papers, biographies, investigations, and extended arguments.

Research has shown that writing, *even very short pieces,* helps kids remember subject matter better than just listening or talking. In a major meta-analysis of studies on writing as a tool of learning, students experiencing frequent in-class writing outperformed conventional students. As researchers reported:

> *In twenty-four of the studies, students completed writing assignments in class, so researchers could record the time spent on the writing tasks. What appears to*

matter more than the amount of time given to an assignment is the nature of the writing task, the kind of thinking that gets done. . . . In general, these studies and other research suggest that writing can benefit learning, not so much because it allows personal expression about subject matter as because it scaffolds metacognitive reflection on learning processes. And the cost need not be great: even relatively brief tasks can boost learning. (Bangert-Drowns, Hurley, and Wilkinson 2004)

Balancing writing to learn with formal pieces is a well-established approach among writing scholars (Zemelman, Daniels, and Hyde 2012) and long practiced by the National Writing Project, through its hundreds of teacher training sites around the country. Pioneers of this balanced approach (Fulwiler 1986, 1987; Countryman 1992; Daniels and Zemelman 1988) developed explicit WTL pedagogies that serve us well decades later.

WHAT MAKES WRITING EASIER

Classroom Conditions That Nurture Young Writers

1. Teachers often compose in front of students, explicitly modeling their own writing strategies.

2. Students engage in short, authentic writing tasks every day, in every class.

3. Students write to explore subject-matter content.

4. Writing topics are interesting, intriguing, significant, surprising, and/or discussable.

5. Writing assignments offer students choices in how to respond.

6. Students' writing products are used during class to advance the lesson.

7. Students regularly write for classmates, to get an immediate audience response.

8. Students use writing as a way to build working relationships with others.

9. Teachers withhold the red pen and focus on the writer's ideas.

10. Teachers assess short writings using the Good Faith Effort standard (see page 9).

11. Teachers periodically collect and review pieces to gauge engagement and thinking.

12. Teachers assign much more writing than they will read; they trust in unmonitored practice.

13. Students may write before, during, and after studying a topic.

14. Students write for purposes and audiences beyond the teacher's inbox.

15. Teachers break longer writing assignments into a series of doable steps.

16. Students recognize and emulate the craft techniques found in mentor texts.

17. Students write with an eye toward voice, creativity, originality, and humor.

18. Students use writing to explore and monitor their own thinking processes.

19. Students use writing to connect with peers.

20. Students use writing to take action in their communities—and around the world.

Mentor Texts: Short Writing Models

For kids to become skillful writers they need to *read* skillful writers, and we have assembled an honor roll of them here. Most of the texts we chose for this book are what we call "one-page wonders" (with the occasional few-page wonder thrown in). What do these OPWs have in common?

- Interesting and relevant to kids
- Surprising, puzzling, funny, quirky, or funky
- Complex enough to justify time and thought
- Invite the reader to visualize places, faces, and events
- Feature people you can get interested in
- Provoke lots of questions
- Contain debatable issues that invite lively written conversations
- Support an array of writing responses and topics

We use the articles in the book in two ways. First, they provide subject matter—rich and relevant content that kids can enjoy writing and talking about. But they also serve as "mentor texts," examples of adult published writing that students can study for their organization, voice, style, vocabulary, sentence patterns, and above all, those special little "moves" that writers make to hook us and keep us reading. We zoom in on several of these in Chapters 11, 12, and 13.

For our first two *T&L* books we found 135 great short pieces, and we didn't have any trouble rounding up more than fifty others for your class this time. Remember, our job is to offer you the first demonstration of each writing strategy—after that, the strategies are yours to exploit with fresh articles from your own subject field. Not to put a curse on you, but we hope you become a nonfiction nerd like us, so you are always adding new pieces to your collection. As you work with these kinds of texts, you'll decide what constitutes a "wonder" for you and your students, and you'll start hoarding your own.

About Reading Levels

You'll notice that the articles, columns, infographics, and book excerpts we have included here are not "leveled." We didn't even look up the Lexile scores. That's because we know how inaccurate this measure can be, and because our lessons support readers so thoroughly that they can handle what's on the page. In this book, we are offering your kids "free range" texts, captured from the wild—which is to say from the diverse world of contemporary nonfiction that people voluntarily read. So this is all "adult" text, and we will make sure your kids can manage and enjoy it, by keeping the interest level high, the text brief (to knock out reading speed as a factor), and the scaffolding abundant.

When you are building your own collection of one-page wonders, you can keep these factors in mind, along with the bulleted list above under "Mentor Texts: Short Writing Models." When you come to creating the kind of bigger, multi-article text sets we feature in Chapters 11–13, look for pieces that link directly to curricular units you need to teach. When you make your own text

"If students are to make knowledge their own, they must struggle with the details, wrestle with the facts, and rework raw information and dimly understood concepts into language they can communicate to someone else. In short, if students are to learn, they must write."
—National Commission on Writing (2008)

set collections to support more extended inquiry, be sure they *are* leveled so kids can specialize: include selections for your students who read at, above, and below grade level.

KEY ELEMENTS OF POWERFUL WRITING EXPERIENCES

The Carnegie Corporation's reports *Writing Next* (Graham and Perin 2007) and *Writing to Read* (Graham and Hebert 2010) identify the elements of current writing instruction found to be effective for helping adolescent students learn to write well and to use writing as a tool for learning:

- **Writing for content learning** uses writing as a tool for learning subject-area material.

- **Writing about text** in ways that include personal response, analysis, interpretation, and summarizing.

- **Collaborative writing** uses instructional arrangements in which adolescents work together to plan, draft, revise, and edit their compositions.

- **The study of models** provides students with opportunities to read, analyze, and emulate models of good writing.

- **Inquiry activities** engage students in analyzing immediate, concrete data to help them develop ideas and content for a particular writing task.

Each of these structures is an integral feature of this book's lessons.

Assessment of Writing to Learn

We live in a world where anything students spend time on is supposed to be graded or awarded points (or deductions). The kids, of course, are totally socialized into this system (except for the ones who have already mentally dropped out) and they will demand to be paid in the coin of numbers or letters if we forget to score them. And on top of that, there is a long tradition (largely perpetuated by parents with poor memories) that student writing in particular needs constant, critical feedback and tough numerical scoring. This is a case of Stockholm Syndrome if there ever was one. So many parents remember their own writing being returned from teachers, dripping with red ink, and somehow reconceptualize this scarring experience as a *good* (or at least a necessary) thing. If you would like to read a whole book chapter containing the research on such "intensive correction" and its utter futility, check out "The English Teacher's Red Pen: History of an Obsession" in Daniels and Zemelman (1988).

But how do you assess your students' writing today without resorting to time-eating and ineffective practices? Here's how to evaluate the kinds of writing-to-learn pieces generated from our lessons:

- Never mark them for mechanics, spelling, or grammar.

- Never grade them summatively, with a letter or number.

- Always use them explicitly in class to advance the work of the course. They might be read by others (silently or aloud), talked about, responded to, posted on the walls, shared online, or quoted by you.

- Intermittently collect and review them to assess their level of engagement, types of thinking, and guidance for future lesson planning.

The "never" items make sense because in assigning these quick writes, we do not provide any time or procedures for revision, rewriting, editing, or polishing. These are by definition first-draft writings and that's it. It would be nonsensical to punish kids for not doing things they weren't asked or given time to do. And no, "bad habits" will not take root in the absence of our red pen.

But we can't forget the kids who are hooked on grades and points. "Good Faith Effort" to the rescue! Our pal Jim Vopat coined this term in his *Writing Circles* (2009, p. 158). The idea is simple and kids understand it well.

> *When we do these writing-to-learn activities, you will be graded on the basis of Good Faith Effort. If you enter the activity with good faith, do the writing, share and discuss with others as asked, shouldering your share of our work together—then you get 10 points. If you don't, you get 0 points. There are no in-betweens, no scores of 3 or 7.5 are available—this is pure binary grading, all or nothing. If your page, paper, notecard, or screen is empty, that's no points. If there is something relevant and ample on that surface, 10 points for you! GFE is easy for us both to recognize: If you jump in and do the work, you'll know it— and I'll know it.*

From a practical point of view, this means we only need to keep track of the few kids who *don't* put forth that GFE, and remember to enter that zero in our gradebook later on.

Still, let's be honest. Giving points is not assessment, it's just grading. When we want to get serious and really scrutinize kids' thinking in these activities, we have to take further steps. As kids do the activities in these thirty-five lessons, they naturally create and leave behind writings, lists, drawings, notes, and other tracks of their thinking. So why pop a quiz? Instead, collect, study, and save the naturally occurring by-products of kids' learning. These authentic artifacts, this residue of thinking, are far more meaningful than a disembodied "72" in your gradebook. The kids' own creations are also far more relevant in a parent conference or a principal evaluation than a string of point totals.

A Final Word

What should a student's day look like in a content-area class? Reading fascinating materials. Doing quick writing pieces. Sharing ideas. Responding to others. Discussing the big concepts, patterns, and processes of the discipline. Debating controversies. Wanting to know more. Becoming an inquirer in the field.

Now that's a class worth attending—and teaching! Let's go to work.

This resource has three main sections: two are in your hands; the third is online. Chapters 3 through 10 present thirty-five strategy lessons for engaging students' content-area reading, writing, and discussion, using thirty-seven short "mentor texts." In Chapters 11, 12, and 13, we offer three text set lessons, using thematically connected assortments of pieces designed to be studied, written about, and debated together. On the web, you'll find downloadable copies of all the texts, articles, forms, prompts, and other projectables for your classroom.

Chapters 3–10: Strategy Lessons

The strategy lessons are each accompanied by at least one "one-page wonder"—an enticing article, essay, argument, or image that engages students in close reading, quick writing, and lively discussion. We selected these pieces with topical relevance, writing quality, and student engagement foremost in our minds. They cover a wide range of genres and themes; only a few were abridged. The lessons accompanying these readings offer specific suggestions and language you can use to teach them. They are written as "generically" as possible, so you can use (and reuse) the steps and language with any other text you choose. And the strategy lessons are quick: most are designed to be completed within ten to forty minutes. All are an investment in future collaboration, writing, and thinking.

The strategy lessons appear in what we'd call a "mild sequential order." For example, it's much easier to support an argument after you've practiced some one-minute writes. The first five lessons would make a terrific set of first-week experiences if the calendar works (and are also helpful if you are bringing in these lessons midyear and want to get a smooth start).

We have grouped the lessons into families based on their thinking and writing focus.

Chapter 3: Setting the Stage for Writing

Chapter 4: Sparking Thinking with Quick Writes

Chapter 5: Writing Before, During, and After Reading

Chapter 6: Taking Note

Chapter 7: Digging Deeper into Texts

Chapter 8: Time for an Argument

Chapter 9: Writing for Understanding

Chapter 10: Closer Writing About Content

Very generally, the lessons become more complex and socially demanding as they unfold. But, that being said, use them in whatever order you like; so far, no fatalities have been reported due to reordering. You can also mix and match any lesson with any reading selection, ours or yours. If a piece looks too easy or hard for your kids, don't give up on the lesson—find an alternative text elsewhere in the book or in your own collection, and carry on. Just remember to always study any potential lesson text carefully to be sure it is appropriate for your students and the community where you would like to continue teaching.

Chapters 11, 12, 13: Text Set Lessons

The text sets are divided by the three most common (and standards-based) nonfiction genres, with one extended lesson each for narrative, informative/ explanatory, and persuasive/argumentative writing.

Chapter 11: Writing an Interview with Paul Robeson

Writing Focus: Nonfiction Narrative

Chapter 12: Creating a Fact Sheet About Edible Insects

Writing Focus: Nonfiction Informative

Chapter 13: Writing a Letter to the Editor About Military Animal Use

Writing Focus: Nonfiction Argument

In each text set, kids encounter two to six coordinated reading selections. Students can now range though multiple texts representing different genres and authors, each of them taking a different angle on a common subject. These lessons focus on rich and fresh topics, offering multiple points of entry for students, and providing for a deep and sustained engagement in reading, writing, and thinking. Each text set leads to a focused writing activity that is based on the subject matter of the text set and also on the close study of a highlighted mentor text, directing students' attention to a particular element of craft essential to writing in the narrative, informative, or persuasive genres of nonfiction.

Always study any potential lesson text carefully to be sure it is appropriate for your students and the community where you would like to continue teaching.

A Word About the Texts

As mentioned earlier, we choose our articles based on interesting events, themes, or trends in the world, especially subjects of curiosity or importance to the young people we teach. Plus, we're always thinking about how these subjects might correlate with a wide variety of content areas.

However, even when we find an amazing topic, we don't always find the perfect article for sharing with students—for instance, sometimes the author assumes a level of background knowledge that most students won't have; other times we find a juicy example but deem it too edgy for school use. Additionally, some of the rights holders of the texts we would have liked to use either would not grant permission to include the texts in this book or insisted on terms that we couldn't honor. Because of these issues, we had some gaps to fill. So when you see an article from the source WrapUp Media, you know that it's a nonfiction piece we wrote ourselves, just for this book. Writing these articles gave us the chance to "find" some pieces that were *exactly* what we wanted for a lesson or text set: they're custom made! In fact, we've heard back from many of our colleagues who have used the first two *Texts and Lessons* books in schools year after year that they've also resorted to the

Steps and Teaching Language: This is the core of the lesson, where all the activities and teacher instructions are spelled out in sequence and in detail. Text that appears in regular typeface indicates our suggestions for the teacher. Text in italic is suggested teaching language that you can try on and use.

Text Type: We've labeled every selection by genre: biography, infographic, opinion column, feature, interview, photograph, map, etc.

Source: Publication information.

Title: Names the teaching strategy.

Time: Tells the expected length of the lesson. Most strategy lessons range from a few minutes to a class period. *For the Text Sets:* Each lesson fills at least one 50-minute class period—and we give you steps and language to dig deeper over several additional periods.

Groupings: Tells the different social structures (pairs, small groups, whole class, etc.) that will be used.

Standards Met: Refers to the Common Core Writing Anchor Standards.

When to Use: Explains situations in which this lesson would be helpful for you and your students.

Introduction: Gives background on the writing strategy and the topic of the text being used, previewing the lesson's value for students.

Preparation: Lets you know what you need to gather, do, or consider before teaching the lesson.

Web Resources: All the texts, images, writing prompts, charts, lists, or forms that need to be projected for any lesson are ready for you at our website (see instructions on page 19). Items that may be downloaded for projection are highlighted with the "download" icon.

Steps & Teaching Language

STEP 1 Prepare kids for the read-aloud. Begin by tossing out a few questions to activate students' background knowledge and engage their thinking. (No writing yet.)

Who here has played a video game?

What are some of your favorite games?

What do you like about the game?

Who do you think plays video games more, boys or girls?

How popular do you think video games are compared to movies, music, or sports? Do you think gaming will grow or fade away?

What do you think of complaints that video games and video game culture is sexist?

STEP 2 Hand out index cards and read aloud. Pass out the index cards and explain that students will use them to do a super-quick write after you read them an article. This is your chance to say something like: *See, when I say a short piece of writing, I really mean it!* Have kids put their names on the cards now.

Now invite students to listen as you read aloud. Be ready to pause if they need thinking time, or if they are reacting aloud (as they may to the finding that women predominate gaming).

Students use cards for quick writes. Next, invite students to write ... the front side of their index card

---

Now that students have co-created and practiced some norms around partner work, kids practice writing short, responsive pieces triggered by nonfiction articles and complex images.

LESSON 6   Card Talk

TIME ▶ 20 minutes

GROUPINGS ▶ Whole class, pairs, individuals

STANDARDS MET ▶ See pages 306–307.

WHEN TO USE ▶ This uber-simple early lesson gets students thinking, writing, and conversing about a complex text.

TEXT	AUTHOR	SOURCE	TEXT TYPE
"More Women Play Video Games Than Boys"	Drew Harwell	*Washington Post*	Feature story

Many kids, whatever the grade, come to us fearful of writing. Our colleague Jim Vopat says that, sooner or later, almost all American school students (and graduates) join the march of "the writing wounded" (2011). Without probing all the causes here, we know the truth of it: many of our students suffer from blank-page fever when asked to write—especially in classes like math, science, and social studies, where they expect to be safe from English teachers and their infernal writing assignments.

To reduce that fear at the start of our course, we can send a concrete signal that we just want *a little* writing. We have kids write on index cards sized to the class writing anxiety level: 3×5 for the abjectly terrified; 4×6 for medium-level trepidation; and 5×7 for the almost-ready-for-a-full-page writers.

To make it even easier, we can read aloud some juicy information for kids to write about—this way, constraints like varying silent reading rates and proficiency with annotation are set aside briefly.

You simply read aloud a relevant, engaging, and surprising article—and then ask kids to jot a quick response on a notecard. This piece from the *Washington Post* really fills the bill.

PREPARATION

1. Practice reading "More Women Play Video Games Than Boys" beforehand, so your smooth and animated delivery will support kids to understand the text without their seeing it (permission rights do not include printing/copying).

2. Download the lists for Steps 3 and 4 and have them ready to project.

3. Have right-sized index cards ready for students to write on in Step 3. We usually start with 4×6.

4. Think about how to handle the card passing at Step 4.

Reading Selection/Mentor Text: Each lesson is built around a short piece of narrative, informative, or persuasive text. For all but one lesson (Lesson 6, in which the text is used as a read-aloud), we have paid the publication for "reproducible" rights, so you may copy and distribute the pieces to students legally. Your kids must be able to write and mark directly on the page, so *make copies for everyone*—not just one set that gets passed from class to class.

Longer writing projects—reflecting the key genres required by the national standards—can be built on the work students have already done in this lesson. As kids continue to explore the topics of our reading selections, we expect that they will bring fresh background knowledge, recent thinking, and genuine curiosity to the task. When you use the lesson above with your own content, you can also use the assignments below as models for extending that content into longer writing projects.

◄ *Research Projects for Extended Writing*

Research Projects for Extended Writing: If you decide to use the work students have done in the lesson as a foundation for an extended research and writing project, consider the suggestions in this section for narrative, informative, and persuasive projects.

Narrative: *Relate your experience with this topic*

Write your own "personal history with video games," if you hav... any other game/sport/hobby you participate in: card player, skat... baseball player, water skier, swimmer. Describe your path from... encountered the game, tell how you developed and got better—o...

Informative/explanatory: *Pitch a related product*

Develop a concept for a new video game. (This doesn't mean... ally marketable product, unless you have lots of time, coding... hundred coworkers.) This is more like a proposal—a few pa... the environment, the players, the goals or conflict, the basic r... levels—and most important, an explanation of why your game... and unique. Drawings of some screens or features would be a...

Persuasive/argumentative: *Take a position on a current, relat...*

Investigate the controversy called "Gamergate." Dig into the... coverage of this issue and you'll find much polarized opinion... mation, then take your own position.

Suggestions for How to Respond

- Make a comment
- Share a connection
- Ask a question
- Agree and give reasons
- Disagree and give reasons
- Make a relevant drawing or illustration

STEP 5 **Whole class shares.** Invite several students to read aloud both sides of the card they just answered, along the lines of: "I got Randy's card, and he said (read text). I wrote back to him and I said . . ." Then invite others to comment or join in ("Jane and I said something similar . . ."). Let the conversation conclude with thoughts about the video game phenomenon and any of its gender issues that interest kids.

STEP 6 **Collect student writing.** Gather all the cards and scan them later for engagement, quality of thinking, and ideas for future minilessons.

Tip ▶ Since this topic and article offer some surprising information, it can lead to a lively, even vociferous discussion among the kids. This is a good thing, of course. But be ready to moderate a spirited exchange, as those students who care deeply about gaming may challenge ideas—and each other.

Variations ▶ Instead of having kids pass cards around the room to achieve a random distribution, gather the cards yourself, shuffle the deck with a flourish, and deal them back out, making sure no kids get back their own cards.

As an intermediate step between 4 and 5, have the pairs who randomly coauthored each card pull their seats together and talk briefly about what they wrote. Then, when you move to the whole class in Step 5, these pairs can each read aloud their own side of the card.

Shoptalk ▶ While we specifically feature a teacher read-aloud here, most of the upcoming lessons have kids reading the texts on their own. But you know your kids best. For any future lesson, if you think reading the text (or part of it) aloud to your students will better scaffold their comprehension, by all means do it.

Tips and Variations: These sections offer different ways of adjusting the lesson to your students, with specific troubleshooting for particular steps.

Shoptalk: We go into shoptalk mode when a lesson reminds us of some broader teaching issue, something that applies beyond this single lesson.

same strategy when necessary. Don't worry—our lovingly homemade pieces are factual: we've cited our references at the end of the book, so you can take a look at our research material if you'd like.

Digital Writing to Learn

As this book comes off the press, we are in a technological transition in American education. In some schools, we see kids using their own devices in every class; for others, it's still notebook paper. And everything in between. We've written these lessons in their baseline form, with kids writing on tree-based surfaces and sharing by handing paper around. There is something basic and human and aesthetic about writing by hand. Besides, paper never crashes, and pencils can be sharpened in a few seconds.

But many of these activities can be duplicated or enhanced on digital devices of many kinds. This has certainly changed our own lives: when we teach now, we can offer the learners a backchannel like TodaysMeet, where they can post their comments as the class goes on, and then we can stop periodically to project those comments and answer questions. Like, wow. And we often visit classrooms where teachers use Edmodo or Google Classroom as a space where kids can compose and share their writing with classmates in limitless conversations. If you are in the lucky position where your students have 1:1 devices, or you have access to these platforms and apps, by all means digitize our lessons.

Just a couple of cautions. For the quick writes and sharing work, every kid must be using the same device or platform and be able to use it with zero friction—as simply as paper and pencil. If you start trying to have kids pass around assorted devices to read and respond, the lesson fails immediately unless you've already explicitly taught kids how to operate every device in use.

MATERIALS AND EQUIPMENT

These lessons are generally pretty low-tech. Mostly, you just make copies of the articles and prepare kids to think, write, and talk about them. But there are a few supplies we like to keep around:

- Post-it notes of various sizes.

- Index cards—3×5, 4×6, and 5×7-inch varieties.

- Large chart paper, newsprint, or rolls of butcher paper, plus tape.

- Fat and skinny markers in assorted colors.

- Clipboards: When kids are working with short selections, they may be moving around the room, sitting on the floor, writing in various locations, meeting in different groups. They'll need to bring a hard writing surface; a weighty textbook works, but feather-light clipboards were made to be portable desks.

- A projector to show the lesson instructions we've parked for you on our website, as well as images, work samples, and web pages related to the lessons.

- Whenever possible, laptops, tablets, or smartphones for everyone, for composing and sharing writing as well as doing quick research.

Student Collaboration

Every one of our lessons has students working with other kids in some way. Collaboration is embedded, first and foremost, because we've seen it work in our own classrooms for an unmentionable number of decades. We consistently observe more student engagement, persistence, enjoyment, and simple retention of content when the work is more sociable than solitary. We're also immersed in the decades of research showing that when kids practice working together in a friendly and supportive way, their achievement goes up (Daniels and Steineke 2013). In fact, we wrote a whole book about this body of knowledge and practice; if you'd like to learn more, check out *Teaching the Social Skills of Academic Interaction* (2014).

These days there are a couple of other reasons why highly collaborative and interactive classrooms are necessary. For one thing, most state standards require us to teach speaking and listening skills, which typically include pair and small-group work. And then there are the classroom assessments that we as teachers face, where someone comes in our room and rates us on a rubric. If you look at these rubrics, including the predominant ones from Charlotte Danielson (2013) and Robert Marzano (2013) as well as the home-grown versions from some individual states, you'll notice great overlap on one factor: you get maximum points for having a highly collaborative, interactive classroom where kids are working with each other much of the time—and even sharing class leadership with you. For example, if you are observed while only a few kids join in a whole-class discussion, you can be rated "Unsatisfactory" on one Danielson four-point scale.

Believe it or not, every class—yes, of teenagers—can collaborate all year long *if we show them how.* Kids are not born knowing how to work effectively in small groups: we have to teach them and give them repeated practice. That's why our lessons are so tightly structured:

- The readings are interesting.

- The instructions are explicit.

- Every kid-kid meeting is highly organized.

- Every lesson follows a "socially incremental" design: kids typically begin working with just one other person (a more controlled scenario than starting in groups of four or five).

- Once collaboration is established, kids can move from pairs to small groups.

- Finally (and always), lessons finish in a whole-class discussion, orchestrated by the teacher.

As you will see, we begin with *pairs* or *partners* in these lessons—and in all our work with young people. When students are meeting with just one other learner, they experience maximum "positive social pressure." That means both persons totally need each other to complete the task. There's no chance to pull back and hope that some other group member will pick up the slack. There are no other members—you two are it! So you have to pay attention, listen carefully, speak up, and take on your share of the work. With pairs, there tend to be fewer distractions, sidetracks, and disputes of the kind we sometimes have to manage in larger groups. Also, pairs can work more quickly and efficiently than larger groups. And since we expected you would be just a little pressed for time, you'll notice that a majority of the lessons use pairs for this very reason.

In almost every lesson, you'll have to decide how to form pairs (or at times, groups of three or four), and there is a lot to think about. You already know what happens when you blithely say, "Everyone find a partner!" Some kids cling to their best friend, whom they've been exclusively partnering with since prekindergarten. These friend partners have plenty to talk about, mostly things other than your lesson. Meanwhile, some kids get left out altogether, while others form groups of five. Instead of letting kids pick their own partners, keep mixing kids up, different partners for every activity, every day. This is part of your community building. Everyone gets to know everyone. No one gets to say, "I won't work with him." To achieve this shuffling, write each kid's name on a Popsicle stick and keep them in a coffee mug; when it's time to pick partners, they draw from the mug. Better yet, use the class list randomizer called "The Hat" (found here: www .harmonyhollow.net/download.shtml) or any one of the numerous randomizing apps available for smartphones and tablets.

Take a look at the following chart, which is adapted from Stephanie Harvey and Smokey's book, *Comprehension and Collaboration* (2015). You'll see seven strategies that skillful collaborators use. All these behaviors are embedded over and over again in this book's lessons. As you conduct the writing, reading, and discussion activities, your kids will get plenty of collaboration practice, and become better partners and group members.

STRATEGY	EXAMPLES/ACTIONS	SOUNDS LIKE	DOESN'T SOUND LIKE
1. **Be responsible to the group**	• Come prepared: work completed, materials and notes in hand • Bring along interesting questions/ideas/artifacts • Take initiative, help people get organized • Live by the group's calendar, work plan, and ground rules • Settle problems within the group • Fess up if unprepared, and take on some other work	"Does everyone have their articles? Good, let's get going." "Let me show you this great website I found . . ." "I'm sorry, guys, I didn't get the reading done." "OK, then today I'll take notes on the meeting."	"What? There's a meeting today?" "I left my stuff at home." "Teacher, Bobby keeps messing around." Arriving late, unprepared, without materials
2. **Listen actively**	• Make eye contact • Nod, confirm, look interested • Lean in, sit close together • Summarize or paraphrase • Use names • Take notes when helpful	"Joe, pull your chair up closer." "I think I heard you say . . ." "So you think . . ." Asking follow-up questions	Not looking at speaker(s) "Huh? I wasn't listening." Playing with pencils, shuffling materials

STRATEGY	EXAMPLES/ACTIONS	SOUNDS LIKE	DOESN'T SOUND LIKE
3. Speak up	• Join in, speak often, be active • Connect your ideas with what others have said • Ask lead and follow-up questions • Use appropriate tone and voice level • Draw upon the notes, materials, or drawings you've brought • Overcome your shyness	"What you said reminded me of . . ." "Can I piggyback on this?" "What made you feel that way?" "Let me show you my drawing."	Silence Whispering or shouting Not using or looking at notes Hiding from participation Only repeating what others say
4. Share the air and encourage others	• Show friendliness and support • Take turns • Be aware of who's contributing; work to balance the airtime • Monitor yourself for dominating or shirking • Invite others to participate • Build upon and learn from others' ideas	"Can you say more about that, Chris?" "We haven't heard from you in a while, Joyce." "I better finish my point and let someone else talk." "That's a cool idea, Tom."	"Blah blah blah blah blah blah blah blah . . ." "I pass." "You guys are so boring." Declining to join in when invited
5. Support your views and findings	• Explain and give examples • Refer to specific passages, evidence, or artifacts • Connect or contrast your ideas to others' • Dig deeper into the text or topic; revisit important ideas	"I think Jim treats Huck as a son because . . ." "Right here on page 15, it says that . . ." "The person I interviewed said . . ." "My thinking was a lot like Jennifer's . . ."	"This book is dumb." "Well, that's my opinion anyway." "No, I didn't consider any other interpretations."
6. Show tolerance and respect	• Receive others' ideas respectfully; no putdowns allowed • Try to restate opposing views • Use neutral language in disagreeing • Offer your different viewpoint; don't be steamrolled • Welcome and seek insight in divergent viewpoints	"Wow, I thought of something totally different." "I can see your point, but what about . . . ?" "I'm glad you brought that up; I never would have seen it that way."	"You are so wrong!" "What book are you reading?" "Where did you get that idea?" Rolling eyes, disconfirming body language
7. Reflect and correct	• Do frequent reflections or "think-backs" on group processes • Identify specific behaviors that helped or hurt the discussion • Talk openly about problems • Make plans to try out new strategies and review their effectiveness • Keep a written record of group processing	"What went well today and where did we run into problems?" "We are not sharing the talk time evenly." "OK, so what will we do differently during our next meeting?"	"We rocked." "We sucked." "It was OK." "Who cares?"

This resource stands on its own, offering immediately usable readings and language for collaborative lessons in writing about nonfiction texts. But it was also created to be used with several recent books by our "family" of coauthors. Over the past ten years, our own collaborative group has created a small library of books focused on building students' knowledge and skill through the direct teaching of learning strategies in the context of challenging inquiry units, extensive peer collaboration, and practical, formative assessments.

Among these resources are:

- *Text and Lessons for Content-Area Reading* (Daniels and Steineke 2011)

- *Text and Lessons for Teaching Literature* (Daniels and Steineke 2013)

- *Upstanders: Engaging Middle School Hearts and Minds with Inquiry* (Daniels and Ahmed 2015)

- *Best Practice: Today's Standards for Teaching and Learning*, 4th edition (Zemelman, Daniels, and Hyde 2012)

- *Best Practice Video Companion* (Zemelman and Daniels, 2012)

- *Comprehension Going Forward* (Daniels 2011)

- *Subjects Matter: Every Teacher's Guide to Content-Area Reading*, 2nd edition (Daniels and Zemelman 2014)

- *Content-Area Writing: Every Teacher's Guide* (Daniels, Zemelman, and Steineke 2005)

- *Comprehension and Collaboration: Inquiry Circles for Curiosity, Engagement, and Understanding,* Revised Edition (Harvey and Daniels 2015)

- *Inquiry Circles in Elementary Classrooms Video* (Harvey and Daniels 2010)

- *Inquiry Circles in Middle and High School Classrooms Video* (Harvey and Daniels 2010)

- *Teaching the Social Skills of Academic Interaction* (Daniels and Steineke 2014)

- *Assessment Live: 15 Real-Time Ways for Kids to Show What They Know—and Meet the Standards* (Steineke 2009)

- *Minilessons for Literature Circles* (Daniels and Steineke 2006)

- *Reading and Writing Together* (Steineke 2003)

Do you have a class that needs extra support to succeed at student-led discussion? If so, the key is to explicitly teach the social skills kids need, *before* they head off into partners or small groups. You can begin with a separate minilesson based around this chart. Use the blank version of the chart on our website and discuss the seven categories of collaboration. Then have kids work in pairs to come up with both positive and negative examples of each, and to be ready to act them out, fishbowl style, for the whole class. As kids provide these demonstrations (expect some good laughs) you'll gradually be populating the chart with examples much like the ones in our filled-in chart. But these will be examples that your kids *own*. Keep your class-created chart visible in the room so kids can refer to it while working with partners. Return to this "anchor chart" as often as needed, like when you want to praise laudable compliance or prevent any backsliding toward incivility.

Ready to Go?

These days, the most common educational exhortations are for schools to add more rigor, higher standards, more complexity, more challenge, more testing— and for kids to show more self-regulation, more compliance, more "grit." But students don't have to pull themselves up by their mental bootstraps if school is engaging and relevant. Instead of more "rigor," we'd like to see schools add more choice, curiosity, exploration, and inquiry. You don't need "grit" if the work is interesting and worth doing. And that's what we are trying to support with this book.

Happy teaching!

**TO ACCESS THE ONLINE RESOURCES FOR
TEXTS & LESSONS FOR CONTENT-AREA WRITING**

1. Go to **http://hein.pub/textsandlessonscaw** and click the **Log In** link in the upper right. (If you do not already have an account with Heinemann, click the **Create Account** link in the upper right.)

2. Register your product by entering the code **T&LCAW**.

3. You will need to have your copy of *Texts and Lessons for Content-Area Writing* with you to complete registration.

4. Once you have registered your product it will appear in the list of **My Online Resources**.

SETTING THE STAGE FOR WRITING

This chapter offers five mostly quick lessons that invite kids to try out short, low-stakes pieces of writing and work repeatedly with a partner. We designed this set for the first week of school—or for any week you decide to plunge into writing to learn. The goals are simple: to build confidence with composing and share writing in a friendly, supportive way. Plus, all of these lessons contribute to community building by helping kids get to know each other while developing positive class norms.

LESSON 1

Quick Write Response

TIME ▶ 20 Minutes

GROUPINGS ▶ Whole class, pairs, individuals

STANDARDS MET ▶ See pages 306–307.

WHEN TO USE ▶ This lesson is perfect when kids are just starting to do short content-area writes and discuss them with a partner.

TEXT	AUTHOR	SOURCE	TEXT TYPE
"Edison Publicly Tortured Animals to Discredit AC Power"	Andrew Handley	www.knowledgenuts.com	News/opinion

How many times have experts, authors, and cognitive scientists repeated some version of the slogan "We are smarter when we write"? It does seem true that when we put our heads down to ponder thoughts and represent them in a graphic form, the results are usually more sensible (and valuable) than when we simply blurt stuff out. This doesn't mean that people haven't been able to write some pretty dumb things throughout human history, but in general, an interval of thinking on paper very often enhances the quality of our reading and our subsequent discussion.

For this first activity, we use a vibrant, opinionated, and slightly sickening hundred-year-old story, retold by a contemporary writer. (Kids seem to love the yucky parts.) In this lesson, all we want is for students to have an engaging easy read, do some comfortable, risk-free writing, and have a supportive conversation with a classmate. The ladder to more sophisticated responses begins here.

PREPARATION

Optional: Google the still pictures and the one-minute film of Topsy the elephant being electrocuted. If you think either is an appropriate supplement to the lesson, grab it for projection. Some kids, of course, love the horror of these images; others are too tender to bear it. Therefore, we use the image occasionally, but the film very rarely. The main thing is that *you* will have watched it, deepening your understanding of the era and the values.

1. Make a copy of "Edison Publicly Tortured Animals to Discredit AC Power" for each student (to be distributed at Step 2).

2. Make sure kids have a full-size piece of paper, a blank journal page, or a powered-up device ready for response writing.

3. Decide how pairs will be formed for Step 5. Whenever kids will be working in pairs, they need to know who their partner is *beforehand*, and they need to move into a good conversation position—face to face, eye to eye, or knee to knee. This setup encourages the use of "indoor voices" and prevents noisy, time-wasting shuffling around midlesson. For pairs, we like to have the kids simply push their desks together or sit directly across a table from each other.

◀ Steps & Teaching Language

STEP 1 **Provide background.** *You've all heard of the inventor Thomas Alva Edison, right? In a minute, we are going to read a story about him. What is he famous for?* Invite kids to offer information, which will probably focus on his many inventions.

Here's some more background that fewer people know about. These days, we take it for granted that we have electricity in our homes. But 120 years ago, there was fierce competition between inventors as to what kind of electricity would be safest and most efficient. And of course, the winning system would make vast amounts of money for its inventor. Edison battled with another inventor, Nicola Tesla, to see whether his own Direct Current (DC) or Tesla's Alternating Current (AC) would be the choice for lighting the cities of America. The press dubbed it "The War of the Currents," and it was quite a throwdown in the 1890s.

STEP 2 **Students read the article.** Distribute the article and invite kids to read it silently. You just might hear some gasps or "yucks" as kids read along.

STEP 3 **Students write or draw their responses.** *OK guys, looking at your expressions and your body language, I think that some people have strong reactions to this piece. So let's quickly capture those thoughts. Get out your writing materials and spend two minutes jotting or drawing your response to the article. Where did this article take you? What did you think or feel or visualize? What questions do you have about it? Jot down words, phrases, sentences, doodles, or drawings—whatever comes to mind. Spelling and grammar do not count—just get your ideas down as fast as you can. Happy writing!*

STEP 4 **Kids write.** Circulate and assist as needed. Watch the time, not so much for the exact two-minute mark, but for level of productivity. If kids are energetically writing or drawing, give more time. If they are winding down, call them back for the next step.

STEP 5 **Pairs share.** *OK, now turn to your partner and talk about the article. Use your notes or drawings however they help you. To explain a thought, you might want to read aloud a short part of your writing or point to a drawing. But don't exchange papers and read silently—we want to be talking out loud for now. I'll give you about three minutes.*

STEP 6 **Whole class shares.** Gather the class and invite pairs to share high-lights of their conversation. To encourage good partner collaboration, kick off the sharing by asking: *Who had a partner with a really interesting thought about the Edison story?*

Orchestrate the sharing, and invite more participation by asking: *Who thought of something different? Who talked about something we haven't mentioned yet? Did someone have an interesting drawing? Who had a question about the story—maybe something you'd like to look up and answer?*

STEP 7 **Discussion and debriefing.** *We could have jumped into talking right after we read the story. But we stopped for two minutes while you wrote or drew your reactions. How did that writing affect your understanding of the article? How did it support the discussion?*

Typically, students will report that the free writing helped them to con-solidate or synthesize their thinking before it slipped away. And when the discussion came, the writing provided kids with more thoughts to "fall back on" if the conversation lagged.

Variations ▶ Only if your kids have a taste for the grotesque (and you have tenure) should you include the final paragraph of the article, which we have appended sep-arately. This section also sheds more light on the author's point of view: his extravagant loathing of Edison and possible exaggeration of details are in full view here.

Research Projects for Extended Writing ▶ Longer writing projects—reflecting the key genres required by the national standards—can be built on the work students have already done in this lesson. As kids continue to explore the topics of our reading selections, we expect that they will bring fresh background knowledge, recent thinking, and genuine curi-osity to the task. When you use the lesson above with your own content, you can also use the assignments below as models for extending that content into longer writing projects.

Narrative: *Write the* whole *story behind the content*

Would it change your thinking about this story if you found out Topsy the ele-phant had previously killed three of her trainers? (She did.) The long story of this particular elephant is remarkably well documented online. Dig into the information and tell the story of Topsy's life, including the major events from her initial capture to her fatal electrocution.

Informative/explanatory: *Find a parallel in today's world.*

In the era of Edison and Tesla, inventors shifted from quiet lab rats to dramatic self-promoters and shrewd businesspeople. Not only did you have to come up with great scientific discoveries, you had to be a larger-than-life public figure, aggressively selling your gizmos to the public, corporations, or the government. Find a person who is taking that inventor-promoter role today and write a short profile of his or her work. *Research clue: The leaders of start-up and high-tech companies often manifest these dual roles.*

Persuasive/argumentative: *Should we trust the source?*

This author obviously has a strong "slant" or a point of view. He's a critic of Edison. But what about the source—www.knowledgenuts.com? Does that sound reliable? Maybe there's another side to this story, one that doesn't make Edison into such a villain. Look into some of the other accounts of his battle with Tesla and his use of animals in demonstrations (there are many conflicting accounts online). Was Edison an animal-abusing sadist (and maybe a sociopath), or simply a scientist doing his work according to the customs and beliefs of his time period? Write to argue your position.

Edison Publicly Tortured Animals to Discredit AC Power

Andrew Handley, www.knowledgenuts.com

The bitter rivalry between Thomas Edison and Nicola Tesla is now the stuff of legend, and it all came to a head during the War of the Currents. On the one side, Edison felt that direct current (DC) was the wave of the future. On the other side, Tesla believed that alternating current (AC) was more efficient for transmitting power over longer distances. Edison launched a massive public campaign to discredit AC, while Tesla partnered with financial mogul George Westinghouse in an attempt to convince power companies to switch over to AC using Tesla's patented AC induction motor.

By this point, the two inventors were old acquaintances, although there was nothing friendly about their relationship. When Tesla moved from France to New York in 1884, the penniless immigrant got a job at the Edison Machine Works as an engineer. Within a year, he was already solving technical problems for the company, and Edison approached him with the task of redesigning the DC generators for the entire company. He famously offered Tesla $50,000 if he could make the generators more efficient, and a few months later, Tesla came back with an improved design. But when he asked for his money, Edison laughed and said, "When you become a full-fledged American, you will appreciate an American joke." Since Tesla had redesigned the generators while working for Edison, he had no claim to the patent, and essentially got nothing out of the agreement (although Edison offered him a raise of $10 per week; Tesla resigned on the spot).

A few years later, Tesla built his AC induction motor, and the War of the Currents began. Edison's main campaign strategy was to prove that AC, which used much higher voltages than DC, was simply too dangerous to use in homes. And to prove that, he went to ruthless extremes. Most famously, he organized demonstrations executing stray dogs and cats, and later cows and horses. One of the first demonstrations took place in 1888, with the electrocution of a large dog named Dash. Edison first sent 1,000 volts of DC through the dog to prove that he would be—if not unharmed—still alive. Then, he hooked the dog up to 300 volts of AC and smoked the pup into oblivion.

And he was just getting warmed up. In 1903, Edison created his largest demonstration yet: He sent 6,600 volts of AC through a circus elephant named Topsy while 1,500 people stood by and watched. The execution was filmed and later released under the name *Electrocuting an Elephant.*

Concluding paragraph of "Edison Publicly Tortured Animals to Discredit AC Power"

Andrew Handley, www.knowledgenuts.com

The real test came in 1890 though, and it was no ordinary animal: The victim was a convicted murderer named William Kemmler. Edison campaigned for the opportunity to create a "more humane" method of capital punishment and, still in the midst of the War of the Currents, he opted to create the electric chair with AC. After all, what better way to prove the dangers of AC than by killing a man with it? And he couldn't have asked for a more visceral demonstration: The first charge burned through Kemmler's insides for a whole 17 seconds, after which he was still gasping for breath. The second charge lasted four minutes, and Kemmler burst into flame before finally dying.

Interviewing an Expert and a Classmate

LESSON 2

TIME ▶ 40 minutes (can be divided into two 20-minute sessions)

GROUPINGS ▶ Whole class, pairs, individuals

STANDARDS MET ▶ See pages 306–307.

 Chapter 11's Text Set

WHEN TO USE ▶ When students are getting started reading, writing, and discussing with a partner. Also, the interview is a frequently used nonfiction structure that students can easily emulate when reporting their own research.

TEXT	AUTHOR	SOURCE	TEXT TYPE
"Here's How You Sell a Haunted House"	Gwynne Watkins	www.vulture.com	Feature story

This longer lesson has multiple purposes. At one level, we are continuing to build friendly and supportive relationships among students so they will be able to collaborate skillfully as the year goes on. And people build friendships as they gradually self-disclose, sharing pieces of their lives and interests with others in a controlled, mutual way. This process is what we often call "getting to know someone better." So in the social dimension, this lesson's payoff comes later, when kids interview a classmate.

But the *interview* is also one of the most common nonfiction text types: people avidly read interviews with top scientists, historians, and other subject-matter specialists.

Of course, we know interviews are a staple of television. Whether it is CNN, Fox, *The Daily Show*, or late night with Jimmy, Jimmy, or Stephen, a substantial portion of any program is devoted to a host or reporter interviewing experts. Now, the subjects might be actors, authors, or politicians, but they all have one thing in common: all could be considered experts on a particular topic. However, an interview is only as interesting as the questions asked.

So, for our students, we need to help them begin to think about the ingredients of a good interview question. How can a question elicit information that

- is detailed
- builds upon previous questions
- "brings out" the interviewee
- creates surprises
- goes in an unpredictable direction

While watching interview videos on the web is helpful, there's another, quicker way to help your students become interview question experts: studying print interviews. In some news stories, interview quotes are woven into a narrative. However, more and more frequently, you can find interview transcripts that retain the order of the questioning. Not only do these interviews provide a quick study into questioning, they also model an excellent nonfiction format that students can use. Without further ado, let's start our interview study with an expert on selling haunted houses!

1. Make a copy of "Here's How You Sell a Haunted House" for each student. Leave the reverse side blank for note taking.

2. Decide how pairs will be formed at the start of the lesson.

3. Consider appointing a student scribe for Step 5 so you can focus on moderating the discussion.

STEP 1 **Turn and talk.** Once students are seated with their partners, pose this question: *What movies have you seen that involve haunted houses or other forms of supernatural inhabitants?* Allow students a minute to orally compare movies with their partners and then call on a few pairs to share some of the movies they've seen. Then ask: *What elements do haunted houses have in common?* Allow pairs to talk for another minute and then hear some responses, which will probably include

◀ **Steps** & **Teaching Language**

- House seems normal at first.
- Someone died there.
- People didn't know the house was haunted when they bought it.
- House was built upon a burial site.
- Ghosts affect some people more than others.
- Ghosts act friendly and then turn evil.

STEP 2 **Distribute the article, introduce it, and give reading instructions.** *Many people believe that haunted houses exist, and people do buy them. As you read this article about a woman who sells haunted houses, please star your two favorite questions and the two most interesting details you uncover as you read.*

STEP 3 **Pairs compare.** *I see that most of you are done, so take a moment and compare your notes with your partner. Try to decide which question got the most distinctive, or weirdest, information.*

STEP 4 **Pairs brainstorm additional questions.** *If you had a chance to interview this realtor, what are some additional questions you would like to ask? Try to think of questions that would get interesting, detailed answers yet not be offensive.*

STEP 5 **Share with the whole class.** *When you discussed the original interview, what was your favorite question, the one you thought was the best? Why?* Listen to answers and explanations.

Then ask: *Let's hear your new haunted house questions.* At this point, it wouldn't hurt to assign a student board writer/digital note taker so that the class can review all of the brainstormed questions, once again deciding which ones would have the greatest potential for uncovering interesting information.

If possible, cruise right on and do the second part of this lesson during the same class period, or schedule it for the following day.

STEP 6 **Present partner interview topic choices.** *The logical follow-up of studying an interview is to then conduct an interview yourself. And the most convenient interview subject is—who else?—your class partner.* Quickly brainstorm some topics on which students could interview each other, or begin with this short list and see what your class can add.

- Pets
- Playing sports
- Accidents
- Vacation
- Amusement park rides

STEP 7 **Partners pick topics.** Both partners do not have to choose the same topic. Each should pick a topic that they could speak on—one in which they have some experience, some expertise.

STEP 8 **Model a quick interview.** Choose a topic and have the class interview you. Answer one question at a time as you coach the class on how to rephrase yes/no or other single-answer questions. Also, coach students on how to base new questions on information given in previous answers.

STEP 9 **Student interviews begin.** Lots of times it's easier to monitor accountable talk by designating who starts: *Rows 1, 3, and 5, you'll be the interviewers while Rows 2, 4, and 6 will be answering the questions.* Also, you might have students jot notes—like real reporters—as they conduct the interviews. They can use the haunted house interview as a model for their own note taking.

As students conduct interviews, monitor pairs, observing interview skills. As interviews wind down (usually two to three minutes), call time and tell students to switch roles.

STEP 10 **Discuss topics and questions as a whole class.** *What were some of the topics you used in your interviews? Tell us the questions you asked. Who thought of a completely new question based on something your partner said?*

Shoptalk ▶ Interviewing is an excellent way for students to get to know each other as they hone skills necessary for the discussion of content-area material. If you can listen and ask follow-up questions in an interview, then you can use those exact same skills in a small-group discussion pertaining to a science text, social studies simulation, or group project.

The interview format is also a great way for kids to demonstrate topic research in writing. Sometimes called "faction," students conduct their research and then present it in the form of an interview. The fun thing about this assignment is that students could be interviewing a historical figure, a fictional character, or an inanimate object such as the pen used by the signers of the Declaration of Independence.

Longer writing projects—reflecting the key genres required by the national standards—can be built on the work students have already done in this lesson. As kids continue to explore the topics of our reading selections, we expect that they will bring fresh background knowledge, recent thinking, and genuine curiosity to the task. When you use the lesson above with your own content, you can also use the assignments below as models for extending that content into longer writing projects.

◀ *Research Projects for Extended Writing*

Narrative: *Research a topic of personal interest and write it up as an interview*

Research another "unusual" career or other topic of interest. Then review your findings and decide who could be the interview subject. While it might be a person, it could also be an inanimate object, animal, plant, etc. Write up the findings as an interview that tells a story.

Informative/explanatory: *Use your own expertise to give others advice in the form of a dos/don'ts article*

While this article is an interview, it also offers some dos and don'ts on how to sell a haunted house. From your own experiences in and out of school, what is something you could give advice on? Start with what you know and then research what advice experts in the field have to say. Write an advice article that focuses on the dos and don'ts of your topic.

Persuasive/argumentative: *Research a controversial topic and argue whether current practices or attitudes should be continued*

Though few have directly encountered haunted houses, most of us have had experience with the violence depicted in film, television, social media, and video games. What effect—if any—do these experiences have on viewers? Research the issue and then write a letter to a purveyor of violent entertainment, either supporting the company's diversionary endeavors or decrying the violence that undermines its viewers.

Here's How You Sell a Haunted House

Gwynne Watkins, www.vulture.com

A family moves into a beautiful, if eerie, new home, only to realize that it's haunted by restless ghosts. It happens all the time in horror movies, but realtor Cindi Hagley does her best to make sure that scenario doesn't play out in real life. A division of her San Francisco–based firm, Past Life Homes, deals properties that have been burdened with "stigmatized pasts." For Hagley, who lived in "several haunted houses" as a child, the business is a labor of love. "I'm always looking for ways to debunk anything I see because I'm very skeptical," Hagley says. "But unfortunately, there's a lot of evil energy out there, and people need help."

How did you get into the business of selling haunted houses?

The majority of homes that I sell are regular residential homes, and there's nothing wrong with them. I might sell maybe only one or two stigmatized, haunted homes a year. One of my very first listings happened to be a haunted home. Almost immediately after, I sold another home where there was a very fresh death—a natural passing, but still a death.

How did you find out that first house was haunted?

It was a beautiful old Victorian home. I was doing an open house, and it was slow one weekend. So I'm sitting there doing paperwork, and I think I see a movement up on the stairs. It hasn't fazed me that there might be a haunting, because the house is kind of creepy. So I continue working, and again I see movement on the stairs. I look up; there's nothing there. The third time it happens, I actually walk upstairs to see what's going on. There's nobody up there, of course, but at that point, there's that kind of cold electricity that you can feel sometimes.

Then what happened?

The seller gets home a couple hours later and I say, "You know, I had a really interesting experience here. Has anyone ever told you your home is haunted?" She says, "Yeah, my boyfriend tells me that all the time. He sees a woman up and down the stairs, and she also hangs out on the back patio."

Is an alleged haunting something that you generally reveal after an offer is made?

I'll usually hold that [information] till the end, because if I put that upfront and it's available to other agents, I get looky-loos, I get creepy people, these ghost-hunting groups want to come through. If people fall in love with a home, there are things that they'll look past. I think an alleged haunting is one of them.

Has there ever been a property that's freaked you out to the point where it affected your ability to sell it?

I've been in homes where the energy has just been so off that I don't want to be in that home, and I've refused listings, or I might go ahead and take the listing, but I won't go back into the home. There's some nasty energy out there, and I just won't be around it.

Your website says that you have a team of clergy, psychics, and mediums. Where do they come into the process?

If it's a bad energy—it sounds so crazy to talk about—but if it's something that's toying with people, then I need to figure out what it is, and I need to cleanse that home. My main guy's name is Mark Nelson, and he's a great psychic. So we go in and we try to figure out what it is, who it is, and we try to get them to pass on. First we'll try a psychic, but some people who are super-religious will have a clergy member come in and bless the home. We also let buyers test-drive the home. If they think it's going to be creepy living there, then we'll let them stay there for two or three nights and test it out.

Analyzing People with Identity Webs

TIME ▶ 30 minutes

GROUPINGS ▶ Whole class, pairs, individuals

STANDARDS MET ▶ See pages 306–307.

Chapter 11's Text Set

WHEN TO USE ▶ We use this lesson early in the writing year, when we are trying to build students' fluency as writers and also their acquaintance with each other, so that they gradually become more friendly and supportive.

TEXT	AUTHOR/SOURCE	TEXT TYPE
"Susan B. Anthony"	The Social Welfare History Project	Biography

One of the most useful writing and sketching tools for kids to acquire is an *identity web*. Once mastered, this graphic + text model allows students to analyze figures from history or characters from literature—or to better understand themselves and their classmates.

In this lesson we begin by supporting students as they web a complex and somewhat neglected historical figure—Susan B. Anthony. Then kids move on to making their own webs, and sharing as they feel comfortable with one partner. We learned this strategy from our colleague Sara Ahmed and from the organization Facing History and Ourselves, where identity webs also are used to build self-knowledge, empathy, and the ability to put yourself in others' shoes.

> ## PREPARATION
>
> 1. Determine how partners will be formed at Step 1.
> 2. Make copies of "Susan B. Anthony" for all.
> 3. Be ready to project the sample identity web.
> 4. Have a student scribe ready to make the list at Step 3.
> 5. Have enough blank paper (legal or ledger, if possible) and markers for the class.
> 6. Be ready to demonstrate making your own identity web, "live."

Steps & Teaching Language ▶

STEP 1 **Form pairs.** Have kids find one partner and get into a high-focus seating position, face-to-face and distanced from other pairs.

STEP 2 **Show the sample web and invite pair talk.** Project the sample and explain. *An identity web is a graphic way to map all the aspects of a person. Taylor, a student in Ohio, made this one about Katniss Everdeen from* The Hunger Games. *Who's read the books or seen one of the movies? Take a look at this web and chat with your partner about what you notice. Whether you already know Katniss or not, what can you say about this person? What connections or overlaps do you see between yourselves and Katniss? What differences? What questions would you ask if she were here?*

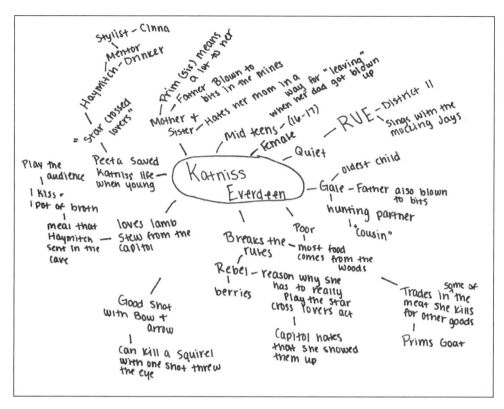

Identity web for Katniss Everdeen in *The Hunger Games*

STEP 3 Find categories. *Now take another look at the sample and decide what categories of information you see.* Expect kids to notice childhood, friends, personality traits, skills, key experiences, family, hometown, jobs, interests, hobbies, turning points, attitudes, beliefs, accomplishments, etc. Have your scribe list these on the board or screen as they are volunteered. Title the list "Identity Web Categories."

STEP 4 Apply the web to Susan B. Anthony. *You guys have probably all heard of—or maybe studied—Susan B. Anthony, one of the more famous women in our history. What do you know about her?* List the key words of students' background knowledge as they share them. No need to critique the range of ideas; even if people volunteer misinformation, you can say, *"We'll see if we can confirm that in a few minutes."*

STEP 5 Students read and annotate the article. Invite students to read the piece, with the Identity Web Categories chart still hanging in view. *After you read this article, you and your partner will collaborate on making an identity web of Susan B. Anthony. So now when you are reading, be sure to mark any places in the text where elements of her identity are revealed.* Turn them loose to read and begin their webs. Circulate to reiterate instructions and monitor progress.

STEP 6 **Share and discuss as a class.** When students have finished their Susan B. Anthony webs, pull the class back together and invite several pairs to share items from their webs. Push for subsequent kids to volunteer new, previously unmentioned elements of her identity until all ideas are mentioned.

This could be a logical time to pause and split the lesson into two sections if time requires. But don't skip the personal webs; these are crucial to the development of your energetic, interactive classroom.

STEP 7 **Teacher demonstrates own web.** Next, get on the computer or document camera and make an identity web for yourself, right in front of the kids. (You may also create it earlier and simply reveal it here.) If you create yours spontaneously, talk about your topics as you write them down, and point out any natural categories or clusters that develop as you write.

STEP 8 **Individuals create their own webs.** *Now it's your turn to create personal webs with the paper and markers I passed out. You can refer to our chart of Identity Web Categories if you need a reminder of topics you might include.* Here's what Taylor Clemons did when she created her own identity web.

Remind kids that they should only write things they will be comfortable sharing later with others. And as you monitor their work, watch for this distinctive dynamic: many times, kids will make a few web entries

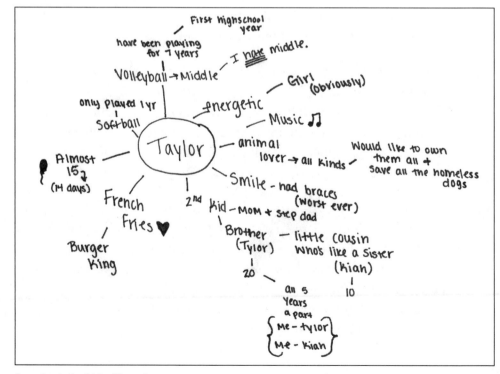

Sample student identity web

and then slow down. But just as you are thinking the activity is winding down, students regain energy and start adding more and more details. There is something about breaking through a first level with this reflective writing, then going deeper. So give them at least five to seven minutes—and let them talk quietly among themselves as they work.

STEP 9 **Students share with a partner as they are comfortable.** Now invite kids to share with their buddy—but first, take steps to be sure kids feel in control of this personal information. We say something like this: *Pick two or three items on your identity web that you feel comfortable sharing with your partner. Then you can take turns talking about the items you have each chosen. If you're both really comfortable with it, you can also just show your webs to each other.*

STEP 10 **Back in the whole group, volunteers report.** Ask a few pairs to report "one cool/interesting/surprising thing I learned about my partner." This is typically quite fun, especially when kids find out things about their classmates they never knew. You can end here, or if kids are eager to share more, go on to Step 11.

STEP 11 **Have a gallery walk.** Have kids hang their identity webs on the walls around the room (evenly spaced, at kid-eye level), and invite students to circulate through the identity web gallery, seeing what new information they can learn about their classmates. For greater accountability, have them carry Post-it notes and write at least one comment/question/reaction at every poster they visit. Visiting four or five webs is plenty for now; they can see others later either officially or informally.

◀ *Variation*

If your kids are connected (and showing good curiosity about Susan B), you could pause for five minutes at Step 6 and invite them to quickly go online and find even *more* information about Anthony that could be added to their webs.

◀ *Research Projects for Extended Writing*

Longer writing projects—reflecting the key genres required by the national standards—can be built on the work students have already done in this lesson. As kids continue to explore the topics of our reading selections, we expect that they will bring fresh background knowledge, recent thinking, and genuine curiosity to the task. When you use the lesson above with your own content, you can also use the assignments below as models for extending that content into longer writing projects.

Narrative: *Create a fictional interview with an important person*

Use the notes on Susan B. Anthony's identity web to write a narrative that includes an imaginary interview with her, building on the interviewing skills you just learned in Lesson 2.

Informative/explanatory: *Report on your own research about the content*

Women were not allowed to vote in America until 1920, less than a hundred years ago. Survey at least twenty-five kids in your class or your school, asking them why they think it took so long for American women to get the vote. (Feel free to tack on related women's rights questions if you like.) Tally the results, analyze the data, and write a report that explains your classmates' responses.

Persuasive/argumentative: *Argue the importance of a historical figure*

While Susan B. Anthony is fairly well known, we don't spend much time studying her in most American schools. Some historians think she has not been given enough credit for the advancement of women's rights in America. Look into some of those arguments, and then use all the evidence you have acquired to make an argument for why Anthony should be more carefully studied in American schools—or that the coverage she currently gets is enough.

Susan B. Anthony
(February 15, 1820–March 13, 1906)

Suffragist, Reformer, Labor Activist, Abolitionist, and Advocate for a Woman's Right to Her Own Property and Earning

The Social Welfare History Project

Early Years: Susan Brownell Anthony was born in Adams, Massachusetts, to Daniel and Lucy Read Anthony in 1820. Susan was the second of eight children. Susan's mother was raised in a Baptist family. Her father, Daniel Anthony, a cotton manufacturer, was a Quaker and active abolitionist. The parents raised their children in a strict Quaker household. For example, the Anthony children were not allowed to experience toys, games, and music, which were seen as distractions from the "inner light." Because Susan was brought up in a Quaker family with long activist traditions, early in her life she developed a sense of justice and moral zeal.

Susan Anthony was a precocious child and she learned to read and write at the age of three. In 1826, the family moved from Massachusetts to Battensville, N.Y., where Susan attended a district school. When the teacher refused to teach Susan long division, Susan was taken out of school and taught in a "home school" set up by her father. Ultimately, Susan was sent to a boarding school near Philadelphia.

Anthony herself taught school from age 17 until she was 29, including three years at the all-female Eunice Kenyon's Quaker Boarding School in upstate New York. Her work experience as a teacher inspired Anthony to help women teachers obtain wages equivalent to those of male teachers. At the time, men earned roughly four times more than women for the same duties.

In 1849 Anthony quit teaching and settled in Rochester, New York, to run her father's farm while he developed his insurance business. During this period, Anthony became alienated from the Quakers after witnessing alcohol abuse and what she perceived as other moral failings among some Quaker preachers.

Career as a Reformer: Anthony's involvement in reform movements began with her attendance at conventions and gatherings related to the temperance movement in New York State. In 1849, at the age of 29, she became secretary for the Daughters of Temperance, giving her a forum to speak out against alcohol abuse. At a temperance meeting in 1851, Anthony met Elizabeth Cady Stanton and their remarkable collaboration on behalf of women's suffrage began at once. Their personal characteristics and societal circumstances helped shape their different roles in their collaboration: Stanton was married and the mother of seven children who chose to stay close to home; Anthony was a single woman and free to travel and earn her living from her reform work. Anthony, it turned out, was also more skillful than Stanton at organizing people to carry out their ideas.

During the 1850s, the women's rights movement gathered steam, but lost momentum when the Civil War began. Almost immediately after the war ended, the 14th and 15th Amendments to the Constitution raised familiar questions of suffrage and citizenship. (The 14th Amendment, ratified in 1868, extends the Constitution's protection to all citizens—and defines "citizens" as "male"; the 15th, ratified in 1870, guarantees black men the right to vote.)

For decades, abolitionists and suffragists had worked together for freedom and justice—for African Americans and women. Then, in February 1869, Congress passed the Fifteenth Amendment (ratified by the states in 1870), guaranteeing that African American men could not be denied the right to vote simply because of their race—but it refused to expand the wording to grant voting rights to women. "One thing at a time," some politicians said.

Some woman suffrage advocates, among them Susan B. Anthony and Stanton, believed that this was their chance to push lawmakers for truly universal suffrage. As a result, they refused to support the 15th Amendment and even allied with Southerners who argued that a white woman's vote could be used to neutralize those cast by African-Americans. In 1869, Anthony, Stanton and other suffragists angry at the collapse of an equal rights convention formed a group called the National Woman Suffrage Association (NWSA) and began to fight for a universal-suffrage amendment to the Constitution. The organization condemned the Fourteenth and Fifteenth amendments as blatant injustices to women. The NWSA also advocated easier divorce and an end to discrimination in employment and pay.

The other association of suffragists was a more conservative group. The American Woman Suffrage Association, centered in Boston, supported the idea that attaining the vote for black men was more important than demanding the vote for women. There were several differences in the positions of the two organizations, and a good deal of personal hostility developed between them. By 1890, however, these problems were overcome, and the two organizations merged into the National American Woman Suffrage Association. Stanton became the group's president. Anthony served as president from 1892 to 1900.

In the early years of the NWSA, Anthony made attempts to unite women in the labor movement with the suffragist cause, but with little success. She and Stanton were delegates at the 1868 convention of the National Labor Union. However, Anthony inadvertently alienated the labor movement, not only because suffrage was seen as a concern for middle-class rather than working-class women, but also because she openly encouraged women to achieve economic independence by entering the printing trades when male workers were on strike. Anthony was later expelled from the National Labor Union over this controversy.

Anthony's pursuit of alliances with moderate and conservative suffragists created tension between herself and more radical suffragists such as Stanton. Anthony felt strongly that the moderate approach to women's rights was more realistic and would serve to gain more for women in the end. Anthony's strategy was to unite the suffrage movement wherever possible and focus strictly on gaining the vote, temporarily leaving other women's rights issues aside.

Although Anthony did not live to see the consummation of her efforts to win the right to vote for women, the establishment of the 19th amendment is deeply owed to her efforts. Susan B. Anthony died of heart disease and pneumonia on March 13, 1906.

Making a "Top List"

TEXT	AUTHOR	SOURCE	TEXT TYPE
"Five Ways to Get Fired from Your After-School Job"	Roger Vector	WrapUp Media	Numbered list

TIME ▶ 30 minutes

GROUPING ▶ Whole class, pairs, individuals

STANDARDS MET ▶ See pages 306–307.

WHEN TO USE ▶ This lesson continues our opening activities that build collaboration around writing and give kids chances to try out common nonfiction text structures—like numbered lists.

One of the most commonly encountered nonfiction types in magazines, newspapers, and especially online is the top ten or top five list. Are you addicted to these like we are? Top Ten Craziest Tattoos, Top Ten Most Dangerous Animals, Top Ten Insane Dictators, Top Ten Crazed Celebrity Stalkers, and more. Irresistible. The best ones combine unexpected or amusing items with sharp, short blurbs that delineate each item and its ranking.

Recent retiree David Letterman probably deserves special credit for institutionalizing this genre, after including a top ten list on his show almost every night for thirty years. But of course, this durable organizational device has been used by writers for centuries. Polonius's famous "neither a borrower nor a lender be" speech in *Hamlet* is a comical Shakespearean top ten list of life advice.

A more lively cousin of the bullet list, top lists have potential for both writing precision and enjoyment. In this lesson, we start with a humorous but negative top five list, and then have kids turn it positive as they list the top five things about themselves.

PREPARATION

1. Make a copy of "Five Ways to Get Fired from Your After-School Job" for each student.
2. Decide how you'll form pairs at Step 1.
3. Download and be ready to project the "Top Five Things About Me List— Categories and Examples" in Step 4.

STEP 1 **Students read the article.** Have kids get with their partners as you hand out the reading. Encourage them to read the article just for pleasure, and to talk with their partner as they read it. Often there are chuckles and some laughs of recognition. When kids are done, offer the next instruction.

STEP 2 **Pairs discuss.** *What did you think of this article?* If kids jump right in, let their responses lead the conversation. If not, prime the pump with these questions:

—*Do you agree that these five "misbehaviors" should result in an employee getting fired? Any excuses?*

◀ **Steps &
Teaching
Language**

—Do you know any kids who've gotten fired from a job? What happened?

—What other things could an employee do to get fired?

Note that we are intentionally letting this reading response be light and easy, and not exercising a lot of control. The goal is an enjoyable, relaxed discussion.

STEP 3 **Consider how top lists work.** *You've probably seen a lot of these numbered lists. They are the backbone of countless magazines, celebrity rags, and gossipy websites. Who can think of ones you've seen? Or that you could imagine?* Take a few volunteers.

Top lists are also easy to write because they follow a simple, fixed formula. You come up with a number of interesting items that fit the space you have, and then write a quick, entertaining explanation of each one and defend its ranking.

Let's try creating our own lists now. The "How to Get Fired" list was really a negative topic, right? It focused on how not *to be a good employee. Now let's try making one of your own, but this time we will definitely accent the positive.*

STEP 4 **Kids create their own lists.** Get kids set up for writing with paper or devices. *A great topic for us to write about at this time of year is ourselves. Since we will be working together all year long, it's important to know what strengths we each bring to the community and to our subject matter.*

You're going to create a Top Five Things list about yourself. So what kinds of things could you possibly put on such a list?

Project the following list and talk kids through it. Stop and mention (or add) the ones that might go on your own list if you were making one (see variations). Emphasize that kids are not limited to these examples and should think of traits that really fit them.

Top Five Things About Me List—Categories and Examples

Personality Traits: Friendly, reliable, creative, hard-working, strong leader, team player, artistic, empathic, energetic, detail-oriented, patient, good time manager, supportive, etc.

Curriculum Background: I have had three prior years of math, can operate TI-85 calculator, have learned to code, have read many books, studied topics on my own time, etc.

General Knowledge: Have traveled, been to shows, movies, museums, cultural attractions, workplaces, have hobbies or collections, have had jobs or volunteered, met many different people, have friends and relatives in diverse fields and places, etc.

Academic Skills: Skilled debater, ace online researcher, strong writer and public speaker, independent worker, can set and monitor goals, can analyze and display data, can run a 3-D printer, etc.

Give kids a minute to study these options, then allow five minutes of quiet work time to get a start on their lists. Remind them that they need to write a two- or three-sentence explanation of each item, just as in the article.

Circulate and assist. Be ready to offer suggestions to kids who have a hard time thinking about a strength they have. Of course, be alert to nonrelevant content, including predictable wish list items like "world's greatest lover." Aren't teenagers hilarious?

STEP 5 **Share with partner and class.** When kids have got their lists going— these will be rough drafts and probably not complete—ask them to turn back to their partners and take turns sharing some strengths. Pull back to the whole group and ask a few volunteers to tell about "one strength on my partner's top five list."

STEP 6 **Going public.** Have students make their rough-draft top five lists into illustrated posters that can go up on the classroom wall, under a banner like "The Assets of Room 106" or "Sixth-Period Strengths."

Remind kids that they can return to their charts anytime to add newly developed or recognized strengths. These can gradually become "Top Eight (or Thirteen) Things About Me" posters.

◀ **Variations**

At Step 4, it is very helpful if you reveal your own top five list, or create one "live," right in front of the kids. Don't worry about making your list perfect. Your willingness to take this risk confers a feeling of safety and confidence to the students, and that feeling is more important than any single item on your list. If the idea of doing this in front of the class makes you anxious, consider making your list ahead of time and showing it to the kids, explaining: *To show you what I mean, here is a top five list I made about myself.*

After kids create posters in Step 6, a gallery walk is a natural next step, just as for identity webs in Lesson 3. If your kids enjoyed and learned from that strategy, by all means do it again. For sure, include the requirement that they leave a written comment beside each poster they visit. "Bradley, I agree, you are a good debater—especially when we disagree about a movie." "Jessie, don't forget that you are an awesome leader in soccer!"

For another publication opportunity, have kids flesh out their draft list into a web-worthy article, using the "Top Five Ways to Get Fired from Your After-School Job" as a model. Post these on your classroom web page or other appropriate spot.

Hang on to the lists and charts from this lesson. You can use them as you develop new partnerships, inquiry groups, and teams in your class.

Research Projects for Extended Writing ▶ Longer writing projects—reflecting the key genres required by the national standards—can be built on the work students have already done in this lesson. As kids continue to explore the topics of our reading selections, we expect that they will bring fresh background knowledge, recent thinking, and genuine curiosity to the task. When you use the lesson above with your own content, you can also use the assignments below as models for extending that content into longer writing projects.

Narrative: *Make a list of the Top Five Childhood Events for yourself or a famous figure*

Start by making a map of the neighborhood where you grew up. Then label each spot where something big happened (e.g., you fell out of a tree, hit a home run, had an adventure, got in trouble). Use these labels to build the list, ranking the events in order of importance. Then write a two- or three-sentence explanation of what happened each time and why it ranks so high in your memory. Or use this same pattern to structure the biography of a famous figure—for example, key early experiences of Einstein, Lincoln, or Fibonacci.

Informative/explanatory: *Verify what you've read with local experts*

Do some research with employers in your community about what they feel are the five most important *positive* traits of workers. You can do this by setting up personal or telephone interviews with several businesses—or by mailing them a survey posing a few simple questions. Be sure you call or mail someone who is either in the Human Resources Department (for a bigger company) or a manager who hires and supervises workers (in a smaller firm). Then tally the results and write a report comparing the employers' desired traits of employees with the negative ones in our article.

Persuasive/argumentative: *Argue from a different perspective*

The article we read was all about employee behavior. But what about *employer* behavior? The success of anyone's employment also depends on the attitudes and behavior of the company. Online you can find many annual rankings of the "top/best companies to work for," created by employees themselves. Check out some of these reports and discover what specific factors lead to high rankings for some companies over others (high salaries, free coffee, whatever you find). Then make your own ranking the top five of these traits and defend each item with a short paragraph.

WrapUp MEDIA

FIVE WAYS to Get Fired from Your After-School Job

Roger Vector, WrapUp Media

These days, 26% of teenagers have after-school jobs, and 32% have part- or full-time jobs during the summer. These numbers are actually record lows; as recently as 1979, almost 60% of teens participated in the workforce sometime during the year.

The bottom line: for young people, getting and keeping a part-time job is harder than ever. Increased competition from older workers remaining in the workforce and declining numbers of entry level jobs mean that if you can snag a job, you'd better protect it carefully.

Reviewing some prominent career-building websites, we discovered several common reasons for teens getting fired from after-school or summer jobs. If you want to get bounced, try these behaviors.

1. **Show up late.** Employers schedule workers for when they are most needed, so when you're late it's immediately disruptive—especially for the people who have to pick up your slack. Plus, many bosses simply feel that promptness is the most basic, nonnegotiable job skill. Be five minutes early every time.

2. **Be a slob.** Even if you work at the Oil Change Pit, there is some standard of dress that you will either be told or can determine by looking at coworkers. If you have a uniform, wear it. If clothing is by choice, dress like the people *one step above you in the organization*, to signal your readiness for a raise and a promotion.

3. **Diss your boss.** Sometimes in entry-level jobs you'll have bosses who are inexperienced, insecure, or not as smart as you. But they are still your boss, and rolling your eyes to their face or joining in break room gossip will not advance your career. For an extra-quick exit, try trashing your supervisor on Instagram.

4. **Play with your phone during work.** Checkers in big-box stores, ushers in movie theaters, day camp counselors, and restaurant servers can earn a pink slip if they get caught texting when they should be taking care of customers. Yes, your job does have boring stretches—so how are you supposed to pass the time? Get to know your coworkers better instead of texting your posse outside.

5. **"Borrow" stuff.** Most employers have some items lying around—paper clips, French fries, or merchandise—that you might like to bring home, using your five-finger discount. Be advised that this is often a firing offense, and some employers will also dial 911.

Creating a Class Constitution

TIME ▶ 30 minutes

GROUPING ▶ Whole class, pairs, individuals

STANDARDS MET ▶ See pages 306–307.

WHEN TO USE ▶ This one caps off our series of five lessons for community building with writing. The classroom compact the kids create is real, and you can put it right to work, posted in the room.

TEXT	SOURCE	TEXT TYPE
Preamble to the U.S. Constitution	http://constitutioncenter.org	Legal; historic, patriotic

When we ask students to work deeply with the "patriotic" historic texts emphasized by many state standards, they often give us blank looks. Fact is, they often don't have much background knowledge to build their thinking on. To compensate, we sometimes preteach content or vocabulary to prepare them to struggle with text that's antique and alien to them.

What we rarely do—and should do more often—is give students an *experiential* base for understanding the words of historic figures, such as the Founding Fathers (and the rarely included Mothers). In this lesson, kids work in groups to create a classroom compact before they ever look at the Preamble to the U.S. Constitution. Then, they are able to connect with the debates and choices that faced, and often divided, our founders. Special thanks to Debbie King, Michele Timble, and Sara Ahmed, whose students inspired this lesson.

PREPARATION

1. Download and prepare to project the Preamble to the U.S. Constitution, which will be used in Step 6.
2. Decide how to pair students for Steps 1–3.
3. Be ready to project prompts at Steps 3, 4, 6, 7, and 9.

Steps & Teaching Language ▶

STEP 1 **Start kids thinking about community norms.** *All of us sitting here have already begun building a new community in this classroom. Sure, some of us knew each other from earlier years, or other classes, or outside of school. But as a unique, newly formed group, we are just starting out, and we will live together for an hour a day for the next nine months. I was thinking we could talk about how to make the best community possible for our work together.*

STEP 2 **Kids turn and talk about ground rules.** *Turn to your partners and talk for a minute: What are some ground rules that would make it more comfortable and fun and interesting to be part of this class? Think back on the best classes you have had in school. What factors made the community work? What were the norms or procedures or rules that made things positive? These might have come from the teacher or the students, or have been negotiated by them together. Be sure to jot down the best ideas you think of—we will be using them shortly.*

STEP 3 **Introduce the "Classroom Compact" template.** *As a way of collecting our ground rules, let's fit them into this template. Have a look.* If needed, you can define compact as a written agreement among a group of people about how to live together.

> ***Classroom Compact***
>
> We, the students of Room ____, in order to form a more perfect classroom, do establish this compact. We promise to:

So each of your best rules will be a bullet point added to a list under this heading. Everybody get this? Now, take a couple minutes and rewrite your rules to fit into this format.

STEP 4 **Build a list of rules.** Now invite students to volunteer the rules they have created. As kids suggest items, write them on an anchor chart, either projected or on paper. Pause with each suggestion, and ask the whole class for some responses. *Who else had a rule like this on their own list? How many agree that this would be a good rule to have? Anyone have concerns? How can we word this best?* For ideas with wide approval, put a star beside them; for ones of dubious unanimity, put a question mark.

Just for your background, here's what one middle school compact looked like.

SAMPLE CLASSROOM COMPACT

We, the students of Ms. King, in order to form a more perfect classroom, do establish this compact.

—We will come prepared to work and do our share every day.

—We agree to speak and listen to each other with respect.

—We will make everyone feel safe to take risks and share ideas.

—We cheer each other on and use supportive language.

—No put-downs!

—We share our brains for power and knowledge.

—Everybody works with everybody.

—We solve disagreements peacefully.

—We helped to create our space and we take care of it.

—We follow what's happening in the world, and take action to help others when we can.

(Signed by 28 students)

If you think kids have omitted rules or ideas they would sincerely endorse, feel free to prompt them by asking: *Do we need a rule about collaboration? About our space? Do you want to add something like that now?*

STEP 5 **Connect to the U.S. Constitution.** *Can you think of anybody else who went through the same process that we just did, creating rules for a new community? Maybe a long time ago?*

When America's founders sat down to create a constitution for America (some nine years after their successful separation from England), their work wasn't so different from what we have been doing here so far.

They also had a new community, and they were looking for the just-right rules and norms and procedures to make sure their new country would be a safe and positive place to live. So, like us, they sat down and drew upon all their background knowledge and came up with a compact.

Let's take a minute and read the Preamble, or introduction, to the U.S. Constitution. It's only ninety-one words.

STEP 6 **Teacher reads aloud.** Project the Preamble and read as students follow along.

Preamble to the Constitution of the United States of America:

We the people of the United States, in order to form a more perfect union, establish justice, insure domestic tranquility, provide for the common defense, promote the general welfare, and secure the blessings of liberty to ourselves and our posterity, do ordain and establish this Constitution for the United States of America.

As you read, clarify vocabulary for *domestic, tranquility, posterity, ordain,* and any other terms that might impede comprehension for some. Rather than simply supplying definitions yourself, invite kids to chime in: *Who knows what* domestic *means? In this context? Probably not just inside a house, but inside a whole country, right?*

STEP 7 **Focus on key topics.** *So, what purposes or categories did the Preamble just enunciate?*

Project the six purposes. *Have a look at these.*

Purposes Enunciated in the Preamble to the Constitution

Form a more perfect union

Establish justice

Insure domestic tranquility

Provide for the common defense

Promote the general welfare

Secure the blessings of liberty to ourselves and our posterity

These were the six issues that the founders were most concerned with.

STEP 8 **Backmap to the classroom compact.** *How do the founders' six concerns compare to what we were doing with our classroom compact? Were you working on the same categories as the founders? Some more than others? Let's compare the Preamble with our Classroom Compact.*

STEP 9 **Share Preamble connections and contrasts.** Project the Preamble purposes again and take it one category at a time.

What rules did you have that were mostly about forming a more perfect union or community? Which ones were about establishing justice?

And right down the list.

There will be plenty of overlap and debates about whether some rule belongs under "more perfect union" or "domestic tranquility." All good discussions to have.

Providing for the common defense doesn't immediately seem applicable to the school classroom, but don't be surprised if kids say, "We have to defend how this class works to other kids, since they might not get it and even make fun of it." Or that they have to defend their right to live in this supportive classroom by adhering to the rules.

So, countries are a little different from classrooms—but all attempts at self-government look a lot alike.

STEP 10 **Implement your classroom compact.** Have kids work on revisions and rewording in light of studying the U.S. Preamble. Then have them come back and affirm a final version by vote. Everyone officially signs the poster, John Hancock style, and it is ceremonially hung in the room. Don't be surprised later on if kids point at it when a rule is breached or an ideal slighted. They are showing you the power of founding documents among human communities.

When kids are brainstorming rules and making the compact, they may get sidetracked into devising elaborately specified "consequences." Unfortunately, most American kids have been raised in authoritarian schools—so when they hear the word *rules*, they immediately think *punishments*—and adolescents LOVE to dream up exotic corrections for peers. Beware and steer them away—unless you can turn it positive. Or point them to the informative/explanatory research project below.

◀ ***Tip***

Longer writing projects—reflecting the key genres required by the national standards—can be built on the work students have already done in this lesson. As kids continue to explore the topics of our reading selections, we expect that they will bring fresh background knowledge, recent thinking, and genuine curiosity to the task. When you use the lesson above with your own content, you can also use the assignments below as models for extending that content into longer writing projects.

◀ ***Research Projects for Extended Writing***

Narrative: *Recall a related event from your own life*

When coauthor Harvey was in fifth grade, he hit a girl on the head with a book, and her barrette caused a five-stitch cut on her scalp. He got into big trouble. Think back on a time when *you* broke a school rule—or knew someone who did. Tell the story of what happened. What was the infraction? Was it something that had been written down or warned about beforehand? What were the consequences for the student? Did it seem fair? How did it end up?

Informative/explanatory: *Find and explain a pattern*

If you search "classroom rules" online you will find a huge array of lists and charts that different teachers have made and hung in their classrooms. You'll also see lots of professional-looking posters that are made and sold by school publishing companies. Looking at many of these lists, try to determine which are the three to five most frequently listed rules. Form these into a list and explain why you think each one is so common.

Persuasive/argumentative: *Argue in support of an informed opinion*

Some educators believe it is vital to start each new class with a clear list of rules and consequences so that kids know the "rules of the game" from the outset. Others say that kids will respect the rules only if they help create them, and thus favor having teachers and students co-create a joint list of classroom rules, as we did in the lesson. To look further into this debate, search some terms like "school discipline rules" and "co-created classroom rules." Finally, take a position on what you feel would be best for most classrooms—a clear set of teacher-made rules, or a process of collaborative rule making.

Now that students have co-created and practiced some norms of collaborative work, they move on to practice writing short, responsive pieces triggered by nonfiction articles and complex images.

LESSON 6 # Card Talk

TEXT	AUTHOR	SOURCE	TEXT TYPE
"More Women Play Video Games Than Boys"	Drew Harwell	*Washington Post*	Feature story

TIME ▸ 20 minutes

GROUPINGS ▸ Whole class, pairs, individuals

STANDARDS MET ▸ See pages 306–307.

WHEN TO USE ▸ This uber-simple early lesson gets students thinking, writing, and conversing about a complex text.

Many kids, whatever the grade, come to us fearful of writing. Our colleague Jim Vopat says that, sooner or later, almost all American school students (and graduates) join the march of "the writing wounded" (2011). Without probing all the causes here, we know the truth of it: many of our students suffer from blank-page fever when asked to write—especially in classes like math, science, and social studies, where they expect to be safe from English teachers and their infernal writing assignments.

To reduce that fear at the start of our course, we can send a concrete signal that we just want *a little* writing. We have kids write on index cards sized to the class writing anxiety level: 3×5 for the abjectly terrified; 4×6 for medium-level trepidation; and 5×7 for the almost-ready-for-a-full-page writers.

To make it even easier, we can read aloud some juicy information for kids to write about—this way, constraints like varying silent reading rates and proficiency with annotation are set aside briefly.

You simply read aloud a relevant, engaging, and surprising article—and then ask kids to jot a quick response on a notecard. This piece from the *Washington Post* really fills the bill.

> **PREPARATION**
>
> 1. Practice reading "More Women Play Video Games Than Boys" beforehand, so your smooth and animated delivery will support kids to understand the text without their seeing it (permission rights do not include printing/copying).
> 2. Download the lists for Steps 3 and 4 and have them ready to project.
> 3. Have right-sized index cards ready for students to write on in Step 3. We usually start with 4×6.
> 4. Think about how to handle the card passing at Step 4.

Steps & Teaching Language ▶

STEP 1   **Prepare kids for the read-aloud.** Begin by tossing out a few questions to activate students' background knowledge and engage their thinking. (No writing yet.)

Who here has played a video game?

What are some of your favorite games?

What do you like about the game?

Who do you think plays video games more, boys or girls?

How popular do you think video games are compared to movies, music, or sports? Do you think gaming will grow or fade away?

What do you think of complaints that video games and video game culture is sexist?

STEP 2   **Hand out index cards and read aloud.** Pass out the index cards and explain that students will use them to do a super-quick write after you read them an article. This is your chance to say something like: *See, when I say a short piece of writing, I really mean it!* Have kids put their names on the cards now.

Now invite students to listen as you read aloud. Be ready to pause if they need thinking time, or if they are reacting aloud (as they may to the finding that women predominate gaming).

STEP 3   **Students use cards for quick writes.** Next, invite students to write a quick response to the text, using just the front side of their index card (the back will be saved for another student's comment later). If kids wonder what they could share, suggest or project the following list:

> ### Suggestions for What You Might Share
> - Your personal reaction to the article
> - What you visualized while I was reading
> - What information stood out
> - What you know about real-life gamers
> - What questions you had or have now
> - What your own video game experience is like
> - Your opinions about video games in general

STEP 4   **Pass the cards around.** After allowing two or three minutes of writing time, say: *Sign your card with your name. Now, pass your card at least three kids away* (down the row, around the circle, however that works for your seating plan). *When you receive a card, read what is written on the front, then turn the card over and write a comment or answer, and sign your name below it.* Again, you can suggest or project some options:

Suggestions for How to Respond

- Make a comment
- Share a connection
- Ask a question
- Agree and give reasons
- Disagree and give reasons
- Make a relevant drawing or illustration

STEP 5 **Whole class shares.** Invite several students to read aloud both sides of the card they just answered, along the lines of: "I got Randy's card, and he said (read text). I wrote back to him and I said . . ." Then invite others to comment or join in ("Jane and I said something similar . . ."). Let the conversation conclude with thoughts about the video game phenomenon and any of its gender issues that interest kids.

STEP 6 **Collect student writing.** Gather all the cards and scan them later for engagement, quality of thinking, and ideas for future minilessons.

Since this topic and article offer some surprising information, it can lead to a lively, even vociferous discussion among the kids. This is a good thing, of course. But be ready to moderate a spirited exchange, as those students who care deeply about gaming may challenge ideas—and each other.

◀ *Tip*

Instead of having kids pass cards around the room to achieve a random distribution, gather the cards yourself, shuffle the deck with a flourish, and deal them back out, making sure no kids get back their own cards.

◀ *Variations*

As an intermediate step between 4 and 5, have the pairs who randomly coauthored each card pull their seats together and talk briefly about what they wrote. Then, when you move to the whole class in Step 5, these pairs can each read aloud their own side of the card.

While we specifically feature a teacher read-aloud here, most of the upcoming lessons have kids reading the texts on their own. But you know your kids best. For any future lesson, if you think reading the text (or part of it) aloud to your students will better scaffold their comprehension, by all means do it.

◀ *Shoptalk*

Longer writing projects—reflecting the key genres required by the national standards—can be built on the work students have already done in this lesson. As kids continue to explore the topics of our reading selections, we expect that they will bring fresh background knowledge, recent thinking, and genuine curiosity to the task. When you use the lesson above with your own content, you can also use the assignments below as models for extending that content into longer writing projects.

Narrative: *Relate your experience with this topic*

Write your own "personal history with video games," if you have one. Or choose any other game/sport/hobby you participate in: card player, skater, Frisbee flinger, baseball player, water skier, swimmer. Describe your path from the day you first encountered the game, tell how you developed and got better—or enjoyed it more.

Informative/explanatory: *Pitch a related product*

Develop a concept for a new video game. (This doesn't mean making a nationally marketable product, unless you have lots of time, coding skills, and a few hundred coworkers.) This is more like a proposal—a few pages that describe the environment, the players, the goals or conflict, the basic rules, the points or levels—and most important, an explanation of why your game would be so fresh and unique. Drawings of some screens or features would be a plus.

Persuasive/argumentative: *Take a position on a current, related controversy*

Investigate the controversy called "Gamergate." Dig into the abundant online coverage of this issue and you'll find much polarized opinion. Study the information, then take your own position.

The Washington Post

More Women Play Video Games Than Boys

By Drew Harwell

The stereotype of a "gamer"—mostly young, mostly nerdy and most definitely male—has never been further from the truth. In the United States, twice as many adult women play video games as do boys, according to the Entertainment Software Association, the industry's top trade group. Male gamers between ages 10 and 25 represent a sliver of the market, only 15 percent, according to Newzoo, a games research firm.

Yet America's 190 million gamers, 48 percent of whom are women, still play in a harsh frontier. About 70 percent of female gamers said they played as male characters online in hopes of sidestepping sexual harassment, according to a study cited by "Hate Crimes in Cyberspace" author and law professor Danielle Keats Citron.

"It's just like playing outside when you're a teenager. It's still a jungle out there," said Peter Warman, the chief executive of Newzoo. Of the women who played as men, he said, "they wanted to be treated equal on the virtual battlefield."

But the average female gamer has played for 13 years, and many are increasingly dedicated. The number of girls and women playing those consoies more than five days a week has grown tenfold since 2011, to 13 million this year, Newzoo said.

"This is the underlying issue: The definition of a gamer is becoming much broader, and it's happening in front of our eyes," said P. J. McNealy, a games analyst and founder of Digital World Research. "It's opened up opportunities for everyone to have contact with gaming, even though they're not the stereotypical 17-year-old male gamer playing 'Call of Duty.'"

As games have expanded from consoles and computers to cellphones and social media, developers and publishers have found whole new niches for attracting a paying audience. "Kim Kardashian: Hollywood," a "red-carpet adventure" with a predominantly female audience, has made $51 million since launching in June and has become one of the highest-grossing apps on iPhone and Android phones.

Women have helped make gaming one of the country's fastest-growing entertainment moneymakers. Americans now spend more

> **About 70 percent of female gamers said they played as male characters online in hopes of sidestepping sexual harassment.**

on video games than at the movie theater. The best-selling game so far, "Grand Theft Auto V," sold faster than any entertainment good in history, notching $1 billion in sales—more than all but a handful of blockbuster films—in just three days.

"You play a game and . . . you get this little, private space where you get to be the master of your own universe, the star of your own movie, whatever that means to you," said Joost van Dreunen, of SuperData Research, a games-market intelligence firm. "That appeals equally to both boys and girls. They all just want to play."

Comparing Images

TIME ▸ 20 minutes

GROUPINGS ▸ Whole class, pairs, individuals

STANDARDS MET ▸ See pages 306–307.

WHEN TO USE ▸ This lesson is a way to include everyone, regardless of reading skill, in standards-based "close reading." Every kid can look at a picture, think, talk, and jot simple notes about it.

TEXT	SOURCE	TEXT TYPE
United States Seen from Space (Day and Night)	National Aeronautics and Space Administration (NASA)	Photographs

A powerful and inclusive way to introduce close reading is to have students study and write about provocative, complex *images* rather than text. When we begin with images, we keep all our students on board, including those learning English, those who are not strong readers, and those with IEPs. Additionally, students are willing to put in the work of looking more deeply, essentially rereading, when the text is a gripping photo or distinguished artwork.

In this lesson we pair two great images of our continent from space with questions that support kids' writing and discussion.

PREPARATION

1. From the book's website, grab the slide set containing the two full-color images, the viewing prompts, and the note-taking form. Make a copy of the form for each student unless you will have kids make their own from a blank piece of paper (see Step 1).

2. Establish pairs for the "turn and talks" at Steps 4 and 8.

3. Decide on a student scribe for Steps 5 and 9.

Steps & Teaching Language ▸

STEP 1 **Distribute note-taking forms.** Hand out the simple two-column form or have students divide a full-size piece of paper into two columns. Label the left column "Day" and the right column "Night."

STEP 2 **Preview the activity.** *In a minute I am going to project an image of the U.S. taken from a NASA satellite during the day. As you view the image, jot down anything you notice in the picture in the left column of your note-taking form. Just use words and short phrases to label what you are seeing. These are some things you might notice* (project the following list):

Some Things You Might Notice About the Daytime Satellite Image

• Things you notice about our country as seen from space

• Specific areas you can identify: states, cities, regions

• Physical features you recognize: bodies of water, mountains, vegetation, human populations

• Questions that come to mind

STEP 3 **Project the daytime image.** After kids have viewed the NASA image for a minute, help them get started with their jotting. Remind any talkers that this stage is a solo/silent activity. They'll get to discuss soon. Keep the image projected as kids write, but you can assist them by quietly reading aloud the suggested topics as you walk the room. Allow about two minutes.

STEP 4 **Kids turn and talk.** *Now, turn to your partner and take turns sharing some things you noticed about the U.S. as seen from space. Use your notes to help you. Take turns and share the time, about two minutes. Look for things you both noticed and things that were different.*

STEP 5 **Whole class shares and begins chart.** *Who had a partner who noticed something really interesting about the picture?* Have a student scribe ready to copy down the ideas shared. Get several pairs to volunteer before moving on. *Who noticed something different? Another pair? Who else?*

STEP 6 **Preview the second image.** *Next, I am going to project an image of the U.S. taken from a NASA satellite at night. As you view the image, jot down anything you notice in the picture in the right column of your note-taking form. Just use words and short phrases to label what you are seeing. Here are a few examples* (project the following list):

> ### Some Things You Might Notice About the Nighttime Satellite Image
>
> - Things you notice about our country seen from space
> - Specific areas you can identify: states, cities, regions
> - Physical features you recognize: bodies of water, mountains, vegetation, human populations
> - Any questions you have about the United States based on this picture
> - What this photo suggests about the use of energy, electricity, and lighting in our country

STEP 7 **Project the nighttime image.** Keep the image projected as kids write, but you can assist them by quietly reading aloud the suggested topics as you walk the room. Or toggle between the image and the list occasionally. Allow about two minutes.

STEP 8 **Kids turn and talk.** *Once again, take about two minutes to share with your partner the most interesting or important things you noticed.*

STEP 9 **Whole class shares and continues chart.** Enlist student scribe again. *Just as we did last time, let's get lots of pairs to tell us what they noticed. Who wants to go first? Thanks. Who had some different ideas?*

Now, let's look over our chart. What are the biggest ideas? Are some of the lingering questions things we might want to investigate further?

Longer writing projects—reflecting the key genres required by the national standards—can be built on the work students have already done in this lesson. As kids continue to explore the topics of our reading selections, we expect that they will bring fresh background knowledge, recent thinking, and genuine curiosity to the task. When you use the lesson above with your own content, you can also use the assignments below as models for extending that content into longer writing projects.

Narrative: *Put a sci-fi spin on the content*

Imagine you are a group of space aliens planning an invasion of the United States. You are looking at these two photos (which you intercepted from NASA), trying to figure out the best places to land and subdue the country. Write a scene in which your invasion team is planning the attack. Develop several characters and use dialogue in which they mention specific information from the two photographs that will factor into the invasion.

Informative/explanatory: *Consider the impact of this issue on the future*

Some cities in the United States have spread so widely that they are now called "megalopolises." Using the night sky map (along with a regular U.S. political map), identify five regions you think might be a megalopolis. Then, look these areas up in other sources, and write an essay on your choice:

1. Explain how this phenomenon of city "sprawl" came to be.

2. Share the distinctive benefits and problems of megalopolises.

3. Predict specific changes that lie ahead for large urban areas in the United States. *Research clue: Google "U.S. megalopolis."*

Argumentative/persuasive: *Support or argue against a published opinion*

Agree or disagree with the following quotation: "NASA's night sky photos show that we waste huge amounts of precious energy needlessly lighting up our country at night. We should take steps to return to the dark, starry sky that we humans were designed to live under." Support your position with specific evidence from your reading, study, and experience. *Research clue: Search "The Dark Side,"* New Yorker *article by David Owen.*

COMPARING IMAGES

DAY	NIGHT

United States seen from space (day)
Source: NASA

United States seen from space (night)
Source: NASA

Interview an Image

TEXT	AUTHOR	SOURCE	TEXT TYPE
Bibb Mill No. 1, 1909	Lewis Wickes Hine	National Archives	Photograph

Whether we like it or not, our students are becoming more and more visually oriented. The rise of Snapchat and Instagram is clear evidence. However, though kids are bombarded with images, how often do they really look at them and think about what they're seeing? And when it comes to content-area images in textbooks or trade books, students often skip them entirely because—in their minds—images are just page fillers that aren't important. Unfortunately, these readers are ignoring the very items that might make the text more accessible! Really slowing down to view a photograph teaches students that there is a wealth of information in an image if one just takes the time to look. This lesson offers viewers the opportunity to do just that. In addition, it demonstrates how one provocative image can spur interest in a topic, resulting in further student-led investigation.

PREPARATION

1. Download the image *Bibb Mill No. 1, 1909*, and determine how you will project it so that the entire class can study it together.
2. Decide how to pair students at Step 2.
3. Decide on a student scribe for Step 5.

TIME ▶ 30 minutes

GROUPINGS ▶ Whole class, pairs, individuals

STANDARDS MET ▶ See pages 306–307.

WHEN TO USE ▶ Most content areas require close visual reading in addition to text. This lesson teaches students how to slow down their viewing, notice details, and make inferences.

◀ **Steps** &
Teaching
Language

STEP 1 **Project the image.** *I'm going to project this image for about one minute. During this time I want you to look at it carefully and notice what you see, think, or wonder. Do not talk. Just study the image silently.*

STEP 2 **Partners share what they noticed.** *Turn to your partner and share what you noticed in this image. Remember to take turns talking. Try to remember the details/ideas that your partner suggested that you didn't notice on your own. Your goal is to see new things that you missed when you were observing individually. Also, as you discuss the image, think about what you wonder: What questions arise about these boys and their environment?* Allow pairs to talk for a couple of minutes. If you are comfortable, encourage pairs to get up and walk closer to the projection, pointing out specific details to their partners.

STEP 3 **Whole class shares.** *Who had a partner that saw or thought of something you didn't? Raise your hands.* Call on some partners to report out. *What questions did you begin to think about as you looked at this photo?* This discussion should be short; the focus should be on noticing photo details that others might have missed, and then questioning the photo.

STEP 4 **Pairs create interview questions.** *Based on your previous pair discussion and what you heard in our large-group share, make a list of questions you'd like to ask these boys. You might think of questions about their work, background, ages, lifestyle, etc. Imagine you are a newspaper reporter assigned to do a story on child labor in 1909. What would you want to ask in order to write an interesting story? Work to come up with ten or twelve questions. Be sure that each of you writes down all of the questions you and your partner brainstorm. Do not assign one partner to be the recorder; you each need your own copy of the questions.*

Give pairs three to five minutes of work time. As you monitor, encourage students to continue looking at the photograph and brainstorm additional questions. Also, require that both students write down the questions they pose. This note taking helps ensure that both students are contributing to the task versus letting one partner do all the work. Also, having the full list of questions will be helpful if you have the time for Step 6.

STEP 5 **Make a class list of the questions.** *Now we're going to make a master list of the questions we've thought of. I'm going to call on each pair to give us a question. If I call on you and all of your questions are taken, say pass, but then try to think of a question to add as you listen to the contributions of the other pairs. After the first round, I'll come back to you to see what you thought of. Oh, and all of you should be adding questions to your original lists. That's why we're writing this on the board.*

To keep you free to monitor the full classroom, ask for a volunteer or designate a student scribe. Remind the rest of the class that it's very hard to write quickly and publicly, so as long as they understand what the scribe is recording, there is no need to point out errors. After the question list is complete, be sure to take a photo of it with your cell phone before it gets erased!

You might get questions like these:

- Why does one child have shoes while the other child is barefoot?
- What is the minimum age for a kid to be employed?
- What are these kids doing?
- How dangerous is their job?
- Why would kids this young be working?
- If these were the jobs little kids had, what kind of jobs did adults have?
- How come kids aren't working in factories today?
- Were there any laws that controlled child labor back then?
- If one of these kids got injured on the job, what would happen to him?
- What other industries in the United States used to rely on child labor?
- Which countries today rely on child labor?

STEP 6 **Conduct mini-inquiries (optional).** Now (if you have the time and technology) these questions can become the basis of a "right here, right now" mini-inquiry. After eliminating or rephrasing any one-word-answer questions, let each pair pick one question to research. Offer ten minutes for kids to jump on devices and do a quick investigation. Reports could take the form of partners speaking to the class as if they were the subjects of the photo, or each pair could write a short, factually based narrative as if they were one of the child mill workers.

◀ ***Research Projects for Extended Writing***

Longer writing projects—reflecting the key genres required by the national standards—can be built on the work students have already done in this lesson. As kids continue to explore the topics of our reading selections, we expect that they will bring fresh background knowledge, recent thinking, and genuine curiosity to the task. When you use the lesson above with your own content, you can also use the assignments below as models for extending that content into longer writing projects.

Narrative: *Invent an interview*

Now that you have studied the two boys closely and thought about questions you'd ask about them and their work, make up an interview you conducted with them. Create a story of you sitting down with them after work (probably late in the day) and asking them some of the questions the class created. Create their answers based on everything you have learned and inferred from the picture.

Informative/explanatory: *Find parallels in today's world*

Is there still child labor in the United States? We certainly seem to have the right laws in place, but how good is the enforcement? Search "child labor in US," "human trafficking," and "migrant labor" and see what you find. Write a report in which you share any evidence of child labor still happening in the United States, list the industries where it is most prevalent, and educate readers on possible ways to stop this abuse.

Persuasive/argumentative: *Argue a related point that touches your own life directly*

While child labor has been outlawed (if not completely prevented) in the United States, it is still rampant in other countries, many of which make items for export to America. As you investigate, you will come across stories of terrible working conditions where workers, often including very young people, work long and dangerous hours to make gizmos for export. Some people have argued that Americans should stop buying products from companies or countries that operate this way. Others claim that while factory life is tough, it is raising millions of people out of abject poverty. Take and support a position: Should Americans actively boycott products that result from exploitative labor practices?

Bibb Mill No. 1, 1909: Macon, Georgia: Lewis Wickes Hine/National Archives, Archive Identifier 523148. Department of Commerce and Labor. Children's Bureau. 1912–1913.

Quotable Quotes

TEXT	SOURCE	TEXT TYPE
"Antibiotic Resistance: From the Farm to You"	Natural Resources Defense Council	Fact sheet

TIME ▸ 30 minutes

GROUPING ▸ Whole class, pairs, individuals

STANDARDS MET ▸ See pages 306–307.

 Chapter 12's Text Set

WHEN TO USE ▸ When you want to help kids zero in on what's important in a text, having them pick out short quotes worth repeating and sharing builds this reading skill.

If you aren't already on Twitter, you should probably check it out. And no, neither of us benefits in any personal way by mentioning this social media site. For teachers, it's a great way to connect professionally with other educators, post a question and crowdsource an answer, or just browse some hashtags. But one thing you'll quickly notice when you dive into tweet reading: it is the perfect medium for distributing a short quote or aphorism—something witty, something important, something to remember, something that warrants a retweet.

Our content-area reading is filled with quotable quotes. After all, we wouldn't give the kids something to read if it wasn't quotable, right? So this lesson encourages student readers to find a quote that stands out to them: something that's important, surprising, contradictory, or controversial. In other words, something tweet-worthy! When this lesson is done, your classroom walls will be festooned with pithy quotes about preventing antibiotic resistance.

PREPARATION

1. Duplicate the first page of "Antibiotic Resistance: From the Farm to You" for each student. (The second page, which contains all the source notes, is available online.)

2. Decide how to pair students for Step 1.

3. Download and be ready to project the list at Step 4. In the concluding steps of this lesson, pairs will need one or two large index cards or some strips of plain 8½" by 11" paper, cut in half lengthwise. Colored markers could add some flair, but pens will work too.

◄ Steps & Teaching Language

STEP 1 **Organize pairs and introduce the topic of antibiotic resistance.** *How many of you have ever needed to take an antibiotic? Sometimes doctors prescribe them when we have a bacterial infection versus a virus like the flu or a cold. Turn to your partner and share what you remember about your experiences with antibiotics.*

STEP 2 **Have a quick whole-class share.** *Raise your hand if you've ever taken an antibiotic.* Quick show of hands. *How did the antibiotic affect you?* Students might discuss side effects such as upset stomach or gastrointestinal distress, but more than a few should also mention that a strep throat or ear infection disappeared rather quickly.

Continue with this question. *Anybody ever know someone whose antibiotic prescription didn't work, and they had to try a different antibiotic, possibly several, before one worked?* Listen to some answers or be ready to tell your own failed antibiotic horror story since that's the reward of being an adult: just about all of us know someone personally who's had a run-in with a superbug or at least can relate a story we've read about.

Finish the introduction with this question: *Why do antibiotics that used to work well stop working? And how does this change affect us? This is the question we're going to think about as we read this short article.*

STEP 3 **Distribute the article and give directions.** First direct students to the three big statistic headings at the top of the page and read each one aloud. *From these statistics, it sure seems like antibiotics are getting weaker while bacteria are getting stronger. I wonder why that's happening.*

I'm going to give you a few minutes to read through the rest of this fact sheet and try to find some answers to this question. Write on the board or project: Why are bacteria getting stronger while antibiotics are getting weaker, and how is this affecting people? *When you find something that explains this phenomenon, underline it. However, try not to underline big chunks of text. Instead look for short, key phrases. And, when you mark something, stop and think for a moment. Be sure you can explain how it answers our question. Finally, aim for one underline per headed section, so you'll have four altogether.*

Now give students a few minutes to read individually and silently. Also, you've probably noticed that this is truly a complex text: small print, dense information. Therefore, before students read on their own, you might choose to read the piece aloud first as they follow along. Then monitor their underlining as they read the piece a second time individually.

STEP 4 **Pairs compare what they've underlined.** *Now turn to your partner and compare what you've underlined. However, instead of just putting your papers side by side and looking, I want you to do some real thinking by following these steps.* Write these steps on the board or project them as you explain.

Protocol for Sharing Quotes

1. Decide who's going to start.
2. Starter reads one of his or her underlined quotes aloud while the partner listens.
3. Listener explains how the quote answers the question: Why are bacteria getting stronger while antibiotics are getting weaker?
4. Quote starter adds additional thoughts.
5. Trade roles (quote starter and listener).
6. Continue switching roles and discussing quotes until I call time.

STEP 5 **Pairs share with the class.** *Who had a partner who found a good quote about antibiotic resistance? Who had a partner that found a really gross piece of information about antibiotic resistance?* Let students share some gems from the article, the funkier the better!

STEP 6 **Create a new quotable quote.** *Now turn back to your partner. Based on the underlined quotes you discussed as well as our class discussion, work with your partner to write a new quotable quote that would grab people's attention and make them aware of what needs to change so that antibiotics remain effective. A slogan that's a little gross is okay, but remember, we're still in school! Work it out on the back side of the handout. When you've got it, show it to me and I'll give you some different paper* (large index cards or paper strips) *to write your final "postable" draft.*

Monitor pairs. Help with wording when necessary. Point out some juicy details to encourage students if needed. Pass out cards/paper strips and markers to pairs ready to write their final drafts.

STEP 7 **Pairs share their quotable quotes.** Once quotes are ready for publication, have each pair stand up, read their quote, and then post it on a bulletin board or tape to a classroom wall. Then remember to invite your other students to read the posts, and possibly entertain the notion of becoming vegans!

◄ **Extension**

You might enjoy pointing out the numerous footnote numbers within the text. Lots of footnotes always gives the appearance of a well-researched document. However, sometimes careful citation sleuthing reveals sources that are rather dubious. Go ahead and project this document's Endnotes page but enlarge sections so that the four-point type is legible. Then have students study the sources and discuss their credibility.

◄ **Research Projects for Extended Writing**

Longer writing projects—reflecting the key genres required by the national standards—can be built on the work students have already done in this lesson. As kids continue to explore the topics of our reading selections, we expect that they will bring fresh background knowledge, recent thinking, and genuine curiosity to the task. When you use the lesson above with your own content, you can also use the assignments below as models for extending that content into longer writing projects.

Narrative: *Tell the story of a related personal experience*

In the lesson, we talked about illnesses we have had. Do you have an especially memorable illness or injury you could tell about? Many times, these events are pretty terrible at the time, but they leave us with stories we remember forever. Pick a time when you were sick or injured and tell about how you first became ill or hurt, what treatment you had, how you got better, and how you look back on it now. If you want to research a childhood illness you had, interview your parents about it.

Informative/explanatory: *Show how this content touches your community*

One of the main ways that antibiotic-resistant bacteria get into our bodies is at fast-food joints. Most of these companies buy their beef, chicken, pork, and turkey from farmers who routinely use antibiotic-enhanced feed so the animals grow heavier and reach maturity more quickly. Look into this issue and see what you can find. Compare the public pledges that different fast-food chains have made about reducing this risk, and also view the results when their food is studied by independent researchers: a few chains get A grades, while most get Fs. Write an article or infographic for your fellow students, sharing what you've learned about the fast-food chains in your community.

Persuasive/argumentative: *Find who's to blame*

If we use too many antibiotics in the United States, whose fault is it? Doctors who prescribe antibiotics for minor illnesses that would resolve themselves? Patients who impatiently demand a pill for every minor ache and pain? Drug companies that lure doctors into overprescribing their profitable medications? Dig into this controversy and develop your position: Who is most to blame? To put it another way, which group most needs to change its behavior and expectations: doctors, drug companies, or patients?

EVERY YEAR IN THE UNITED STATES:

2 MILLION PEOPLE
CONTRACT ANTIBIOTIC RESISTANT INFECTIONS.

23,000 PEOPLE
DIE AS A RESULT OF THE INFECTIONS.

$55 BILLION
LOST DUE TO EXCESS HOSPITAL COSTS AND LOST PRODUCTIVITY.

Antibiotic Resistance: From the Farm to You

Antibiotic resistance is one of our most serious health threats. Antibiotic use in both humans and animals contributes to that threat. Antibiotic-resistant bacteria from poultry and livestock production contribute to rising rates of antibiotic resistance in humans in a number of ways.

"Scientists around the world have provided strong evidence that antibiotic use in food-producing animals can harm public health."[1]
Centers for Disease Control and Prevention (CDC)

RESISTANT BACTERIA ON FOOD THREATEN OUR HEALTH

Scientists and governmental agencies routinely find antibiotic-resistant bacteria on animals at slaughter[2] and on raw meat[3] in grocery stores. The World Health Organization (WHO) and the CDC have implicated antibiotic use in food animals as a contributor to the emerging threat of antibiotic-resistant infections[4] and have deemed antibiotic-resistant infections from food pathogens a serious threat.[5] Preliminary research indicates that poultry may be contaminated with resistant bacteria that cause urinary tract infections.[6]

RESISTANT BACTERIA FROM ANIMAL FACILITIES SPREAD THROUGH AIR, WATER, AND SOIL

Resistant bacteria can travel via air[7] or water[8] and can wind up in the soil when manure is applied to crops,[9] allowing them to end up on fruits and vegetables.[10] Even insects[11] and rats[12] can carry resistant bacteria away from farms.

RESISTANT BACTERIA SPREAD TO AND THREATEN WORKERS AND THEIR COMMUNITIES

People who work in the meat industry are more likely to carry resistant bacteria on their bodies and into their communities.[13] In addition, they are more likely to get sick from bacterial infections than the general public,[14] putting them at higher risk from antibiotic-resistant bacteria.[15] Similarly, communities near livestock facilities or fields treated with livestock manure, are more likely to be exposed to and infected by Methicillin-resistant *Staphylococcus aureus* (MRSA), an antibiotic-resistant bacterium.[16]

RESISTANT BACTERIA CAN PASS ON RESISTANCE TRAITS TO OTHER BACTERIA

Resistant bacteria can pass their resistance genes onto other bacteria.[17] Some of these genes can confer resistance to other antibiotics that were not used on the animals.[18] Researchers have shown that resistance genes can be passed from bacteria in soil (including manure) to pathogenic bacteria in the community,[19] and that ingested resistant bacteria can share resistance genes with other bacteria inside the human gut.[20] More than ever scientists refer to a growing "reservoir" of antibiotic resistance in our communities and environment.[21]

For more information, please contact:

Carmen Cordova, Ph.D.
ccordova@nrdc.org
(415) 875-6100
switchboard.nrdc.org/blogs/ccordova

www.nrdc.org/policy
www.facebook.com/nrdc.org
www.twitter.com/nrdc

CHAPTER 5 WRITING BEFORE, DURING, AND AFTER READING

Once exposed to the fun of "short writing," students are ready to use it as an integral learning tool for reading. When they record their ideas before, during, and after reading, students increase their retention of important content-area information and can also see tangible evidence of how their thinking changed as a result of content study.

LESSON 10

Kickoff Write

TIME ▸ 15 minutes

GROUPINGS ▸ Whole class, pairs, individuals

STANDARDS MET ▸ See pages 306–307.

WHEN TO USE ▸ When you want to get kids immediately engaged, start off class with a quick write on your topic.

TEXT	AUTHOR	SOURCE	TEXT TYPE
"10 Things People Will Miss Most Without Electricity at Home"	Ken Jorgustin	www.modernsurvivalblog.com	Blog

This is the first of several lessons where we use short writing-to-learn activities to start, extend, and finish class periods during which kids encounter lots of content—doing science experiments, working math problems, examining primary source materials, watching instructional videos. Whatever the day's curricular agenda, we get more student buy-in (and more writing practice) when we use brief writing tasks along the way. These beginning, middle, and ending writings help engage kids in the subject matter, make them accountable for staying focused, and support lively, clarifying conversations with classmates.

For this lesson, we will use the topic of electricity as the content. But, as always, feel free to substitute a great short article that's closer to your subject matter.

> ### PREPARATION
>
> 1. Decide how pairs will be formed for Step 3.
> 2. Make copies of "10 Things People Will Miss Most Without Electricity at Home" for the class, to be distributed at Step 5.

Steps & Teaching Language ▸

STEP 1 **Introduce the lesson and list making.** *Good morning, guys* [or friends, students, scholars, eighth period—whatever you call your kid-dos]. *Today we are going to start a new unit and we are going to kick it off with some writing that I think you'll enjoy.*

Here's the scenario: Imagine that one day the electricity fails around here, including at your house, and it stays off for days or weeks. We know that we depend on all sorts of electric-powered devices—but the question is, which ones would you actually miss the most?

STEP 2 **Kids write individual lists.** *Everyone please grab* [some paper, a laptop, your tablet] *and make your own list, ranking the electrical devices you would miss most in the order of their importance to you. So this is kind of like making a list of the "Top Ten Electric Things I Could Not Live Without."*

Happy writing, everyone. I'll be around to help if you need me. In a couple of minutes, you'll get to compare your list with an author who has studied this topic.

While students compose their lists, you'll probably be busy answering questions. Kids may not realize which home appliances or systems use electricity (like central heating, for one thing). Remind them that they need to be number-ranking their items as well as listing them.

STEP 3 **Partners compare lists.** *OK, get with your buddy and compare your lists. In a minute we'll see what are some of your most cherished electrical appliances.*

STEP 4 **Whole class shares.** Invite pairs to share some of their most essential devices as well as, on second thought, the ones that maybe they could live without. Keep probing for different, fresh ideas. There are lots of defensible rankings of these tools of "modern" living.

STEP 5 **Read and annotate the blog list.** *Next we are going to read a top ten list from someone who has made a study of this topic. The author is a survivalist and "prepper," which is someone who worries that our society might suddenly collapse, and who is actively preparing for that eventuality. As far as losing electricity is concerned, people like Ken fear that a war, a terrorist attack, a computer hack, or a simple failure of our outdated power grid might cut off power at any time.*

You'll see that Mr. Jorgustin's list contains a lot of information and also a lot of his own opinions. He's talking about how a power shutdown might affect him—but what about you?

Read his list and annotate it. Use + and – codes to mark entries you agree or disagree with.

STEP 6 **Kids revise lists.** *Now make a final list of the items you and your family would miss most if there were a long-term power outage. You can keep your own ideas from your first list, add some of Jorgustin's ideas, move the rankings around, or throw things out. Write your final list in the same format as the author: rank and number each item, and jot a short explanation of why you would miss this electrical item.*

Give three or four minutes of writing time. If kids are still actively writing, extend the time.

STEP 7 **Whole class shares.** Invite kids to share their rankings and reasons one item at a time. *OK, let's see what people ranked as the number one electrical device they would miss at home. . . . Now, who ranked something else as number one? Another? What did you rank last and why? Who else bottom-ranked a different device? Who added something new to the list? Who took something off the list completely?*

STEP 8 **Collect writing.** Gather all lists and annotated articles. Flip through them to gauge engagement, monitor thinking, and spot possible future minilesson ideas.

Variation ▶

This is the full version of an activity that could be shorter. For the two-minute version, have kids read the blog list, then invite them to renumber the items in an order that better fits their own lives. In editing the original piece, they're not only showing their comprehension, they're considering how the text applies to their own lives.

Research Projects for Extended Writing ▶

Longer writing projects—reflecting the key genres required by the national standards—can be built on the work students have already done in this lesson. As kids continue to explore the topics of our reading selections, we expect that they will bring fresh background knowledge, recent thinking, and genuine curiosity to the task. When you use the lesson above with your own content, you can also use the assignments below as models for extending that content into longer writing projects.

Narrative: *Imagine yourself facing these conditions*

Most of us have experienced power outages a few times during our lives (or seen them in horror movies). Sometimes, the lights go out because of an obvious storm, and other times the darkness comes on suddenly and mysteriously. Write a story about the power going off and the problems that follow. Your characters and events can be based on an experience of your own, or you can completely make it up. Either way, try to work in what happens when some of the devices we have just been studying stop working. You could think of this as a public service brochure: "What could happen to your family in a power outage if you are unprepared."

Informative/explanatory: *Investigate a related cover-up*

One risk factor often cited by doomsday predictors is an EMP, which stands for electromagnetic pulse. In this scenario, an enemy force (or even an alien ship) generates a sudden electromagnetic surge that destroys our power system for good. But is this real or even possible? There is tons of information online about EMP and EMP weapons, and much more info seems to be classified by the U.S. Department of Defense. Try to come up with a one-page explanation of what EMPs really are and what they might—and might not—be capable of.

Persuasive/argumentative: *Take a side on a current controversy*

How safe is the American power grid? Survivalists and some infrastructure critics think that we are in urgent peril of going dark for good, perhaps even reverting to primitive, hunter-gatherer tribes. On the other hand, most experts think that prompt repairs and better security will keep the lights on. Research the claims and evidence on both sides, and take a position: How close are we to losing power for good? Should we really be prepping for disaster?

10 Things People Will Miss Most Without Electricity at Home

Ken Jorgustin, www.modernsurvivalblog.com

To go without electricity for a couple of hours is a bad enough experience for most, but imagine the horror if the power grid were to stay down for days, or even weeks! The resulting shock to today's modern family would not only be an emotional jolt, but could quickly turn into a life-threatening reality for those who have not prepared for such an occurrence.

Without electricity (even for a short time), these ten things will be high on the list for most people; the things that will be missed the most based on the modern lifestyle of today.

LIGHTS: The most basic of luxury that electricity provides is our light at night, and even during the day. How long will your batteries last in your flashlights? Then what? Do you have a plan for that?

CELL PHONES: Most of today's communications revolve around our cell phones/smartphones. They are the lifeblood of our social networks and the primary means of communicating with our family and friends. How will you cope without that ability to communicate?

INTERNET AND COMPUTER: This category should almost go without saying . . . it is probably the most relied upon resource in our modern lives today. It is crucial to our communications, our finances, our economy, and our entertainment. Many people won't know what to do without it.

TELEVISION: The average adult watches 4 hours of television a day while the typical child watches 6 hours TV per day including their video-games. It will be a shock to the (emotional) system without this distraction.

iPODS, STEREO, MUSIC: I mention this category due to the observation of so many people walking around with ear-buds attached to their iPod (and other) devices while listening to their music. There will be no recharging these little entertainment devices. Like television, music is a major part of the background (and foreground) entertainment for many people.

AIR CONDITIONING, FANS, AND HEAT: Many modern buildings will be completely uninhabitable without it, due to modern day HVAC design in large multi-story buildings. We have lived for many decades with the convenience of air-conditioning, and being without it will be a shock. Not sure how many could survive without it these days. If electricity were to fail in the winter, there will be even more grave consequences!

REFRIGERATOR AND FREEZER: This appliance is in its own category due to the important role it serves in keeping your food fresh longer and the ability to keep you supplied with fresh food for a time. Without electricity your frozen foods will be thawed within 24 hours and will need to be consumed immediately or tossed out. Then what?

KITCHEN APPLIANCES: How will you handle first thing in the morning without a cup of coffee brewed in your electric coffee pot? Think about ALL of your kitchen appliances that run on electricity and how you would manage without them. No dishwasher? No appliances to assist?

STOVE, OVEN, AND MICROWAVE: The majority of people rely on an electric stove, oven, or microwave for cooking their food. Let that sink in a moment . . .

CLOTHES WASHER AND DRYER: Keeping our clothes clean is something that we completely take for granted. It would not take long for this situation to become unhealthy.

Hopefully these thoughts have given you something to think about. If you are inclined to become better prepared for such things, spend a day keeping track of everything that you do and see how many of those activities involve the requirement of electricity. Then imagine life without it. Figure out ways to survive without it.

Writing Breaks

TEXT	AUTHOR	SOURCE	TEXT TYPE
"Job Survival in the Age of Robots and Intelligent Machines"	David Tuffley	www. theconversation.com	Feature story

TIME ▶ 30 minutes without extension

GROUPINGS ▶ Whole class, pairs, individuals

STANDARDS MET ▶ See pages 306–307.

WHEN TO USE ▶ If you notice students skimming text as if it were just one more Internet page to glance at briefly, use this lesson to get kids to slow down and begin monitoring their thinking as they read.

Have you noticed how the act of reading is changing? While students still expect to read novels word for word (or expect to read quiz prep summaries on Spark-Notes), they have grown to see nonfiction reading as a skim/scan activity, probably because that is the way reading often occurs on an Internet search. When you think about it, skim/scan is the perfect skill for searching, but once you find the right information, it's time to read carefully and really think about the text. Writing breaks encourage students to do just that because they demonstrate how one needs to slow down reading by stopping, thinking, and even jotting down some notes. These breaks also encourage students to respond to text in chunks, paying attention to the organization of the information and thinking about what's already been said as the article subtly moves forward.

Writing breaks are particularly useful when reading assignments become longer or more challenging. Breaks help students remember what they've read as well as monitor their comprehension. Breaks enable kids to notice how much or little they are interacting with the text. If a reader stops for a break, he or she either has some thoughts/connections/reactions about the information or, oops, has nothing due to a "reader space-out," a signal that it's time to do some rereading. However, breaks help students to detect a "space-out" sooner than later! Better to have to reread a few paragraphs or pages versus an entire chapter.

PREPARATION

1. Make a copy of the article, "Job Survival in the Age of Robots and Intelligent Machines," for each student.
2. For this lesson you will also need to project the article on a white/smart board or via a document camera, so that students can see your modeling as well as some of the notes taken by their classmates.
3. Determine how partners will be formed at Step 3.

Steps & Teaching Language ▶

STEP 1 Pass out the article and model your own thinking. *Today we're going to read an article about robots, but instead of reading the entire article in one shot, we're going to be taking some writing breaks. You'll see that, in this article, there are dots to note places where we can do this. Follow along as I read the first part of the article aloud and then take a "writing break" myself.*

Read the first section and stop. Then think out loud as you write. Of course, go ahead and share your own thoughts, but here are some responses that would fit:

- *I think the jobs that will be lost first are those that require a lot of repetition. We're already seeing this in factories.* (Thought)

- *I've seen a ton of movies that feature robots* (Star Trek, Star Wars, Blade Runner, The Terminator, Transformers) *but it seems lots of movie robots fall into just two categories: helpful or destructive.* (Connection)

- *If Australia thinks they will lose 500,000—half a million—existing jobs to robots, I wonder how many jobs the U.S. will lose?* (Question)

As you think out loud and write down your own thoughts, remind students to copy your ideas onto their own papers.

After sharing your thinking: *When I took a writing break, what did you notice?* Students may say:

- You stopped reading.
- You remembered something else you read or saw or experienced.
- You asked a question.
- Your writing was specific.
- You used your imagination.
- You wrote in complete sentences.

It is your call whether to ask students to write in complete sentences or "bullet points." Forgo complete sentences if it interferes with kids' ability to record their thinking, and they instead obsess about correct spelling and grammar.

STEP 2 **Students silently read the article and respond to the writing breaks.** *Does anyone have any questions? This article has three writing breaks left. Remember that a writing break only works if you take the break, so I do want you to interrupt your reading when you see the dot and notice your thoughts, connections, or questions. Stop, think about what you just read, and then respond with some specific notes just like I did. It's okay if you focus on only one of those three ways to think about the text, but it's not okay to read the whole article without doing any writing and then go back. Think of this stopping as a skill drill for expanding the way your brain works as you read!*

As students read, your main job is to monitor for those writing breaks. Do not hesitate to intervene if a student is not following the directions. If you find any students finished far before the others, scan their notes for the least detailed entry and then quietly confer by asking a few elaboration follow-up questions. When you move on, encourage those student to add all of those conversation details to their notes.

STEP 3 Students meet with partners and compare their thinking.
Now it's time to share your thinking with your partner. Rather than just putting your papers side by side, I want you to keep your notes hidden from your partner. Instead, as you stop to examine each writing break, I want you two to have a conversation about your reactions to the text. TALK to each other about your thoughts, because just reading them off the page prevents you from thinking of more ideas; plus, it's super boring! Work to see how your reactions to the text were similar and different. Use those differences to create some sustained discussion by asking questions that get your partner to explain his or her thinking further.

This time as you monitor, you'll want to look for conversation versus taking turns reading off the page. Do not hesitate to intervene if students are moving through too quickly or are failing to create some dynamic conversation. When necessary, jump in and do some mini-modeling of how to use notes to spur interesting conversation.

STEP 4 Pairs share their notes and conversations with the whole class. *Who had a partner with some interesting thoughts?* If students are not forthcoming, it's perfectly all right to call on some pairs. After all, you've already previewed much of what they wrote and discussed as you monitored during Step 3. Invite pairs to step up, place the pertinent writing break response under the document camera (if available), and report on some of their discussion highlights.

Extension ▶ Students can interview an article as well as an image (see Lesson 8). If your class posed many questions about the information brought up in this article, a quick mini-inquiry might be in order. Have pairs choose one question, allow ten minutes for research on available devices, and then give each pair about thirty seconds to orally share their results. Or if time is short, put a copy of the article on the board or wall, and have students neatly write down their questions and answers on big sticky notes that they then affix around the article.

Tip ▶ Writing breaks are easy to include even when an article isn't set up that way. Project the article and mark writing break locations with consecutive numbers. Your students can write numbers in the text margin, but use a journal page or piece of loose leaf paper to record their writing break thoughts. That way no one has to worry about writing in miniature or fitting everything into a too-narrow margin.

Research ▶ Projects for Extended Writing Longer writing projects—reflecting the key genres required by the national standards—can be built on the work students have already done in this lesson. As kids continue to explore the topics of our reading selections, we expect that they will bring fresh background knowledge, recent thinking, and genuine curiosity to the task. When you use the lesson above with your own content, you can also use the assignments below as models for extending that content into longer writing projects.

Narrative: *Invent a related character*

If you could design your own personal robot, what would it look and sound like? What functions would it perform? (Yeah, sure, homework, but what else?) Would it be a friend, a "task rabbit," or a status symbol? How would it interface with other electronic devices (phone, TV, computer)? In a short story, explain how your robot would affect your life, perhaps including a drawing of your robot, using labels to show its parts and captions to tell how it works.

Informative/explanatory: *Consider the impact of the content on your future*

Think of three careers you have considered entering someday. Write them down. Now reread the article section labeled "Virtual Environments." Here are more than twenty-five jobs that will still be in demand when robots have taken over other occupations. Compare your career interests with these prospects—which ones look most promising for you and why? Maybe they aren't even careers you've ever thought about. Choose three from the list in the article and write a report titled "My Top Three Post-Robot Jobs" that explains why each one attracts you.

Persuasive/argumentative: *Take a side on a related "insider" controversy*

Just about every historical, technical, scientific, and mathematical field has its own controversies, which the rest of us often know little about. These days, there is a raging debate in some scientific circles about "the Singularity"—the date when artificial (or robot) intelligence will finally surpass the human brain. Some very prominent businesspeople, scientists, and inventors are excited about this event and eager for its arrival. Others, just as famous, are encouraging us to prevent it and predicting doom if we don't. Look into these opposing positions, examine their evidence, and offer your own "take." Should we fear smarter-than-us machines, or accelerate their creation?

Job Survival in the Age of Robots and Intelligent Machines

How to protect your employment prospects as robots take over more jobs

David Tuffley, theconversation.com

In Australia, there are reports that up to half a million of existing jobs could be taken over by robotics or machines run by artificial intelligence.

So with smarter computers taking on more of the work that people currently do, we are left to wonder what jobs there might be left for us humans.

●

Could a robot do your job?

Almost any job that can be described as a "process" could be done by a computer, whether that computer is housed in a robot or embedded somewhere out of sight.

So if intelligent machines can take over many of the jobs of today, what can you do to ensure your job prospects in the future?

Some jobs will always be done by people. The reasons can vary greatly: economic, social, nostalgic or simply not practical for robots to do.

If we consider that many of the jobs of the future have not been invented yet, we cannot be sure what those future jobs will actually look like, though futurists are not shy of making predictions.

While we may not know what outward form these jobs will take, we can still make a catalogue of the generic skills that will be valued highly.

Thinking skills for future workers

In his book *Five Minds for the Future*, the Harvard professor Howard Gardner makes the case for cultivating a disciplined mind, being someone who can bring their attention to a laser-like focus and drill down to the essence of a subject, perceiving the simple truth of it.

Then taking this clarity to the next level by combining multiple ideas in new ways to create something interesting and perhaps useful. This is done by a synthesizing mind and the creative mind.

Gardner describes the respectful mind that values diversity in people and looks for positive ways to interact, thus overcoming the "us and them" instinct that still creates so much conflict in human affairs.

Building on this is the ethical mind, one who thinks about the big picture and how their personal needs can be brought into alignment with the greater good of the community. Skills for a globally connected world.

●

Mastering the new media

The future will see a host of new technology for creating and communicating content. In-demand workers will be able to critically assess this content and find ways to communicate it to good effect. Communication skills have always been important and will remain so.

Knowing how to deal with large data sets will be a handy skill: finding ways to make sense of the data and turn it into useful information. This could involve devising new, multi-disciplinary and perhaps unconventional approaches to the challenges.

Managing the information

We already filter a deluge of information every day. Our grandparents were lucky, they had to deal with a lot less. People will need to be even better at managing the cognitive load; they will have the thinking skills to filter the deluge and find optimum solutions to problems.

When good collaboration tools exist for virtual project teams, there are few limits to what can be achieved. More projects will be done by such teams because the technology that supports them is getting better every year. It allows the right people, with the right skills at the right price to be employed, regardless of where they live. So it will be the people with the right virtual team skills who will be in high demand.

Virtual environments

Speaking of the virtual, Procedural Architects will be at a premium. These are people who can design virtual environments and experiences that allow people to get things done and perhaps have some fun. This is what the minds behind Google, YouTube, Facebook, Amazon, Wikipedia, Twitter, eBay, LinkedIn, Pinterest, WordPress, and MSN have done.

All of this leads us to the question: what actual jobs are likely to be in demand? Employment specialists compile lists of what they think will be in demand, based on trends. These are some of the jobs that appear on multiple lists.

The IT sector is likely to need: information security analysts, big data analysts, artificial intelligence and robotics specialists, applications developers for mobile devices, web developers, database administrators, business intelligence analysts, gamification designers, business/systems analysts, and ethicists.

In other disciplines, there will be a need for: engineers of all kinds, accountants, lawyers, financial advisers, project managers, specialist doctors, nurses, pharmacists, physical therapists, veterinarians, psychologists, health services managers, schoolteachers, market research analysts, sales reps, and construction workers (particularly bricklayers and carpenters).

Both lists are not exhaustive.

On the downside, occupations likely to shrink in demand include: agricultural workers, postal service workers, sewing machine operators, switchboard operators, data entry clerks, and word processor typists.

●

The bottom line

To position yourself favorably for the jobs of the future, become someone who can look at problems in unorthodox ways, seeing different angles and finding workable solutions.

Be a multi-disciplinary, insatiably curious person who knows how to use the tools to model ideas and create prototypes. Possessed of an open mind and few fixed ideas about how things should be done, you nonetheless have a strong conscience and can operate outside of your comfort zone to achieve win-win outcomes. You are known for your integrity and resilience.

All of these qualities can be cultivated or perhaps rediscovered, since children often exhibit them in abundance. They have always been the way for creative, high-achieving people and they are still the way today and into the future.

In the brave new world of the coming age of intelligent machines, it is these essentially human qualities that will be more important than ever. Some things will never change because human nature is what it is.

●

Finding the Takeaway

TEXT	AUTHOR	SOURCE	TEXT TYPE
"How Much Water Do You Waste?"	Anne Leigh	WrapUp Media	News/quiz

TIME ▶ 20 minutes

GROUPING ▶ Whole class, pairs, individuals

STANDARDS MET ▶ See pages 306–307.

WHEN TO USE ▶ These quick writes help students to synthesize their subject matter "takeaways." Once students have learned how to write them, save a couple of minutes at the end of class periods for students to do these final quick writes.

Any author always hopes that the reader leaves with something, hopefully something important. Would Dickens' *A Tale of Two Cities* have had the same lasting impact without this phrase: "It was the best of times, it was the worst of times . . ."? And how about Patrick Henry's declaration: "Give me liberty or give me death"? Yes, authors want readers to carry a morsel of their text with them, a sentence or phrase that will keep them thinking long after they've finished reading the full text.

"Finding the Takeaway" asks students to read a short piece of text and then think about what they learned and what others should know. But, instead of just copying down something from the text, students have to write an original "takeaway" that grabs the reader and informs him as well. Not only is this an effective—and quick—comprehension assessment, it also is a great way to conclude a lecture, film, or even a student speech.

PREPARATION

1. Decide how to form pairs at Step 1.
2. Make a copy of the article "How Much Water Do You Waste?" for each student.
3. Have a supply of 3x5 sticky notes (enough for one per student).

STEP 1 **Introduce the concept of water usage.** *I bet everyone in this room has used water in at least a dozen different ways in the past twenty-four hours. Turn to your partner and talk about all of the activities you and your families participated in that required water.*

Give students a minute to talk and then quickly call on each pair to offer up an activity no one has yet mentioned.

STEP 2 **Pass out the article for students to read.** *When you stop to think about how much we depend on water for so many different activities, it's amazing that we just sort of take it for granted. Believe it or not, there are lots of ways that we waste water as well. Take a minute to read through this article silently and try to find one especially important piece of information that is worth remembering and even passing on to others.*

◀ **Steps & Teaching Language**

Give students a few minutes to read. If you run across any students who finish ahead of the pack, encourage them to revisit the article in order to better remember the details.

STEP 3 **Pass out sticky notes and explain directions.** *Okay, turn the article over and let's see what you remember. On your sticky, write down something you think others should know about water waste. If you have several ideas, pick the one that you think is most important, something that might give others pause for thought or encourage them to change something in the way they use water. These are your takeaways.*

Monitor the room as you encourage students to work from memory. Explain that it is very valuable to put key ideas into their own words—it requires them to synthesize the ideas they're reading. Also, by working from memory, they are more likely to jot down something big and important versus a startling, but ultimately less important statistic.

STEP 4 **Pairs compare stickies and then share with the class.** *Turn to your partner for a quick pair share. How similar or different are your takeaways? Who had a partner that wrote something similar to you?* Hear a few of the responses. *Who had a partner with something different?* Call on some of these pairs as well.

After concluding the discussion, post all of the water-use stickies on the wall or board and encourage students to share what they've learned about water waste with those beyond the classroom.

Research Projects for Extended Writing ▶ Longer writing projects—reflecting the key genres required by the national standards—can be built on the work students have already done in this lesson. As kids continue to explore the topics of our reading selections, we expect that they will bring fresh background knowledge, recent thinking, and genuine curiosity to the task. When you use the lesson above with your own content, you can also use the assignments below as models for extending that content into longer writing projects.

Narrative: *Put yourself in a related situation*

Reading the article, we were reminded of all the ways we depend on water every day. Using all that information, write a story titled "The Day the Water Stopped." Imagine waking up one morning and discovering that all the running water in your house has stopped. Describe what happens as you discover each missing water device. Tell how you'd cope. How would life have to change if the water never came back on? Of course, millions of people around the world have never had running water in their homes, so our lives might come to resemble theirs. You could study how they live to help you write your scenario.

Informative/explanatory: *Explain an essential service in your community*

To help other people in your community understand where their water comes from, write an explanation of the path taken by the water that comes out of the faucets in your community or school. Go and look at the infrastructure if you can. How is the water captured, stored, treated, distributed, and paid for? How stable or reliable is this resource? Are there any threats to the water supply in your area? In most places, there is a government water department (city, county, or regional) whose website you can browse for background information. A phone interview with a water official can also yield information that you might not have thought to ask about.

Persuasive/argumentative: *Consider a related regional controversy*

Coauthor Harvey lives in the high desert of New Mexico, amid a catastrophic long-term drought that also affects Arizona, Texas, California, and Nevada. Nancy lives in Chicago, beside the largest source of fresh water in North America—the Great Lakes. Some people in Harvey's arid Southwest want to pipe water from Lake Michigan and Lake Superior, more than a thousand miles away, to solve their drought. Do the southwestern states have any right to ask this? Dig into this topic and find what arguments are being made by politicians, scientists, environmental groups, and others—and then take your position. Under what terms, if any, should Midwest water supplies be shared with drier regions of the United States?

How Much Water Do You Waste?

Anne Leigh, WrapUp Media

On average, Americans waste about a trillion gallons of water every year. How much is that?

- **Enough to fill 24 billion bathtubs**

- **Enough to fill 40 million swimming pools**

- **Enough to fill the Rose Bowl stadium in Pasadena, California, 12,000 times**

- **Enough to meet the yearly water needs of over 11 million households**

Though activities like a long shower or a running faucet while brushing one's teeth do waste water, much of our water waste goes unnoticed.

A faucet that drips only once a minute will waste 34 gallons in a year. That doesn't sound like that much, but think about how many homes have at least one leaky faucet that drips five or more times a minute—34 gallons quickly turns into millions of gallons of wasted water.

Is there a running toilet in your own home or a friend's? That toilet could waste between 1,000 and 4,000 gallons of water per day!

Now start to think about all the other places in your house that might harbor a leak: garden hose, water pipe, dishwasher, washing machine, or swimming pool.

What's to be done? Start by noticing leaks and taking steps to fix them. Most leaky faucets can be repaired by replacing a few worn parts. The same can be said for leaky toilets. Not handy? Then watch some home repair videos on YouTube or hire a plumber. Even the initial expense of a plumber will be outweighed by the costs of the leaks. A running toilet can easily cost $14 per day, which adds up to $420 a month, or $5,040 in a year!

Another way to start conserving water is to capture or reuse it. Many people already harvest rainwater for their gardens, and the equipment needed is relatively low tech and affordable.

More elaborate systems can even capture wastewater for reuse. Did you know that all of your wastewater is not the same? The water flushed from your toilet is called blackwater; it is highly contaminated and must be processed at a sewage treatment facility. However, two-thirds of household water use falls into the category of greywater. This is the water that drains from your dishwasher, washing machine, or shower. It is far less contaminated and can be reused for watering the lawn or flushing the toilet. Though installing a plumbing system that separates and stores greywater for repeated use is more expensive, imagine if you could reuse two-thirds of your water? The system might pay for itself over several years. Plus, you would be doing your part to conserve water, a truly precious resource.

Flip the Card

TIME ▶ 20 minutes

GROUP SEQUENCE ▶ Whole class, pairs, individuals

STANDARDS MET ▶ See pages 306–307.

WHEN TO USE ▶ A good reader always thinks about a text topic *before* reading in order to access useful background knowledge. "Flip the card" teaches kids how to do this while also enabling them to compare changes in their thinking after reading.

TEXT	AUTHOR	SOURCE	TEXT TYPE
"What Can a Robot Bellhop Do That a Human Can't?"	Walter Frick	*Harvard Business Review*	Interview

The most important resource any student brings to a text is background knowledge. Anytime kids start reading, their first inclination should always be to ask themselves, "What do I know about this topic? Have I heard of it before? Where? Have I read something about it or seen a movie?" Unfortunately, it is not unusual for students to just barrel into a text without taking that first step or even reading the title! Of course, if they do have sufficient background knowledge, they will comprehend the text. On the other hand, if they actively worked to connect prior knowledge with new knowledge, they would remember even more. Flip the card helps to nudge students in their thinking with just a little information before reading, coupled with a quick reflection on what they've learned.

> ### PREPARATION
>
> 1. Make a copy of "What Can a Robot Bellhop Do That a Human Can't?" for each student.
> 2. You will also need one 3×5 index card for each student.
> 3. Decide how you will form pairs for Step 2.

Steps & Teaching Language ▶

STEP 1 **Pass out the index cards and give writing directions.** *Today we're going to read an article about robots doing a job that used to be done by humans. But before we read the article, I want you to think for a minute about what you already know about robots. Your background knowledge might be from other reading, television, movies, or personal experience. I'm going to give you a minute or two to jot some notes on just one side of the index card. See how much you can think of and try to keep writing until I call time. Remember to just use one side of the card; we're saving the second side for something else later.*

As students write, monitor the room. Do your best to read over shoulders. That way you can find some interesting ideas that should be shared with the rest of the class.

STEP 2 **Partners compare notes and quickly share with the whole class.** *Looks like everyone has a lot written on their cards. Go ahead and turn to your partner. Each take a turn talking about what you wrote down. Keep a mental tally of ideas you had in common as well as where you diverged.*

As students compare cards, monitor and listen in on conversations.

We're just about ready to read the article, but first let's hear from a few pairs. Who had a partner with some interesting ideas or knowledge about robots? Usually, students are more than willing to volunteer their partners for a little sharing, but if the kids are reticent, you already have a few pairs to call on based on your diligent eavesdropping!

STEP 3 **Pass out the article and explain reading directions.** *Grab your article and read it silently on your own. Be on the lookout for details that confirm ideas you previously had, but also look for details that teach you something new or show that you might have been initially mistaken about something. You can mark on the text if you want, but the main thing is to just pay attention to the information and your thinking on the topic.*

Students will be thrilled that they don't have to do any annotation. The monitoring goal now is to keep students reading and nudge those who have finished early to reread and see if they notice something new. When most students have finished (usually noticeable when there's an uptick in off-task conversation), move on to the next step.

STEP 4 **Explain postreading directions.** *Looks like everyone has finished reading, so grab those cards again. First, read what you wrote down a few minutes ago. Then flip your card over to its blank side. On the side we've been saving, I want you to write down your new thoughts about robots taking human jobs. Just like before, your goal is to fill that side of the card. If you run out of ideas, it's perfectly okay to go back to the article for a detail you can riff on. If you fill your card before I call time, reread it so that you can make sure it makes sense to you.*

STEP 5 **Partners compare notes.** *Go ahead and get back with your partner and share what you wrote on the "card flip." To make it more interesting and conversational, try to talk about what you wrote versus just reading it verbatim. And just like the last time, listen to your partner's ideas and notice where your thinking is similar and where you two differ. Part of the fun of talking with someone else about a text is when the other person notices or thinks of something that completely passed you by!*

Remember to keep eavesdropping as you monitor so that you have a few pairs in mind to call on just in case the upcoming class share gets off to a slow start.

STEP 6 **Whole class shares.** *Who had a partner with an interesting idea related to robots taking human jobs?*

As you finish up sharing, the class will probably notice that some kids view the advent of robots optimistically while others view their increasing use as a threat to mankind.

Research Projects for Extended Writing ▶

Longer writing projects—reflecting the key genres required by the national standards—can be built on the work students have already done in this lesson. As kids continue to explore the topics of our reading selections, we expect that they will bring fresh background knowledge, recent thinking, and genuine curiosity to the task. When you use the lesson above with your own content, you can also use the assignments below as models for extending that content into longer writing projects.

Narrative: *Envision a related disaster*

What could happen if the Botlr goes off its programming? Write a short story where a hotel guest requests some service from the robotic bellhop and things go terribly, terribly wrong. You could create this story in either a comedy or a horror framework. Try to make the Botlr's breakdown relate to specific tasks it is designed to perform.

Informative/explanatory: *Trace the portrayal of an issue in entertainment media*

A recent World Bank report reminds us that "robots have been a part of our mythology for thousands of years, the emphasis alternating between their positive transformative power over human society and acting as agents of great destruction. Our image of robots has been shaped to a large extent by Hollywood and literature." In an essay, explore our society's varying attitudes toward the "robot revolution." You might hunt up some school-appropriate robot movie/TV show trailers to view and compare or check box office results to see which robot tales make the biggest bucks.

Persuasive/argumentative: *Consider the downside*

In the article, nobody loses their job when a robot joins the team. But not all experts are predicting such a rosy outcome. There are sharply conflicting prognostications about whether robots (and other forms of artificial intelligence) will actually steal jobs from Americans, and if so, how many and how soon. Some economists foresee big and rapid job losses, while others predict minor, longer-term impacts that we'll have plenty of time to prepare for. Look at the evidence and make your best prediction: How much will robotics eat away at U.S. jobs, and how fast? *Research clue: Search for "jobless future" and "robots and employment."*

What Can a Robot Bellhop Do That a Human Can't?

By Walter Frick, *Harvard Business Review*

Years ago, I worked briefly as a hotel bellhop, greeting guests, bringing luggage up to their rooms, and helping them haul it back down again when they checked out. It was social and dexterous work—hoisting skis, snowboards, bags of all sizes; navigating narrow hallways; making small talk and angling for a tip. In other words, the kind of thing that is supposedly hard to automate.

So I was intrigued to read last week about a robotic "butler" being tested at Starwood Hotels' Aloft line, at its Cupertino location. The "Botlr" can deliver toothbrushes, razors, and similar items to guests' rooms, replacing the need for human staff to do so. I reached out to Aloft, and spoke with Brian McGuinness, Aloft's global brand leader, to hear about the motivation behind the pilot.

Tell me about the origin of the idea to use a robot in the hotel.

Something like five years ago we created the Aloft brand to appeal to the tech-savvy, the early adopters, the next-generation traveler. One of our key locations is Cupertino, so, essentially on the Apple campus. And part of our facility there is testing next-generation technology. And Savioke, which is a robotics company, was reading about us and our push for technology around what the future of hotels looks like. They contacted us, and said, "We're working on a robot, would you be interested?" And we said, "Absolutely."

What will the Botlr be doing—and how will it know where it's going?

With our help, [Savioke has] mapped the hotel. The robot is essentially going from the front desk, navigating through the lobby, onto the elevator—it actually has a two-way communication with the elevator system. So, calling the elevator, the elevator [informs the Botlr that] it has arrived and the door is open. The Botlr is boarding the car, going up to let's say, the fourth floor. The elevator says, "You are now on the fourth floor, the doors are now open," the Botlr exits, goes to the room. Because of the mapping technology, it calls the guest room and says, "I'm out here, I have your delivery." [The] customer opens the door, there's a steel container or compartment, the lid pops open, the customer retrieves their item. The lid actually closes on its own, they get finished, thank you very much, and the Botlr returns and navigates back to the front desk. So, that's where we are today. It has done many runs to guest rooms from the front desk and back.

What's been the reaction from the staff?

It's a relief. This isn't going to replace associates or our talent. We don't have doormen or bellhops. Just the front desk agent. Essentially, this is doing the tasks that they would have to leave the front desk and run upstairs [for]. Sending the Botlr on that journey simply means that they're at the front desk serving a customer in a better way. You all have seen those clocks in windows or at the desks that say I'll be back in five minutes. We're essentially negating the issue. And quite frankly, it's better work. They're working more closely with our customers from a personalization perspective of the guests' stay.

Many traditional note-taking strategies are boring for kids, ineffective for remembering content, and energy-draining for everyone. This chapter offers five alternative ways for kids to track what they are learning by writing about ideas immediately as they encounter them.

Alphabox Jigsaw

TIME ▶ 40 minutes

GROUPINGS ▶ Whole class, pairs, individuals

STANDARDS MET ▶ See pages 306–307.

WHEN TO USE ▶ If your kids' note-taking efforts result in copying text word for word, alphaboxes—which demand brevity—will break them of the habit. Readers can record only key words to help them remember the important details connected with each alphabox entry.

TEXT	AUTHOR	SOURCE	TEXT TYPE
"People and Dogs: A Genetic Love Story" (parts 1 and 2)	Virginia Hughes	*National Geographic*	Feature story

When we talk about comprehension, we're really thinking about two things: how well we understand what we're reading *and* how well we remember it later. While text annotation is a very important way to accomplish both of these comprehension tasks, students often balk at having to do more than underline or possibly code important or interesting information. Luckily, the alphabox note-taking form is a way to get students to reread their underlining and distill it into key words or *very short* (three-word maximum) phrases that will serve as a summary tool and memory trigger for revisiting the information later.

As this lesson will hopefully show you, there is something almost magical about this way of taking notes—by jotting single words, arranged by their first letter. If you think about it, this is an arbitrary, not categorical order, and yet kids generally love doing it, and it spurs memory strongly. Big thanks to Linda Hoyt and her nationwide crew of alphaboxers for inspiring this lesson.

> ### PREPARATION
>
> 1. Duplicate the two-page article "People and Dogs: A Genetic Love Story" so that half of your students will get the first page and half will get the second page.
> 2. Duplicate the alphabox handout, one per student.
> 3. Prepare the model alphabox for projection in Step 3.
> 4. Read (or reread) "How Much Water Do You Waste?" (page 84), paying special attention to the ideas and terms on the model alphabox.
> 5. If you like, download some projectable photos of domesticated dogs, wild African painted dogs, and wolves that you can use in introducing the article.
> 6. Decide how to pair students in Step 6.

STEP 1 **Introduce the topic.** If you've chosen to project some photos, do this as you orally introduce the topic. *Some researchers think that dogs might have been companions to humans for 33,000 years. Though it is established that dogs evolved from wolves, how that evolution occurred is still being investigated. The article you're about to read will discuss this.*

STEP 2 **Pass out the article halves.** *Rather than having you read the entire article, I have split it in two, so you and your partner will each have to read only half of it! Don't worry, even if you have the second half, it will still make sense. But, since your partner will depend on you to find out what is in the other part, you're going to have to pay close attention. So as you read, be sure to underline the interesting and important information you run across. Any questions? Before we read, double check with your partner to make sure each of you has a different half.*

As you monitor, read over shoulders and quickly move in on students who appear to be underlining everything. Coach these students individually or, if you find that many students are making the same mistake, call a "teacher time out" for an underlining reset announcement: *I can see that you're working really hard on this, and that's great. I just wanted to remind you that you don't have to capture* everything *in your underlining—just the most important points. Remember, all you need to underline are the most important/interesting phrases, not entire sentences. When you underline everything, it's like you've underlined nothing at all.*

STEP 3 **Introduce alphaboxes.** *Now you have your key ideas underlined. But, if you were looking for a way to see those key ideas easily or if you were planning to add more information from another source, it would be pretty difficult to have to scan this article over and over again to remember the important points. Instead, you can organize your notes with alphaboxes, a tool that lets you see just the important ideas from the article.*

Project an empty alphabox and explain: *To complete this alphabox, you'll need to go back and reread the underlines. After you reread an underline, think: What are the key words that summarize it? Then write those words in the appropriate alphabox square. Alphaboxes give you a place to record important terms alphabetically. You only have to use the boxes that you need.*

Project the filled-in alphabox sample. *Here's a sample of an alphabox that includes the important ideas from an article called "How Much Water Do You Waste?" See how there are only a few terms on it, and how some of the boxes don't have anything written in them? The point of an alphabox is to help you remember the important stuff in a way you can reference easily, not to fill in a lot of boxes.*

STEP 4   **Let students work on their alphaboxes.** Pass out an alphabox sheet to each student. *Now it's your turn! Take a look at what you've underlined in the article, and use the alphabox sheet to record the important terms and ideas.* Look over shoulders as students work, reminding students that only one to three words can label a piece of article information. The goal is for those words to trigger memory, so that students can talk about the information without having to return to the original article. If any students finish super early, encourage them to reread and add to the alphabox.

In subsequent use of alphaboxes, this step of reading and underlining first can be skipped as long as students understand that the goal of alphaboxes is to telegraphically capture entire ideas in one or two memory-triggering words, versus skimming an article and jotting down important-looking words.

STEP 5   **Model alphabox interviewing.** *Because this is our first time using alphaboxes, let's try an alphabox interview together so we can see how it works.* Project the filled-in sample alphabox. *Here's my alphabox from the other article again. Take a moment to jot down two or three ideas from my notes that are the most interesting to you.* Give the students a minute to do this. *Now, let's try this out: interview me to find out more about the topics you've listed.* Let students take turns asking you questions. Remind them to ask follow-ups if they don't fully understand your responses. Also, prompt them to notice that you have your back to the projection and you are working without the original article. Good alphabox note taking enables the researcher to remember a lot of the information with minimal notes.

STEP 6   **Pairs meet and discuss alphaboxes.** *Now let's see what you remember from your reading. Get together with your partner, trade alphaboxes, and look over your partner's sheet. Which words or phrases are you most curious about? Pick out four or five and put stars by them.*

Here's your chance to find out what was in the other half of the article about dogs. Raise your hand if you had the first page of the article. You're going to get interviewed first. Interviewers, base your interview questions on the words you starred on your partner's alphabox. Your job is to get them to explain the information without *looking back at the article.*

I'm going to give you a couple of minutes for this interview and then we'll switch. If you cover all of your starred words and I haven't called time, just continue the interview with some other alphabox words on your partner's sheet. Any questions?

Monitor for following the directions and working from memory versus returning to the original article. After a couple of minutes, call time and tell partners to switch roles.

Pairs share with whole class. *What were some interesting things you found out about the evolution of dogs?* Be sure to call on a few students who read each part.

You might also like to engage the class in a short discussion about the process. *How did the alphaboxes work for you? Did you remember the information when your partner interviewed you, or did you feel like you needed to go back and look at the article? How could you change your initial reading and underlining of your alphabox notes so that you remember more next time?*

We have mentioned mini-inquiry extensions throughout the book. Alphaboxes are a wonderful note-taking tool for all these investigations. While students enjoy the brevity of the note taking, this same concision forces them to think about the information and to use—for the most part—single words to summarize key pieces of information. Also, the alphaboxes provide individual accountability since each student creates one and then is further responsible for being able to articulately discuss her topic with others using only the alphabox for reference.

◀ ***Shoptalk***

Longer writing projects—reflecting the key genres required by the national standards—can be built on the work students have already done in this lesson. As kids continue to explore the topics of our reading selections, we expect that they will bring fresh background knowledge, recent thinking, and genuine curiosity to the task. When you use the lesson above with your own content, you can also use the assignments below as models for extending that content into longer writing projects.

◀ ***Research Projects for Extended Writing***

Narrative: *Write from another's perspective*

Most communities have an animal shelter or pound where lost or abandoned dogs are kept, and (we hope) claimed by new owners. Check the web for animal adoption resources (or an animal control officer) in your area and identify someone there who would do a phone or in-person interview with you. Then prepare a list of questions you would like to find out about. Some other kids have asked: "Why do some people abandon their dogs?" "What kind of dogs are most likely to be in the pound?" "Which ones get adopted soonest?" "Are there types of dogs nobody wants?" Make your own questions about whatever really interests you. After your interview, write up several of the most interesting or surprising things you learned. Use your research to write a narrative from the perspective of an abandoned dog in a shelter.

Informative/explanatory: *Share useful information with a specific audience*

While most pet dogs have been well domesticated, some breeds are still prone to sudden violence. Every year in the United States, there are 10 million dog bites and about sixty people are killed by dogs. Do some research into dangerous dogs and investigate which breeds most commonly attack humans. Then, write a handout or blog post about what can be done by owners to protect family, friends, and neighbors from dogs that bite. *Research clue: "Dogs bite" and "pit bull lovers."*

Persuasive/argumentative: *Defend a theory*

As our article suggests, there are several theories of how humans and dogs bonded, perhaps as long as thirty thousand years ago. Dig further into this debate and examine the several different theories. Then write a defense of what you think is the best-supported scenario. If you like, you can write this as a debate between scientists holding different views, being sure to have them quote the strongest research or expert opinion.

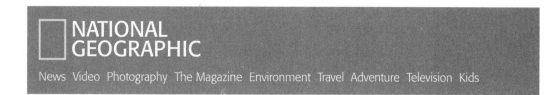

People and Dogs: A Genetic Love Story (*Part 1*)

A Blog by Virginia Hughes

Here's a possibly true story about the first friendly dog. It's dusk on a human settlement some ten thousand years ago. After a long day of farming, a family gathers around a campfire. Suddenly they hear rustling coming from the shadows. They turn around and see the glowing eyes of a wolf.

The people are surprised, maybe, but not scared. For many years they've noticed an odd group of wolves loitering just outside the village, rummaging up food scraps from the dump pile. The animals have never caused any harm and keep to themselves. But this is the first time a wolf has dared to come so close. It slowly approaches the fire, sits down, and cocks its head. Somebody tosses out a bit of bread.

As a recent dog owner, I love this story: Dogs are the wolves that mooched. They needed us, approached us, and ultimately wooed us into being best friends forever. This is a popular scientific theory—the 'scavenger hypothesis'—of how dogs came to be. But it's not the only one, not by a long shot.

Treats, do you have treats?!

Another theory says that people went out into the woods and deliberately trapped wolf pups, with the goal of training them to be sentinels or hunters. Still other scholars say the co-evolution of wolves and humans was mutually beneficial, with humans learning to hunt by watching wolves. "There are as many specific scenarios as there are people working in this field. We're looking back at such a long time ago, it's a matter of speculation," says Bob Wayne, professor of evolutionary biology at the University of California, Los Angeles.

Most genetic evidence says that dogs emerged in the Neolithic period, just as humans were transitioning from a hunter-gatherer lifestyle to one of agricultural settlements. But some dog fossils are much older, dating as far back as 33,000 years ago. Where canine domestication happened is also up for grabs. It could have been in the Middle East, China, Siberia or several places at once.

Erik Axelsson and colleagues at Uppsala University in Sweden tried to learn more about the evolution of canines by comparing the genetic sequences of modern-day dogs and wolves. They've found that dogs show distinct differences from wolves in genes involved in two key functions: starch digestion and brain development. Brain development genes are interesting because of the well-known behavioral differences between dogs and wolves—namely that as wolves mature they become aggressive while dogs don't.

People and Dogs: A Genetic Love Story (*Part 2*)

A Blog by Virginia Hughes

"Wolves and dogs are actually quite similar when they're very young: They both do the same playful behavior, run around in circles, and generally look cute. Little wolf puppies will even bark like a dog," says Nicholas Dodman, a professor in the veterinary school at Tufts University. "But suddenly the wolf grows up and becomes aloof and lean and suspicious."

Many animals seem to take on a more juvenile state as they are domesticated, getting bigger eyes, smaller faces and less aggressive demeanors. "One common way of achieving a domesticated form of a species might be to slow down the development of the animal," Axelsson says. "So the finding here, that it's the development of the nervous system that's affected, gives some support to this theory."

Most of his new study, though, is devoted to digestion genes. Dogs break down starch in three digestive stages, and the researchers found genetic differences related to each. AMY2B is a gene that makes alpha-amylase, an enzyme in the pancreas used to convert starch into maltose. The wolf genome carries 2 copies of AMY2B, whereas dogs carry anywhere from 4 to 30 copies. In other words, dogs have evolved a mechanism for digesting starches that wolves don't have. Axelsson says his findings fit well with the scavenger hypothesis. If wolves had wanted to get human food, they would have needed to evolve both trusting behaviors and mechanisms for digesting starch.

Other experts point out, though, that these changes could have easily come about at different times. It's possible, even likely, that wolves started hanging around our dumps a few thousand years before we had any starches to speak of. In order to know for sure, future studies will need to compare DNA from a wider range of dog breeds as well as from dog fossils.

Amidst all the speculation, I'm taking two broader points from this study. One's a practical tip for dog owners. Should you try that trendy (and expensive) raw-meat diet? "This suggests no," Wayne says. "Dogs have special digestive equipment for handling carbohydrates."

The second is that dogs can teach us about our own history and genetic evolution. Get this: Human studies suggest that we, too, picked up extra copies of the alpha-amylase gene during the agricultural revolution. "We have evolved, co-evolved, in parallel to the same environmental change, which was the development of agriculture," Axelsson says. "It makes you realize how big a change it must've been."

ALPHABOXES TOPIC: _____

A	B	C	D
	Blackwater	Costly Conservation	Dripping Drought
E	**F** 4,000 gal. $5,040	**G** Greywater	**H**
I	**J**	**K**	**L** Leaky hose
M Money	**N**	**O**	**P** Plumber
Q	**R** Rainwater Reuse	**S** Sink	**T** Trillion gal. Toilet
U	**V**	**W** Waste	**XYZ** YouTube

ALPHABOXES TOPIC: _____

A	B	C	D
E	**F**	**G**	**H**
I	**J**	**K**	**L**
M	**N**	**O**	**P**
Q	**R**	**S**	**T**
U	**V**	**W**	**XYZ**

May be photocopied for classroom use. *Texts and Lessons for Content-Area Writing* by Nancy Steineke and Harvey "Smokey" Daniels, © 2016 (Portsmouth, NH: Heinemann).

Conceptual Annotation

TEXT	AUTHOR	SOURCE	TEXT TYPE
"Choking the Oceans with Plastic"	Charles J. Moore	*New York Times*	Editorial

TIME ▶ 40 minutes

GROUPINGS ▶ Whole class, pairs, individuals

STANDARDS MET ▶ See pages 306–307.

 Chapter 12's Text Set

WHEN TO USE ▶ When we want students to notice key details related to important concepts, annotation while reading helps students monitor their comprehension and catch their thoughts—or confusion—immediately.

Whenever students read nonfiction text, they have to determine what's important while simultaneously—and mentally—categorizing, organizing, and chunking the information for understanding and recall. This aforementioned reading sophistication is compounded even further when the text has few reader road signs such as headings, bullet points, or pullquotes. Real-world text often requires readers to construct text organization along the way. Wow, no wonder kids sometimes glaze over when we hand them a content text and then later respond with, "Yeah, I read it, but I don't remember any of it." When students say that to you, it's their code for "I need a strategy that will help me understand and follow the text." Teaching students how to monitor and record their thinking with annotation is a pretty sure way to help move students beyond this "reader space-out" roadblock. Using conceptual annotation is a way to offer students further guidance for organizing the information and their thinking under some bigger important ideas. As you might imagine, conceptual annotation is a tool for reading most nonfiction texts.

The article we've offered for students to begin practicing conceptual annotation is a fascinating—and chilling—description of the Great Pacific Garbage Patch, a gigantic island of plastic pollution located in the Pacific Ocean. While it rarely comes up in conversation or in the media, plastic pollution poses catastrophic consequences for humans and ocean inhabitants. This article offers students the opportunity to examine this problem conceptually: What caused this convergence of plastic trash? What are the effects of ocean plastic pollution? What are the possible solutions?

PREPARATION

1. Download the NOAA illustration of the largest Pacific Ocean garbage patches and the conceptual annotation instructions in Step 3; determine how you will project them.

2. Make a copy of "Choking the Oceans with Plastic" for each student.

3. Establish pairs for Step 2.

Steps & ▶ Teaching Language

STEP 1 **Introduce the topic.** *Who has something with them that is made out of plastic or has a plastic component? Raise your hand. Okay, now think for a moment. How many different items that contain plastic are you wearing or do you have in your pockets, bag, purse? Silently count them up.* Then start taking a poll by a show of hands to see how much plastic each person carries around with him on a daily basis: *How many of you have more than five items using plastic? More than ten? More than fifteen? More than twenty?* Of course, depending on your students' enthusiasm for counting plastic items, this examination could expand to their classroom, lunchroom, or homes. The point you want to drive home is that we are absolutely inundated with plastic products.

STEP 2 **Project the NOAA illustration.** *Study this graphic. What does it show?* Either immediately take responses or have students do a quick turn and talk with their partner. Depending on where your students live, they may or may not be familiar with the Great Pacific Garbage Patch, so you might have to add a little background to what students have said. *Believe it or not, there are actually numerous huge areas in the Pacific Ocean where floating plastic collects. What do you think causes this plastic pollution?* Take some ideas and then move on to Step 3.

STEP 3 **Pass out the article; project the questions and directions.** *This article does a great job explaining how plastic has accumulated in these "garbage patches" but also makes it clear that this pollution endangers humans, not just ocean inhabitants. As you read, I want you to look for information that answers three questions* (project the questions and instructions):

> ### The Great Pacific Garbage Patch: Causes, Effects, and Solutions
> 1. What caused these garbage patches to occur? Underline and mark this information with a **C** for **cause** in the margin.
> 2. What effects is this plastic pollution having on our environment? This includes ocean inhabitants as well as humans and other living creatures. Underline and mark this information with an **E** for **effects** on the environment in the margin.
> 3. What are the solutions to this plastic pollution problem? Underline and mark this information with an **S** for **solution** in the margin.

STEP 4 **Students read and annotate individually.** Monitor individual reading, coaching recalcitrant annotators to mark the text as they read rather than reading the whole article first and then going back to annotate. This real-time annotation is critical because it requires students to read more carefully and actively monitor their comprehension. Annotation is the antidote to that often-heard student explanation, "I read it, but I don't remember anything."

As some students finish while others need more time to work, quietly prod those "sprinters" to review the article and their annotations to see if they can add to or refine their thinking further. This article contains much information, so time for a second reading could uncover some new thoughts or noticings.

STEP 5 **Pairs meet and discuss the causes and effects of ocean plastic pollution.** *When you get with your partner, decide who wants to lead the discussion on what causes these gigantic patches of plastic in the ocean. Who's taking charge of this part of the discussion? Raise your hands. Great. It's your job to get your partner talking about what they marked as **C**'s first. Encourage him to read really important underlined parts aloud. Rather than just add anything he missed, ask a question or two that gets your partner to explain his personal reaction to this information.*

Monitor pairs. You should notice one person initially doing all of the talking while the other person listens or asks questions. However, both people should be looking at the article and referring back to underlined information in the article. When the class conversation quiets, tell pairs to trade roles and continue their discussion on the effects of this pollution; this is the information they underlined and marked with **E**'s.

Continue monitoring for the same discussion behaviors.

STEP 6 **Pairs review and rank solutions.** *Now please focus on the last part of the article, the section that included solutions. Together, review the solutions presented. Then pick the three that you think would be most effective at solving the problem as well as being the most doable. Don't be afraid to debate with your partner a bit. Also, are there any solutions that this writer didn't consider? Talk about those as well.*

STEP 7 **Pairs share top solutions with the class.** *Which solutions did you decide had the most potential?* Take volunteers or call on pairs to explain their discussions.

Longer writing projects—reflecting the key genres required by the national standards—can be built on the work students have already done in this lesson. As kids continue to explore the topics of our reading selections, we expect that they will bring fresh background knowledge, recent thinking, and genuine curiosity to the task. When you use the lesson above with your own content, you can also use the assignments below as models for extending that content into longer writing projects.

◀ ***Research Projects for Extended Writing***

Narrative: *Tell the story of a related journey*

Take a common plastic object and trace its (possibly worldwide) journey from its manufacture, transportation, point of sale, use by consumer, and discarding to, somehow, the ocean. Using your research, tell the story of this journey, reporting as a narrator or as the plastic object itself. You might find some inspiration in Heal the Bay's mockumentary, *The Majestic Plastic Bag*, narrated by Jeremy Irons. *Research clue: Search for "How does plastic get into the ocean?"*

Informative/explanatory: *Describe a location or situation*

While this article is informative, it does not convey the enormity of the problem in the same way an attention-grabbing visual can. Check YouTube for Great Pacific Garbage Patch footage—there is a ton. Then, use what you read and the video to write a description of the garbage patch.

Persuasive/argumentative: *Raise public awareness*

There is wide agreement that plastic pollution in our oceans is serious and out of control. But the problem is so enormous—and so hidden from view—that it's hard to galvanize the public, countries, or industries to take action and spend money. They need to see it and feel its enormity. The article mentions several promising strategies to end the flow of discarded plastic into the ecosystem. Choose one you find promising and develop a public service announcement or print or viral media ad to raise awareness, generate a sense of urgency, and encourage people to tackle this threat to the planet.

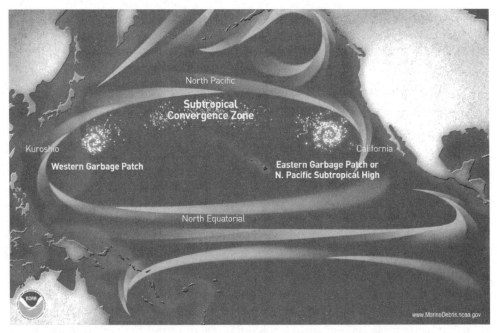

Source: NOAA.

The New York Times

Choking the Oceans with Plastic

By Charles J. Moore

LOS ANGELES—The world is awash in plastic. It's in our cars and our carpets, we wrap it around the food we eat and virtually every other product we consume; it has become a key lubricant of globalization—but it's choking our future in ways that most of us are barely aware.

I have just returned with a team of scientists from six weeks at sea conducting research in the Great Pacific Garbage Patch—one of five major garbage patches drifting in the oceans north and south of the Equator at the latitude of our great terrestrial deserts. Although it was my 10th voyage to the area, I was utterly shocked to see the enormous increase in the quantity of plastic waste since my last trip in 2009. Plastics of every description, from toothbrushes to tires to unidentifiable fragments too numerous to count floated past our marine research vessel Alguita for hundreds of miles without end. We even came upon a floating island bolstered by dozens of plastic buoys used in oyster aquaculture that had solid areas you could walk on.

Plastics are now one of the most common pollutants of ocean waters worldwide. Pushed by winds, tides and currents, plastic particles form with other debris into large swirling glutinous accumulation zones, known to oceanographers as gyres, which comprise as much as 40 percent of the planet's ocean surface—roughly 25 percent of the entire earth.

No scientist, environmentalist, entrepreneur, national or international government agency has yet been able to establish a comprehensive way of recycling the plastic trash that covers our

> *Plastics are now one of the most common pollutants of ocean waters worldwide.*

land and inevitably blows and washes down to the sea. In a 2010 study of the Los Angeles and San Gabriel Rivers, my colleagues and I estimated that some 2.3 billion pieces of plastic—from polystyrene foam to tiny fragments and pellets—had flowed from Southern California's urban centers into its coastal waters in just three days of sampling.

The deleterious consequences of humanity's "plastic footprint" are many, some known and some yet to be discovered. We know that plastics biodegrade exceptionally slowly, breaking into tiny fragments in a centuries-long process. We know that plastic debris entangles and slowly kills millions of sea creatures; that hundreds of species mistake plastics for their natural food, ingesting toxicants that cause liver and stomach abnormalities in fish and birds, often choking them to death. We know that one of the main bait fish in the ocean, the lantern fish, eats copious quantities of plastic fragments, threatening their future as a nutritious food source to the tuna, salmon, and other pelagic fish we consume, adding to the increasing amount of synthetic chemicals unknown before 1950 that we now carry in our bodies.

We suspect that more animals are killed by vagrant plastic waste than by even climate change—a hypothesis that needs to be seriously tested. During our most recent voyage, we studied the effects of pollution, taking blood and liver samples from fish as we searched for invasive species and plastic-linked pollutants that cause protein and hormone abnormalities. While we hope our studies will yield important contributions to scientific knowledge, they address but a small part of a broader issue.

The reality is that only by preventing synthetic debris—most of which is disposable plastic—from getting into the ocean in the first place will a measurable reduction in the ocean's plastic load be accomplished. Clean-up schemes are legion, but have never been put into practice in the garbage patches.

The National Oceanic and Atmospheric Administration in the United States supports environmentalist groups that remove debris from beaches. But the sieve-like skimmers they use, no matter how technologically sophisticated, will never be able to clean up remote garbage gyres: There's too much turbulent ocean dispersing and mixing up the mess.

> We suspect that more animals are killed by vagrant plastic waste than by even climate change—a hypothesis that needs to be seriously tested.

The problem is compounded by the aquaculture industry, which uses enormous amounts of plastic in its floats, nets, lines and tubes. The most common floats and tubes I've found in the deep ocean and on Hawaiian beaches come from huge sea-urchin and oyster farms like the one that created the oyster-buoy island we discovered. Those buoys were torn from their moorings by the tsunami that walloped Japan on March 11, 2011. But no regulatory remedies exist to deal with tons of plastic equipment lost accidentally and in storms. Government and industry organizations purporting to certify sustainably farmed seafood, despite their dozens of pages of standards, fail to mention gear that is lost and floats away. Governments, which are rightly concerned with depletion of marine food sources, should ensure that plastic from cages, buoys and other equipment used for aquaculture does not escape into the waters.

But, in the end, the real challenge is to combat an economic model that thrives on wasteful products and packaging, and leaves the associated problem of clean-up costs. Changing the way we produce and consume plastics is a challenge greater than reining in our production of carbon dioxide.

Plastics are a nightmare to recycle. They are very hard to clean. They can melt at low temperatures, so impurities are not vaporized. It makes no difference whether a synthetic polymer like polyethylene is derived from petroleum or plants; it is still a persistent pollutant. Biodegradable plastics exist, but manufacturers are quick to point out that marine degradable does not mean "marine disposable."

Scientists in Britain and the Netherlands have proposed to cut plastic pollution by the institution of a "circular economy." The basic concept is that products must be designed with end-of-life recovery in mind. They propose a pre-cycling premium to provide incentives to eliminate the possibility that a product will become waste.

In the United States, especially in California, the focus has been on so-called structural controls, such as covering gutters and catch basins with screens. This has reduced the amount of debris flowing down rivers to the sea. Activists around the world are lobbying for bans on the most polluting plastics—the bottles, bags and containers that deliver food and drink. Many have been successful. In California, a new statewide law prohibits grocery and retail stores from providing single-use plastic bags.

Until we shut off the flow of plastic to the sea, the newest global threat to our Anthropocene age will only get worse.

Charles J. Moore is a captain in the U.S. merchant marine and founder of the Algalita Marine Research and Education Institute in Long Beach, California.

Closely Reading an Image

TIME ▶ 30 minutes

GROUPINGS ▶ Whole class, pairs, individuals

STANDARDS MET ▶ See pages 306–307.

WHEN TO USE ▶ Whenever you have to introduce a new topic, unit, or concept, think about using images. You can start with an image study like this one or show a series of images in order to get kids thinking and talking.

TEXT	AUTHOR	SOURCE	TEXT TYPE
The Age of Brass/Or the Triumphs of Women's Rights	Currier and Ives	The History Project, University of California–Davis	Political cartoon

As we've mentioned earlier, being able to read and interpret images is an explicit goal in the Common Core and many state standards. More importantly, images are a way to spark interest and evoke background knowledge. Even better, images speak a universal language. Our students may come from a variety of backgrounds, languages, and ethnicities, but everyone can look at and talk—or gesture animatedly—about a picture.

This strategy offers you and your students a way to look at an image's details more closely by breaking it down into sections. This mockery of women's rights activists is arguably one of the most famous political cartoons in U.S. history, published by no less an American institution than Currier and Ives.

PREPARATION

1. Download images for *The Age of Brass/Or the Triumphs of Women's Rights* and determine how you will project them.
2. Make a copy of the Image Reading handout for each student.
3. Decide how to pair students for Steps 1 and 7.

Steps & Teaching Language ▶

STEP 1 Introduce the topic. *How many of you know someone who didn't vote in a recent election? What kept them from voting?* Hear some responses. *While some people didn't vote because work, family, or other serious obligations kept them away from the polls, a lot of you said in one way or another that some people you know didn't vote because they just weren't interested. For a variety of reasons the desire just wasn't there.*

Did you know that before 1920, women did not have the right to vote? Prior to ratification of the Nineteenth Amendment, women's voting rights were determined by each state. In some states, particularly in the West, women had full voting rights. Elsewhere voting rights ranged from none whatsoever to being able to vote only in school board, municipal, or presidential elections. And just because you could vote in one election, it didn't mean you could vote in another. What do you think of that? Check in with your partner and see what they think. Give pairs a minute to talk and then move on.

STEP 2 **Project full image of *The Age of Brass/Or the Triumphs of Women's Rights*.** *This is a political cartoon depicting women's rights prior to the Nineteenth Amendment. Let's take a closer look.*

STEP 3 **Distribute the Image Reading handout.** *On the line at the top of this sheet, write in "Women's Rights Cartoon."*

STEP 4 **Project the image divided into thirds.** *In order to notice more details in this cartoon, we're going to look at it in thirds, starting with the piece on the left.*

STEP 5 **Project the left third of the image.** (The remaining cartoon is blacked out). *Grab your paper and fold it so that you can write only on the left third. Now study this part of the picture carefully. First of all, just jot down everything you see. What do you notice? Include people, gestures, posture, facial expressions, clothing descriptions and details, objects, foreground and background details.*

Give students a minute to look and take notes. Monitor their progress. When most have run out of steam, give the next instruction. *Go back and reread what you wrote down. Now, before we move on to the next part of the picture, record your response to these details. What do they make you think about, wonder about?*

Give students another minute to reflect and add to their notes.

STEP 6 **Project the center image and the right.** Show the remaining thirds separately. Repeat the steps and language outlined in Step 5 for each of the remaining image portions. Have students refold their handouts so that just the column they are using is visible.

STEP 7 **Pairs meet and compare their observations.** Project the image with divider lines. *Get together with your partner and compare what you saw, thought, or wondered. Pay particular attention to how your noticings differed because that is what will make this discussion really interesting. If your partner is trying to point something out that you just can't see, it is perfectly fine for both of you to get out of your seats to take a closer look at the projection, but then return to your seats to finish the discussion.*

Monitor the pair discussions. When partners are on task you will see shared talking, references to notes, and a lot of pointing and looking toward the projection.

STEP 8 **Pairs share discussion highlights with the class.** *Let's get back together and share some discussion highlights. Who had a partner that noticed something interesting?* Take volunteers or call on pairs randomly. If students were engaged in on-task conversations, they should all have something to contribute.

STEP 9 **Project the original image again.** *What conclusions can you draw from looking at this cartoon? What was the message the artist was trying to convey? How might a female viewer's reaction be different from a male viewer's reaction? Turn back to your partner and discuss this.*

Monitor the pair discussions. As discussion quiets, pose this final question. *Based on your discussion of this cartoon's message, what should it be titled? Talk it over with your partner and write the title on your sheet.*

STEP 10 **Pairs share their titles with the class.** *Let's get back together and hear some titles. When I call on you, give us your title and explain your reasoning behind it.* First, call on some pairs randomly. Then open the discussion up to volunteers who are *dying* to tell everyone the title they thought of.

Wow, those were some great titles. You know what the real title of this cartoon is? Actually there were two titles. The first one is The Age of Brass. *What do you think that has to do with women's rights?* Take some ideas. You may need to tell students about the archaic definition of *brass* as excessive self-assurance, impudence, or effrontery. *The second title is* The Triumphs of Women's Rights. *We usually think of a triumph as a success. Do you think the artist is celebrating women or implying something else?* Take some ideas. *Anybody have a guess when this cartoon was published? 1869. That was a little over fifty years before women in the United States got the right to vote. As you can see, this was an equal rights issue that was not resolved quickly.*

Research Projects for Extended Writing ▶

Longer writing projects—reflecting the key genres required by the national standards—can be built on the work students have already done in this lesson. As kids continue to explore the topics of our reading selections, we expect that they will bring fresh background knowledge, recent thinking, and genuine curiosity to the task. When you use the lesson above with your own content, you can also use the assignments below as models for extending that content into longer writing projects.

Narrative: *Write from another's perspective*

What was it like for a woman living in 1869? While this cartoon depicts the women's suffrage movement, were there other rights men enjoyed but women lacked? Investigate this 1869 civil rights issue and create a diary entry for one of the female or male characters in the cartoon based on what you discover. Be sure that your diary character reflects the attitude and concerns of the figures in the cartoon.

Informative/explanatory: *Summarize an issue*

What was the newspaper article that might have accompanied this cartoon? Investigate how women's roles and rights evolved over the previous one hundred years, from 1769 to 1869. Describe the progress (or lack thereof) and give specific examples.

Persuasive/argumentative: *Use a historical perspective to consider a contemporary issue*

Though women now have the right to vote, work, and own property, in what ways do women still struggle for equality in the United States? Is there a need for further passage of equality laws or constitutional amendments? Investigate current women's equality issues and use the information to write a letter to the editor concerning additional federal intervention. Do you support new laws or not? Defend your stance with accurate facts and specific details.

The Age of Brass/Or the Triumphs of Women's Rights: Library of Congress Prints and Photographs Division; Call no. 90708465. PGA—Currier & Ives.

IMAGE READING: _____

As you view each section, observe the image details carefully and jot down what you see, think or wonder

Two-Column Video Notes

TEXT	AUTHOR	SOURCE	TEXT TYPE
"Megadroughts Projected for American West"	Ben Cook	NASA, Goddard Space Flight Center	Informational video

TIME ▸ 30 minutes

GROUPINGS ▸ Whole class, pairs, individuals

STANDARDS MET ▸ See pages 306–307.

WHEN TO USE ▸ Many of the subjects we teach in school now have countless related videos that can introduce kids to topics, offer vibrant images, and make real-world relevance clear. But we can't just "show movies." When we start screening our content, students need more than popcorn—they need well-structured tools to capture their thinking as they view.

If you've ever shown a film in class, you might have noticed many different student reactions: total engagement, polite viewing, subtly off-task behavior (secretly texting, trying to complete the assignment due next hour), or blatantly off-task (sound asleep and snoring). Of course, if you're like us, the first course of action is to turn the lights back on. But, as Peggy Lee laments, "Is that all there is?" Actually, no. We've found that taking some notes during a video, whether it's long or short, increases attention, accountability, comprehension, and engagement because the notes give students specific conversation starters after viewing. Though we've chosen a short NASA clip for this lesson demonstration, two-column notes work just as well with full-length feature films. Also, you can customize the headings, depending on what you want students to notice and think about.

PREPARATION

1. Make a copy of the two-column notes handout for each student, plus an extra copy for yourself if you decide to work alongside students in Steps 1 and 2.

2. Use a search engine to find the NASA video "Megadroughts Projected for American West." Download the video and determine how you will project it to the class.

3. Determine how pairs will form at Step 4.

4. Download the conversation steps instructions used in Step 5.

5. Have enough 3x3-inch sticky notes to give one to each pair.

6. Having a document camera for some quick note-taking modeling would be useful as well, but not absolutely necessary.

STEP 1 **Pass out the two-column notes handout; introduce the video and note taking.** *Today we're going to view a short video about droughts in the western half of the United States. While we watch, you'll use this handout to take some notes. Fold the paper in half lengthwise so that just the column that says "Information: Narration/Dialogue/Images" is visible. The video is pretty short and packed with information. Watch carefully and see how many pieces of information you can jot down in that left-hand column. You can jot down details from the narration, or information that is conveyed from the images. Don't worry about trying to write in complete sentences; words and phrases will work just fine. Any questions? Okay. Get ready to view carefully and take some notes along the way.*

◀ **Steps &
Teaching
Language**

STEP 2 **Show the video and take notes.** Show the video and, if you like, take notes yourself. Since the video is short, you might even choose to show it a second time, similar to when a text needs a second reading. During this time, monitor the class and observe the note taking.

STEP 3 **Respond to the video details.** *Let's take a couple of minutes to think about what we just saw and heard. Open up the handout so that the right column labeled "Thoughts and Questions" is visible. Now go back and read through the notes you took on the video and think about your own personal response to each piece of information. What do you think, remember, picture, wonder? Work to capture a personal response to each of the information details you jotted. I'll give you a couple minutes to work silently.*

If you took some viewing notes yourself, project them on the doc cam and model what a thoughtful response looks like. This step will help steer students toward more detailed, specific responses.

As students work, monitor their progress and read over their shoulders. For the kids who are writing furiously, suggest that they number their info entries so that they can write corresponding responses further down on the page or on the other side. For the kids who are writing vague one-word responses, ask some guiding follow-up questions to probe their thinking. For example: *What made that surprising? How did you think differently before? How do you think this affects the people who live there? What would you be willing to give up to turn climate change around?*

STEP 4 **Students reread their entries and choose three with conversation potential.** *Before you compare notes with your partner, go back and put a star by the three details that spurred the richest thoughts for you.*

STEP 5 **Pairs share their starred entries.** *When you get together with your partner, I want you to have some conversation about this video instead of just putting your notes side by side and seeing what you each wrote. Instead, keep your notes to yourself and make use of them as a conversation starting point.*

> ### Conversation Steps
>
> 1. Tell your partner about one of your three starred info details.
> 2. Instead of then explaining the response you wrote in the right-hand column, have your partner explain his or her reaction to that information while you listen carefully.
> 3. After your partner has explained, either ask a follow-up question to get more details or share what you were thinking on the topic.
> 4. Switch and let your partner start the next round of conversation. Keep this pattern going until I call time. And if you run out of starred items to talk about before time's up, it's okay to talk about any of the other items on your note-taking sheets.

When most pairs have covered at least four of the six possible starred items between them, call the class back together.

STEP 6 **Pairs share discussion highlights with the whole class.** *Who had a partner that jotted down a piece of information that you also recorded? What was it? Anybody else have that jotted down? Why do you think that piece of information stood out to you?*

Who had a partner that came up with an idea or response you hadn't thought of yourself? What was it?

What were some of the questions or wonderings that arose as you watched this video and thought about it on your own and with your partner? Pass out a sticky note to each pair. *Talk this over with your partner and write down a drought question that remains unanswered.*

Finish with a quick round robin where each pair reads its question aloud to the class. Discuss patterns in the questions asked and what the questions might say about the students' interests and background knowledge. If students are burning with curiosity, seize the moment for a quick inquiry. Get out the laptops, tablets, or smartphones and see what answers students can dig up on their question in ten minutes.

◀ ***Research Projects for Extended Writing***

Longer writing projects—reflecting the key genres required by the national standards—can be built on the work students have already done in this lesson. As kids continue to explore the topics of our reading selections, we expect that they will bring fresh background knowledge, recent thinking, and genuine curiosity to the task. When you use the lesson above with your own content, you can also use the assignments below as models for extending that content into longer writing projects.

Narrative: *Use data to create a setting*

In the science of drought, there are specific worsening stages—or degrees of dryness—that affect plants, animals, and humans over time. Look up some of the common scales used to describe degrees of drought. Then create a story about a group of humans, historical or contemporary, who are living through a deepening drought. Use the details from your research to tell how your characters are affected as the drought deepens—possibly over several decades.

Informative/explanatory: *Share solutions from another culture*

If you look at the climate history of the southwest United States, you will find that the region has been characterized by periodic multidecade droughts for many centuries. These dry cycles had very specific human consequences for the native peoples living there. Dig into the migration patterns of Navajo, Pueblo, and/or Apache Indians and see what lessons we can learn about how to adapt to drought.

Persuasive/argumentative: *Develop a policy*

People who live in other parts of the country often criticize residents of the Southwest for foolishly building cities in a perennially dry region. After Hurricane Katrina in New Orleans, some critics from elsewhere thought the city should not be rebuilt in such a flood-prone area. And what about San Francisco and Los Angeles, with their earthquake risks; Oklahoma City, Indianapolis, and all the other cities in "Tornado Alley"; Florida with its hurricanes; Washington State with its wildfires; and so on? Study these and other high-risk habitations and develop a public policy on how much Americans from other parts of the U.S. should be required to help rebuild other peoples' homes after predictable disasters.

TWO-COLUMN VIDEO NOTES

Information (narration/dialogue/images)	Response (thoughts and questions)

Carousel Annotation

GROUPINGS ▶ Whole class, multiple silent partners, individuals

STANDARDS MET ▶ See pages 306–307.

WHEN TO USE ▶ This is the just-right structure when you want kids to have a wide-ranging conversation about a rich topic with many other classmates— but also to keep it quiet and reflective.

TEXT	SOURCE	TEXT TYPE
"Most U.S. Middle and High Schools Start the Day Too Early"	Centers for Disease Control and Prevention	Health report/infographic

We've taught several different forms of text annotation already, and next comes a version that most kids especially enjoy. The underlying structure is the same: we show students a specific way of marking content-area material in order to capture and understand particular themes, concepts, or evidence. These annotations later support kids to write about the subject matter far better than if they had simply skimmed the selection.

The topic for this lesson is American teens' lack of sleep. What, that again?! We have been hearing for decades that our students don't get as much sleep as they should. (Neither do most teachers, but there are no studies on us.) This is all well-intentioned stuff, but doesn't a single researcher understand how school buses are scheduled in this country? The first run gets the big kids in the dark, and then goes back for the little guys on a sunny second round later. What are you gonna do? Buy a second barn full of buses and drive everybody in at 9:30? Have kindergartners stand in the dark on subzero Minnesota mornings? But we digress.

PREPARATION

You'll need to do a little more prep for this lesson than for most of the others, but once you see the value, you'll want to keep these supplies on hand.

1. Make copies of the CDC infographic and report, "Most U.S. Middle and High Schools Start the Day too Early," for use in Step 3.

2. Be ready to project the photo of students doing this work (page 119).

3. Cover tables (or a group of desks, pushed together) with butcher paper or chart paper and attach the CDC article or the infographic to the center of each table. The large paper will become the "margins" of the central texts where kids will have lots of space to write. An alternative setup is single sheets of chart paper, each with an article, hung from the walls. In this version, kids would be doing the writing standing up, so you tend to get less stamina and focus in the writing and minor management issues as kids jostle around the walls. Be sure to hang charts a good distance from each other so that students have room to move around them.

4. Put out assorted colors of dark, skinny markers (no yellow or orange—they're too hard to read).

Chart paper variation of carousel annotation. Students are having a written conversation about factoring binomials.

The photograph shows one way to set this up. You can use it to plan the activity; you can also project it for the kids so they see what the idea is. The teacher has placed several prompts on the chart paper.

◀ **Steps** & **Teaching** **Language**

STEP 1 **Guide the students to find a spot in the room.** To minimize confusion, greet students at the door. *The room looks a little different today. As you come in, find a seat near one of the texts that's on display.*

STEP 2 **Explain the room setup and goals.** *Today we are going to read two short texts about the same topic, as we often do. But this time we are going to move from seat to seat and then from table to table, having a written conversation with each other as we go.* Project the photo of the students doing this work.

Look at what the kids are doing in the picture. The idea is to first read through the text you are sitting in front of, and then pick something on the page you want to write about. These students are using "carousel annotation" to practice factoring polynomials in Algebra 2, by doing their own problems and then affirming or correcting others' work as they circulate around the chart. There are four problems on the chart. When the kids have responded to each one, they'll move to another table and jump into other students' work.

So today, we have our own topic, which is already planted on the chart paper for you. When we start, you can just sit down and read one item. Then out in the margin, write a comment, reaction, suggestion, or some questions. Every two or three minutes, I'll invite you to move to another article or another table. When you get there, look at what someone else has written and comment on that comment. Or you can pull out another idea from the text and talk about that in the margin.

STEP 3 **Kids read the text and write first comments.** *Everyone pick a pen from the table. You will bring it with you to all of the tables, and it will be your signature color. Okay, have a look at the text in front of you. Half of you have an article from the Centers for Disease Control, and the other half have an infographic that accompanied the same article. The topic is you—teenagers—though you don't have to agree with what these documents say. In fact, we don't know if any of these experts ever talked to any kids about their sleep habits.*

Once you've had a chance to write your initial comments, move to another spot at your table and comment on someone else's comments. Keep going until you've worked around your table. Then, move on to commenting on the papers at the other tables until I tell you to stop. Be sure to sign every note you write.

Happy reading and writing. I'll be writing comments too, but grab me if you need any help. I'm looking forward to joining some rich big margin conversations!

Allow plenty of time for the initial reading and writing of each text; later visits will become quicker. While you can shift students around by calling out "move," we prefer to let kids set their own pace, relocating when they are ready. If you choose this approach, you'll be actively moving some kids along, and encouraging others to stay and write more.

STEP 4 **Have kids move to additional seats and extend the conversations there.** As the paper margins fill up with notes, you'll be busy managing and making suggestions. At this stage, kids have already read the article, so at each sitting, more time should be devoted to writing—either new thoughts on the content or comments to the students who have already made interesting notes in the margin.

If lines of conversation peter out, remind kids that they can respond to a different comment on that page, or start a new chat-line by leaving a fresh and engaging comment.

STEP 5 **Gallery walk.** Now have students circulate through some tables/conversations they were not part of, not writing comments this time, but reading to find out what other students talked about. Have them visit three or four displays before returning to their own "home text," where they began.

STEP 6 **Concluding whole-class conversation.** *After doing all this writing, what ideas have you developed about your sleep patterns and how they fit with school? Does everyone have the same biorhythms? How much sleep do people need to feel really alert the next day? Are some people fine with starting early? Did you see some solutions that people proposed? Could school change in ways that would make you less sleepy?*

STEP 7 **Collect all student writing.** With this activity, taking photos with your cell phone may work better than rolling up all that big paper, with handouts coming unglued and falling off. You can do that once or twice, but the corners of the room may fill with tubes of written conversations, making them hard to easily access again. As always, you can look at these samples for kids' participation, their thinking about the topic, and for ideas about what they need next.

The most obvious variation is to place different articles on the same table. Pro and con pieces about the same topic are always engaging, and help kids practice writing argument and persuasion. Profiles of different fictional characters or historical figures allow students to contrast the different qualities of persons. Our pal Sara Ahmed has had her kids do carousel annotation with classic black-and-white photographs of school integration in the 1950s. Sixth-grade teacher Ben Kadish has used eight different texts about civil rights issues, so kids could travel deep into the content as they moved around the room.

◀ *Variations*

Longer writing projects—reflecting the key genres required by the national standards—can be built on the work students have already done in this lesson. As kids continue to explore the topics of our reading selections, we expect that they will bring fresh background knowledge, recent thinking, and genuine curiosity to the task. When you use the lesson above with your own content, you can also use the assignments below as models for extending that content into longer writing projects.

◀ *Research Projects for Extended Writing*

Narrative: *Consider how this issue affects your own life*

Write up a description of your typical day, as if you were telling it to a friend: when you get up, go to school, do other activities, come home, go to sleep. If it changes from day to day, tell how and why. Do you feel like you get enough sleep? Or would you want more? Does your family influence your sleep habits? Most days in school, do you feel alert and tuned in, or are you fatigued?

Informative/explanatory: *Investigate an issue on a global scale*

Investigate school starting times around the world. Find data for as many countries as you can, and make a chart showing start times for a comparable grade level. For example, there is lots of international data on fifteen-year-olds, since that is the age when some big educational studies are done. Then, research how countries with different school starting times compare on international educational rankings. In a brief report, explain any patterns you see in the correlations of start times and rankings. *Research clue: OECD.*

Persuasive/argumentative: *Petition for a change in your school*

According to the CDC article, the average American high school starts at 8:03 a.m., while the recommended time is 8:30. An even more recent study from the American Academy of Pediatrics suggests that teens should not start school until 10:00 a.m.! However, critics of this idea cite the difficulties and costs of transportation for late-starting schools: Who would ensure that teenagers get to school if parents are already at work long before the day begins? Would school districts need to buy new buses to get teenagers to school at the same time as elementary students? And of course a midmorning start would mean school ends too late for prized after-school activities like sports, drama, and music practice. Research this issue (including costs, downstream effect, and long-term outcomes for students) and decide what you think is best for the community as a whole: traditional early start times or later start times. Then, work with a group of classmates who have the same opinion to write a letter to your school board supporting your side of this argument.

Most U.S. middle and high schools start the school day too early

Students need adequate sleep for their health, safety, and academic success

Centers for Disease Control and Prevention

Fewer than 1 in 5 middle and high schools in the U.S. began the school day at the recommended 8:30 AM start time or later during the 2011–2012 school year, according to data published today in the Centers for Disease Control and Prevention's Morbidity and Mortality Weekly Report. Too-early start times can keep students from getting the sleep they need for health, safety, and academic success, according to the American Academy of Pediatrics.

Schools that have a start time of 8:30 AM or later allow adolescent students the opportunity to get the recommended amount of sleep on school nights: about 8.5 to 9.5 hours. Insufficient sleep is common among high school students and is associated with several health risks such as being overweight, drinking alcohol, smoking tobacco, and using drugs—as well as poor academic performance.

"Getting enough sleep is important for students' health, safety, and academic performance," said Anne Wheaton, Ph.D., lead author and epidemiologist in CDC's Division of Population Health. "Early school start times, however, are preventing many adolescents from getting the sleep they need."

Key findings:

- 42 states reported that 75-100 percent of the public schools in their respective states started before 8:30 AM.
- The average start time was 8:03 AM.
- The percentage of schools with start times of 8:30 AM or later varied greatly by state. No schools in Hawaii, Mississippi, and Wyoming started at 8:30 AM or later; more than 75 percent of schools in Alaska and North Dakota started at 8:30 AM or later.
- Louisiana had the earliest average school start time (7:40 AM), while Alaska had the latest (8:33 AM).

In 2014, the American Academy of Pediatrics issued a policy statement urging middle and high schools to modify start times to no earlier than 8:30 AM to aid students in getting sufficient sleep to improve their overall health. School start time policies are not determined at the federal or state level, but at the district or individual school level.

The authors report that delayed school start times do not replace the need for other interventions that can improve sleep among adolescents. Parents can help their children practice good sleep habits. For example, a consistent bedtime and rise time, including on weekends, is recommended for everyone, including children, adolescents, and adults.

Most U.S. middle and high schools start the school day too early

 5 out of **6** U.S. middle and high schools start the school day before **8:30**AM

The American Academy of Pediatrics has recommended that middle and high schools should aim to start no earlier than 8:30 AM to enable students to get adequate sleep.

 Teens need at least **8** hours of sleep per night.   Younger students need at least **9** hours.

 **2** out of **3** U.S. high school students sleep less than **8 hours** on school nights

Adolescents who do not get enough sleep are more likely to

be overweight   not get enough physical activity   suffer from depressive symptoms   engage in unhealthy risk behaviors such as drinking alcohol, smoking tobacco, and using illicit drugs   perform poorly in school

For more information: www.cdc.gov

National Center for Chronic Disease Prevention and Health Promotion
Division of Population Health   **CDC**

DIGGING DEEPER INTO TEXTS

Here, lessons ramp up in the complexity and depth of the readings and in the writing structures used. Students are taking more time, engaging in more extended partner interactions, and becoming more metacognitive as they comprehend and compose.

LESSON 19 Teacher and Student Think-Aloud

TEXT	AUTHOR	SOURCE	TEXT TYPE
"My Atom Bomb Is in the Shop"	Roger Vector	WrapUp Media	News article

TIME ▶ 30 minutes

GROUPINGS ▶ Whole class, pairs, individuals

STANDARDS MET ▶ See pages 306–307.

WHEN TO USE ▶ When we want students to "close read" increasingly complex texts and then write about them, we have to *show them how first.* That means we model the cognitive processes ourselves and then coach them through their initial attempts.

Why do we see such disappointing results when American kids' reading is assessed (especially when the scores wind up in newspaper headlines and we teachers get the blame)? There are countless causes of weak reading comprehension, but here's one big one: we have failed to *show* kids how to read. Sure, we've assigned plenty of reading, upped the complexity of the reading selections, and graded zillions of postreading quizzes. The trouble is, we haven't spent enough time *demonstrating* how effective readers think.

To many kids, the act of reading is a mystery, a black box, a magic formula, a gift only given to a few "good readers" who seem to comprehend effortlessly from the beginning to the end of any printed material. But as proficient adult readers, we know that reading isn't a gift; it is the product of hard, recursive mental work. Creating meaning from challenging text is a construction project that requires all the cognitive tools (strategies) and materials (subject-matter background knowledge) we can muster.

To help kids better understand what reading actually entails, we teachers have to demonstrate it "live" in the classroom. And we need to model our reading not just generally, but in our specific subject fields—in science, math, literature, history, and all the rest. Students need to see proficient readers in various disciplines show how they read the distinctive, specialized texts found in each subject field.

The baseline, number one lesson for delivering this modeling is the think-aloud, which we introduce here. This demonstration structure is infinitely adaptable, as we'll show in several later lessons that use the same basic process.

1. Prepare your think-aloud for the first three paragraphs of the article. Do this by reading the piece and noticing where you experience authentic connections, questions, inferences, visualizations, or uncertainties along the way. Then choose a few of these spots where you'll stop during your read-aloud and open up your thinking to students. Think about what you'll say and what quick notes you will leave in the margin to mark the "tracks of your thinking." We suggest at least one stop with the title and then one for each paragraph.

2. Make a copy of "My Atom Bomb Is in the Shop" for each student, ready to hand out at Step 3. The paragraphs are numbered to facilitate taking turns. Choose how to project the article so that you can write your notes directly on the projected image. This usually means using a document camera, a smart board, or a projector aimed at a whiteboard where you can use a marker.

3. Decide how you will form partners in Step 1.

4. Appoint a student scribe to help out at Steps 5, 9, and 11.

Steps & Teaching Language ▶

STEP 1 **Kids turn and talk.** *What do you know—or think you know—about atomic bombs? Chat with your partner for two minutes, sharing any background knowledge you have about nuclear or atomic weapons.*

STEP 2 **Pairs share out.** Invite a few partners to share one piece of background knowledge. As pairs share, access the full range of kids' schema by requesting: *Who knows something different? Who has some other information? Who thought of something we haven't mentioned yet?*

STEP 3 **Introduce the article and strategy.** Project the article and hand out copies to all students. Explain: *In a minute, I am going to read part of this article aloud and I will be stopping along the way to show you some of my thinking. I'm going to "open up my head" and show you how I react, think, and make decisions while I read. Your job is to listen to me reading, and when I stop to share my thinking, jot some quick notes about what you hear me saying. Later, you'll get to try this "thinking aloud" with a partner. Ready?*

STEP 4 **Model thinking aloud.** Offer the think-aloud as you planned it for the first three paragraphs. Each time you stop reading and switch to sharing your thinking, be sure to look up from the text and mark the shift with your voice. You can also directly address the students, using language like, "You know, I just had a question here," or "Guys, I'm getting a little confused, I think I better go back and reread this section." As you think aloud, jot notes in the margin to quickly label your thinking, using words, codes, symbols, or doodles.

STEP 5 **Invite comments.** *Take a minute to look over your notes.* After a brief interval, say: *Who can share what you noticed about my thinking at some points in the article?* Invite several pairs to mention what they noticed, and have a student scribe record their observations on a chart/screen. Likely comments might include "You talked to yourself," "You talked about what you were seeing," "When you were having trouble understanding, you did something about it," "You talked about your feelings about the text," "You mentioned related information you knew," "You asked questions about the author or the information."

STEP 6 **Establish roles for student pairs.** *Now let's set this up so you can take turns trying this with a buddy. Turn to your partner and share birth dates; just month and day is fine. For the first round, the person with the earliest birthday will think aloud paragraphs 4 and 5, and the partner with the later birthday will be the listener/note taker. After we debrief the first round, you'll switch roles for paragraphs 6 and 7.*

STEP 7 **Students silently read the remaining sections of the article.** So they can prepare for their think-alouds, give students a couple of minutes to read the remaining four paragraphs. *As you read your assigned paragraphs, think about what you can share about your own reading strategies when it's your turn.*

STEP 8 **Students think aloud, round 1.** Advise "think-alouders" that they do not need to write notes in the margin as you did; doing so can be cognitive overload for first-timers. "Listeners" should jot a few words beside the place in the text where their partners stopped to share their thinking. The goal is just to get a sense of what the reader says about his/her thinking. Finally, remind kids that this is not a two-way conversation about the text, but a read-aloud by one person to a silent note taker.

Now cue the first student to think aloud paragraphs 4 and 5, while the partner takes notes on the shared thinking strategies.

STEP 9 **Debrief the first round.** Have your student scribe ready to add to the chart when you ask: *Listeners, what did you notice about your buddy's thinking? Thinkers, what did you notice about your own thinking? How did it feel doing this?* Kids may report that this activity feels mechanical or artificial. You can comment that it feels odd mostly because they haven't done it before. With more experience, this kind of metacognition (thinking about our own thinking) feels more natural and comfortable—plus it helps us to develop a conscious awareness of the mental moves we can select from to enhance our comprehension.

STEP 10 **Students think aloud, round 2.** Now invite the later birthday students to think aloud the last two paragraphs, with their partner taking notes.

STEP 11 **Debrief the second round.** Have your student scribe ready to add to the chart. *Listeners, what did you notice about your buddy's thinking? Thinkers, what did you notice about your own thinking? How did it feel doing this?*

STEP 12 Review the strategies list. *What we have been developing here is a list of ways that readers can make sense of text even when it is hard. We could also call these "strategies for comprehension."*

Let's leave this chart up in the room so we can refer to it when you are reading on your own. We will be doing more think-alouds with future readings, and we can add to our list as we discover more of the moves smart readers can make. Below is a sample from one class.

Comprehension Strategies We Can Use

Pay attention to your brain while you are reading

Slow down

Read it again (sentence, paragraph, the whole thing)

Make pictures (or sounds) in your head

Notice when you have a question

Underline important parts

Use codes or notes in the margin

Look up hard words (or ask someone)

Make connections to what you already know

Make predictions about what's coming next

Stop and think often while you are reading

Look for the important stuff, key words

Don't sweat minor details

Try to put everything together

Talk to a buddy

STEP 13 Pairs discuss lingering content questions. The important work in this lesson isn't just to name reading strategies, it's to put them to use. Let students see how much they were able to absorb from this article as a result of their work in this lesson: have pairs meet one last time to list some questions they now have about atomic bombs, having read and discussed the article.

STEP 14 Whole class shares. Invite each pair to share one question about nuclear weapons. Keep going until all unique questions have been heard.

STEP 15 Collect writing. Review students' annotated articles and their atomic bomb question lists for thinking, engagement, and any clues they offer for follow-up lessons.

Tip ▶ Making marginal notes while doing a think-aloud is pretty challenging for anyone. It is something you get comfortable with after doing a few think-alouds. So we consider it optional for you, and especially for the kids who are thinking aloud for the first time.

Longer writing projects—reflecting the key genres required by the national standards—can be built on the work students have already done in this lesson. As kids continue to explore the topics of our reading selections, we expect that they will bring fresh background knowledge, recent thinking, and genuine curiosity to the task. When you use the lesson above with your own content, you can also use the assignments below as models for extending that content into longer writing projects.

Narrative: *Personify an object to share its history*

"I am a model B61 atomic bomb warhead, and I was born, I mean made, in 1968. For the past few years, I have sat on top of a missile in an Ohio-class submarine patrolling the Pacific Ocean. Today, I have just arrived back at Los Alamos National Laboratory in New Mexico to be refurbished. Here is what they are going to do to me before I go back to my duties . . ." Find out what it means to "refurbish" an atomic bomb. Then complete this first-person narrative, speaking in the voice of an atom bomb, up through the redeployment of the warhead. *Research clue: Begin with the four sources listed for this in the WrapUp Media Sources section at the end of the book.*

Informative/explanatory: *Analyze related costs and funding (AKA follow the money)*

Research and compare the amount of money spent on atom bombs to the costs of other government programs and services. Create an infographic that uses bar graphs, pie charts, or other features to show comparisons between nuclear weapons spending and other possible federal priorities. (Spending on nuclear weapons comes out of the military budget, the Department of Energy, and classified sources, so search hard.) *Research clues: U.S. budget priorities, federal spending breakdown.*

Persuasive/argumentative: *Argue the content's relevance to today's world*

Some experts argue that there is a "new arms race" between the United States and Russia, with the modernization of weapons yielding more powerful arsenals without increasing the actual number of warheads. Meanwhile, there is another nuclear arms race among currently non-nuclear countries seeking to develop a nuclear weapon of their own (e.g., Iran). And there is also an arms race among "nonstate actors," such as terrorist groups seeking to buy, steal, or build an atomic bomb of their own. Investigate these developments and take a position on the following statement: The danger of nuclear warfare is higher today than it has ever been. True? Exaggerated? *Research clue: "Doomsday Clock."*

My Atom Bomb Is in the Shop

Roger Vector, WrapUp Media

1. Did you know that just like any appliance in your kitchen, an atom bomb can wear out? And, just like that old toaster might fail to brown your bagel one morning, an aging warhead might fizzle when someone pushes the button.

2. So, on a regular schedule, every single atomic bomb the United States owns, whether it is deployed on a missile, a submarine, or a bomber plane, must be returned to its birthplace in New Mexico and given a tune-up. At Los Alamos National Laboratory, where the original Hiroshima and Nagasaki bombs of WWII were also built, the scientists call this regular warhead checkup "refurbishing."

3. Most of America's 5,000-plus warheads were built back in the sixties and seventies, and they have now become "Baby Boomers," just like the generation of Americans that built them: creaky, cranky, scuffed up, dried out, and at imminent risk of failure.

4. Constructed of such diverse materials as plastic, aluminum, uranium, rubber, plutonium, dynamite, and copper wires, these complex weapons wear out as components age at different rates. Humidity, vibration, and temperature variability are just some sources of deterioration.

5. While regular nuclear "life extension" visits have been quietly going on for years, something new has recently been added. Instead of just getting a routine tune-up, bombs are now getting an extreme makeover. According to the International Arms Control Association: "The U.S. military is in the process of modernizing all strategic delivery systems and refurbishing the warheads they carry. These systems are in many cases being completely rebuilt with essentially all new parts."

6. So these weapons will return to service with more killing power than ever. Our current intelligence suggests that Russia is also supercharging its warheads. Some scholars have labeled these destructive upgrades "a new arms race," drawing parallels with the 1960s when the United States and the Soviet Union were in a mad competition to build ever bigger arsenals. By 1970, both countries had stockpiled enough weapons to destroy life on earth hundreds of times over. (We still retain enough bombs to do the job dozens of times.)

7. One thing we know for sure, arms races aren't cheap. The U.S. is committed to spending $53 billion a year (that's $150 million a day) to keep this modernization "boom" going.

Pen Pal Pairs

TEXT	AUTHOR	TEXT TYPE
"Bye-Bye Bake Sales"	Lester Johnson, WrapUp Media	Opinion
"Smart Snacks in School"	U.S. Department of Agriculture	Infographic

TIME ▸ 30 minutes

GROUPINGS ▸ Whole class, pairs, individuals

STANDARDS MET ▸ See pages 306–307.

WHEN TO USE ▸ So far, we have been developing a long sequence designed to support kids' writing about subject-area topics with partners. This next version offers a versatile peer writing structure you can use *every day*.

Here we introduce a world-class writing-to-learn strategy: Pen Pals (AKA Written Conversations, AKA Dialogue Journals, AKA Digital Discussions). Smokey and his teacher-wife Elaine have written a whole book arguing that this is the single most important teaching strategy that any of us will ever learn, whether we teach chemistry, keyboarding, Spanish, or world history (2013).

Everyone complains about school lunches, so why not take up that all-time favorite topic again? Over the past several years, the USDA has been working to implement the Healthy, Hunger-Free Kids Act, passed in 2010 with a big boost from Michelle Obama's "Let's Move" anti-obesity campaign. But as the regulations took full effect in 2015, controversy erupted over nutritional imperialism, soaring lunch waste (mostly composed of those newly added fruits and vegetables), and the elimination of long-established pizza and candy bar fund-raisers—not to mention special-occasion treats in the classroom. There are even a few sarcastic Twitter/Instagram hashtags some high schoolers use when posting pictures of their low-enjoyment school lunches.

We kick off with this lunchroom controversy now, and return to the topic in Lesson 21, where your students can do a little in-house research.

PREPARATION

1. Make a copy of "Bye-Bye Bake Sales" and the "Smart Snacks in School" infographic for each student. It's fine to print them back to back.

2. Determine how pairs will form in Step 1.

3. Make sure students have ready access to pens and paper. Pen pal letters can also be written on digital devices, but *only* if everyone has the same devices and can use them fluently, with zero technological friction.

4. Be ready to project the infographic at Step 2, the rules at Step 3, the letter-starter stems at Step 4, and response options at Step 5.

STEP 1 **Partners prepare.** Have kids sit next to their partner. *Get in a good position for both writing and talking, and be sure you can still see any materials I project on the screen. Everyone please get out a full-size blank piece of paper. Put your name in the upper left-hand margin.*

◂ **Steps** & **Teaching Language**

Then, just below your name, write a "salutation" to your partner, as in "Dear _____." Now you are ready to have a pen pal conversation with your pal.

STEP 2 **Students read the article.** *I'm passing out an article about school lunches that includes an infographic. Take a few minutes to read both of them on your own. Later, you'll be discussing this information with your partner.* To assist kids in their reading, project the image of the USDA infographic on the screen, nice and big. Circulate and make sure kids are engaging with both the article and the infographic.

STEP 3 **Explain the rules.** *Interesting article, right? Plenty to talk about, but we are going to have a pair discussion in writing instead of out loud. Here are the rules of pen pal notes.*

Guidelines for Pen Pal Notes

1. Use your best handwriting, so your partner can understand you.
2. Don't worry about spelling and grammar. Just get your thoughts out. No erasing—cross out any errors and go on.
3. Draw pictures, diagrams, or cartoons if that helps you make your point.
4. Use all the time I give you for writing. Keep that pen moving until I tell you to exchange letters.
5. No talking. This is a silent activity.

So, you are all going to write your buddy a letter about our article, and then "mail it" by exchanging notes. When you get your buddy's letter, you'll write a response right under where he or she left off writing. Then, you'll pass it back to your buddy, and you'll respond to what he or she just wrote on the other letter.

The writing time will be pretty short, just about 1½ minutes per letter. We will write back and forth three times. You are both going to be writing letters at the same time. You're not waiting or watching your partner, you're both writing all the time.

I will give you a warning when you have fifteen seconds of writing time left with each letter.

STEP 4 **Support students as they write letter #1.** *If you have any trouble getting started, use one of these possible starters to get your letter going.* Be clear that they are not being asked to write a little bit about each of these topics but to use one only if they don't already have their own reactions to start with. Project the following list.

Questions to Help You Get Started

- Are any of these changes happening at our school?

- How have the lunches changed?

- Are there restrictions on certain foods? Something you miss?

- Do you think kids' choices should be restricted in these ways?

- What would happen if kids could eat whatever they wanted?

- Is it the school's job to make students thinner?

- What would be on your ideal menus?

- How do you feel about your school's lunch program now?

Go ahead and write your partner about your thoughts, reactions, questions, or feelings about the article. Happy writing, pen pals. I will let you know when there are fifteen seconds left.

We mention the "just 1½ minutes" figure mainly to lower kids' anxiety. Most often we will have them write longer, as long as we carefully observe how it is going. Don't look at your watch; walk around and watch kids write. When most students have filled a quarter of a page, it is time to pass.

STEP 5 **Students exchange letters and write responses.** *Okay, time to "mail" your letters. Swap letters with your partner. Now read your buddy's note, and think about it a little bit. Then, just beneath where their letter ended, write back for 1½ minutes. If you're not sure what to say, take a look at this list of possible responses.* Project the following list.

A Few Ways You Might Respond to Your Pen Pal

- Share your reactions

- Make a comment

- Ask a question

- Share a connection you've made

- Agree and give reasons

- Disagree and give reasons

- Raise a whole new idea about school lunches

Just keep the conversation going! Walk the room, looking over shoulders to get the timing right.

STEP 6 **Kids exchange second letters and write a final note.** Around this point in the lesson, some kids may be complaining of sore wrists. We usually jokingly invite the gripes, falsely promising to bring in a physical therapist next time.

Pass again, please. This will be your last piece of writing, so look over the whole conversation so far, and then write your partner one more time. You have the same choices as before and 1½ minutes to write. Just keep that conversation going.

Project choices again if needed. Monitor as usual.

STEP 7 **Kids read whole conversations.** *Pass back your letters one last time, and read that last entry your partner just made. When you are done reading, go ahead and talk out loud for a minute or two; just continue the conversation.*

STEP 8 **Whole class shares.** *Let's gather as a whole class and see what new learning or questions came out of these letters. Will a few pairs please share one highlight, one thread of your discussion? Something you spent time on, something that sparked lively discussion, maybe something you argued or laughed or wondered about?* Seek a wide array of responses and approaches. Since kids almost always enjoy this form of discussion, we feel safe in advising you to end the lesson by saying: *Did you like doing this? Great, because this is a conversation structure we can use over and over all this year.*

STEP 9 **Collect student writing.** Gather all the pen pal letters and review them later for engagement, quality of thinking, and ideas for future minilessons.

Variations ▶ ### Digital discussions

If you are an Edmodo or Google Classroom user, you already know you can put kids in pairs (or groups of any size) and have them converse right on the platform. And when this tool gets revved up, the conversations can really go viral, ramping up to lively whole-class discussions—and offering students the chance to engage with kids across the hall or around the world.

"Takeaway" dialogue journals

Live dialogue journals, as described above, are usually done by the whole class at once, with the teacher doing the timing, and the letters being written, received, and answered immediately—kind of like texting. Takeaway dialogue journals are more leisurely, and operate more like regular letters or emails. Language arts teachers may be familiar with this letter style from Nancie Atwell's *In the Middle* (2014).

Kids write their partner a note when their schedule permits (sometimes as homework), taking whatever time they need to offer a thoughtful missive. Typically, these notes are longer and more carefully composed than the speedy live pen pal letters in this lesson. They are "mailed" by simple hand delivery, via email, or by placing them in the partner's classroom mailbox—a system that teachers who use this strategy often set up.

Recipients answer these dialogue journals when they have time to think about and thoughtfully respond to their partner's notes. They return them through the same channel they arrived. These "takeaway" dialogue journals sometimes go on for weeks, or longer. Many teachers start these more sustained conversations a bit later in the year, allowing students to request their own long-term partners by submitting a written application explaining why they will work well together (another great writing assignment).

Longer writing projects—reflecting the key genres required by the national standards—can be built on the work students have already done in this lesson. As kids continue to explore the topics of our reading selections, we expect that they will bring fresh background knowledge, recent thinking, and genuine curiosity to the task. When you use the lesson above with your own content, you can also use the assignments below as models for extending that content into longer writing projects.

◀ *Research Projects for Extended Writing*

Narrative: *Tell the story of a typical day*

Get a cook's-eye view of national lunch policies. Prepare a list of questions about how the new guidelines are affecting your own school's food program. Then, make an appointment to interview a school cook, food service director, or supervisor. Take careful notes during your interview (video it, if permitted) and write a description of a workday for one of these people (with video clips, if possible), with an emphasis on how lunch laws and district constraints affect the folks who put food in your lunchroom every day.

Informative/explanatory: *Analyze related legislation*

Investigate the specific student health concerns targeted by the USDA. Dig into the Healthy, Hunger-Free Kids Act. Try to determine how the law aims to improve student wellness. What specific health concerns do the law and its rules try to address? Make a bullet list of the main health and wellness goals of the law.

Persuasive/argumentative: *Argue for a change in your school related to this content*

Pick one new item that you think should be *added* to your school's lunch menu—or an item that should be *subtracted* from the current offerings. Be ready to defend your menu revision with evidence: expert opinions, nutrition information, student polling data, menus from other schools, cost effectiveness, or other information.

Bye-Bye Bake Sales

Lester Johnson, WrapUp Media

Some of my own favorite school memories revolve around delicious snacks. Chocolate cake when a classmate had a birthday, a candy frenzy at Halloween, ethnic meals delivered by classmates' families, bake sales before Homecoming, PTA-funded pizza parties, and the chocolate-bar fund-raisers that paid for our field trips.

But all those toothsome treats are banned from school now, thanks to the sugar-buzz killers at the U.S. Department of Agriculture, the agency with jurisdiction over public school chow. Based on a law passed in 2010 but not fully implemented until 2015, even the beloved Girl Scout cookie table will be thrown off campus for peddling "junk food." How did it come to this?

The USDA has been reporting for years about the poor eating habits of Americans and especially of kids in school. The facts are undeniable: schools have been serving young people too much salt, sugar, and fat to keep them trim and well-nourished. Driven by these health concerns, the USDA set new standards for many foods served in school cafeterias— and in classrooms, vending machines, and bake sales.

The accompanying USDA infographic shows how different "snack food" items are being classified, replaced, and in some cases, banned from schools.

Though the USDA allows school districts special-occasion days when old-school calorific treats may be sold, many districts are taking a hard line, deciding to simply ban unhealthy foods all year long.

All this culinary correctness is a little over the top. Of course we don't want to cultivate prediabetes in school. But human beings celebrate with food all around the world. Do students really need to swap all forms of edible enjoyment for 180 days of nutritional correctness? As this column goes to press, it looks like school kids aren't thrilled with the new healthier menus either. A new study shows that students are actually eating about 13 percent fewer fruits and vegetables than before the regulations took effect—and throwing away 56 percent more food.

The study didn't investigate whether kids might be smuggling fun food into the classroom. But if I were going back to school today, I'd be stuffing my pockets with contraband Oreos right now.

United States Department of Agriculture

SMART SNACKS IN SCHOOL

The Healthy, Hunger-Free Kids Act of 2010 requires USDA to establish nutrition standards for all foods sold in schools — beyond the federally-supported meals programs. This new rule carefully balances science-based nutrition guidelines with practical and flexible solutions to promote healthier eating on campus. The rule draws on recommendations from the Institute of Medicine, existing voluntary standards already implemented by thousands of schools around the country, and healthy food and beverage offerings already available in the marketplace.

● Equals 1 calorie   ○ Shows empty calories*

Before the New Standards

286 TOTAL CALORIES	249 TOTAL CALORIES	242 TOTAL CALORIES	235 TOTAL CALORIES	136 TOTAL CALORIES
Chocolate Sandwich Cookies (6 medium)	**Fruit Flavored Candies** (2.2 oz. pkg.)	**Donut** (1 large)	**Chocolate Bar** (1 bar-1.6 oz.)	**Regular Cola** (12 fl. oz.)
182 Empty Calories	177 Empty Calories	147 Empty Calories	112 Empty Calories	126 Empty Calories

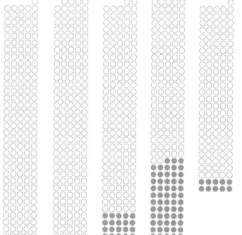

After the New Standards

170 TOTAL CALORIES	161 TOTAL CALORIES	118 TOTAL CALORIES	95 TOTAL CALORIES	68 TOTAL CALORIES	0 TOTAL CALORIES
Peanuts (1 oz.)	**Light Popcorn** (Snack bag)	**Low-Fat Tortilla Chips** (1 oz.)	**Granola Bar (oats, fruit, nuts)** (1 bar-.8 oz.)	**Fruit Cup (w/100% Juice)** (Snack cup 4 oz.)	**No-Calorie flavored Water** (12 fl. oz.)
0 Empty Calories	17 Empty Calories	0 Empty Calories	32 Empty Calories	0 Empty Calories	0 Empty Calories

*Calories from food components such as added sugars and solid fats that provide little nutritional value. Empty calories are part of total calories.

LESSON 21

Gathering and Summarizing Data

TIME ▶ 30 minutes, across 2 days

GROUPINGS ▶ Whole class, pairs, individuals

STANDARDS MET ▶ See pages 306–307.

WHEN TO USE ▶ Real writers are by definition *researchers*, gathering and interpreting information, whatever their field. This lesson puts students directly into that investigatory mode.

TEXT	SOURCE	TEXT TYPE
"Smarter Lunchrooms Self-Assessment"	B.E.N. Center, U.S. Department of Agriculture	Observational/scoring rubric

If your kids enjoyed the school lunch investigation in Lesson 20, you might want to follow it directly with this one. This time, instead of having written conversations, kids use a formal instrument to assess their own school's lunchroom and then write a three-paragraph summary of its best features, recent changes, and areas for improvement.

Now, don't worry—we've learned to keep this topic positive. A few years back, Smokey's sixth graders surveyed schoolmates who offered some carelessly critical comments about their school's food service. When the cooks saw the survey results, there were some tears behind the counter—and some hasty apologies from the young researchers. The only thing our "cooks" were actually doing was transferring pans of precooked (terrible) food from the truck to the serving line. But the kitchen employees still felt pride in their work and their loving treatment of the kids, so it was easy to hurt feelings with casual slanders of the menu. What a good lesson about being responsible researchers, and remembering that "subjects" are human beings, not just numbers.

PREPARATION

1. Download the USDA scorecard and make a copy for each student. Read the scorecard and examine the school schedule to figure out when your kids would be able to complete the scorecard. With various class schedules and campus events, you may need to allow several days to complete the survey. Be ready to firmly establish the day you will return to this lesson, at which time all kids should have their completed surveys in hand.

2. Alert the cafeteria staff that this project is happening and invite them to contact you with any questions. Your being knowledgeable about the latest USDA mandates may earn their trust and enthusiasm. They may even ask you to share the kids' results.

3. Determine how to form pairs for Step 2.

4. Be ready to project the summary structure in Step 3.

Steps & Teaching Language ▶

STEP 1 **On day 1, introduce the scorecard and schedule the research.** Have a copy of the scorecard on everyone's desk when the first brief class meeting begins. *Take a look at this document and try to figure out what we might do with it.* Let kids talk with neighbors as they read. Invite them to share guesses.

Yes, we are actually going to use this form to rate our own lunchroom. But we can't do it by just sitting here and trying to remember everything; the survey is far too detailed for that. So you are each going to take a little in-school field trip, all the way to the cafeteria, some time in the next couple days. You'll find a time when you are not actually eating to walk around, observe, and fill out the form.

Then we will come back here on [chosen day] *and take it from there.*

I've told the cafeteria staff that we are doing this project, and you should be respectful of them when you're scoring.

If you recently did Lesson 20, you might add: *As you can see, this document comes out of the same USDA program we talked about in our bake sales pen pal letters. So you already have some good background knowledge about the topic.*

STEP 2 **On day 2, pairs compare their lunchroom scorecards.** Give kids three or four minutes to look at each others' rankings and compare notes.

STEP 3 **Students write a summary of their lunchroom's performance.** *Look over your scorecard, which offers a huge amount of data. Also think about your own experience with the lunchroom and its staff day in and day out.*

Next, you are going to write a three-paragraph summary of your findings, divided like this. Project the following list.

> Paragraph 1: Some things I really like about our lunchroom: the atmosphere, the staff, the menu, my favorite items, positive changes going on, etc. (You might have been reminded of these by doing the survey, or just from memory.)
>
> Paragraph 2: Some key ways in which our lunchroom seems to be meeting the new USDA standards for nutrition.
>
> Paragraph 3: Some key ways in which our lunchroom might not yet meet the new USDA standards for nutrition.

Allow a good chunk of work time, perhaps three minutes per paragraph.

If you see kids having difficulty transferring info from their scorecards into the three categories, slow down and break the work into two steps. First, have them go through and code their scorecard entries 1, 2, or 3 to match the suggested paragraph contents. Then, turn them loose on the summary writing.

STEP 4 **Kids share summaries with the whole class.** You can ring-lead this with a sequence of prompts: *Who can read aloud their paragraph 1 about some things you like about our lunch service? Another? Who has a paragraph 2 about how the lunchroom is moving toward USDA standards? Another one? Now, who can share their paragraph 3 about what* *further steps the cafeteria needs to take reach USDA standards, whether you agree with them or not. Another?*

STEP 5 **Share findings with school food officials (optional).** We always want kids to have a real audience for their writing, whether it is a classroom partner or a student across the country.

With this topic, you need to first make sure that you have a food manager who actually wants the feedback. Then, you have to monitor the kids' writing for appropriateness and balance. If you need to just send along a few samples of kids' summaries, so be it.

STEP 6 **Collect all writings.** The scored rubrics mainly reassure you that kids completed the on-site assessment. The summaries are much more useful; they offer a window into kids' ability to weigh lots of information, find the most important ideas, and then put complex information into their own words—concisely.

Research Projects for Extended Writing ▶ Longer writing projects—reflecting the key genres required by the national standards—can be built on the work students have already done in this lesson. As kids continue to explore the topics of our reading selections, we expect that they will bring fresh background knowledge, recent thinking, and genuine curiosity to the task. When you use the lesson above with your own content, you can also use the assignments below as models for extending that content into longer writing projects.

Narrative: *Tell a personal investigation story behind the data collection*

Have kids use their scorecards to help reconstruct a chronological account of their evaluative visit to the lunchroom. For example: "When I first walked in, I noticed how colorful the room really is." "As I approached the salad bar, I noticed that it was really crowded and people were moving slowly through there. Some kids gave up and went to the pizza line." "As I was leaving, I saw Mrs. Wilson looking at me, so I showed her my survey. She was really curious about it."

Informative/explanatory: *Synthesize data for a new audience*

A team of kids might want to dig deeper into the rich data yielded by the scorecard. They could calculate averages for some key questions, then incorporate them into an "executive summary" of survey results.

Persuasive/argumentative: *Take a political side*

When you take a deeper look at the survey, you realize it is really measuring school's ability to "steer" kids toward the government's preferred (and maybe entirely wholesome) choices. At the same time, compliant lunchrooms purposely hide other choices, making it hard for kids to make those selections. Then there is the menu language; school cafeterias advertise food flavors just like fast-food businesses do in their ads (and perhaps just as deceptively). The question to write about: Is all this "steering" actually manipulation and deception—or is it benign social engineering for our own good?

Smarter Lunchrooms Self-Assessment

2014 Scorecard

©The B.E.N. Center 2014

Since its founding in 2009 the Smarter Lunchrooms Movement has championed the use of evidence-based, simple low and no-cost changes to lunchrooms which can simultaneously improve participation and profits while decreasing waste. This tool can help you to evaluate your lunchroom, congratulate yourself for things you are doing well and and identify areas of opportunity for improvement

Instructions

Read each of the statements below. Visualize your cafeteria, your service areas and your school building. Indicate whether the statement is true for your school by checking the box to the left. If you believe that your school does not reflect the statement 100% do not check the box on the left. After you have completed the checklist, tally all boxes with check marks and write this number in the designated area on the back of the form. This number represents your school's baseline score. The boxes which are not checked are areas of opportunity for you to consider implementing in the future. We recommend completing this checklist annually to measure your improvements!

It's not nutrition ...until it's eaten!

Important Words

Service areas: Any location where students can purchase or are provided with food

Dining areas: Any location where students can consume the food purchased or provided

Grab and Go Meals: Any meal with components pre-packaged together for ease and convenience – such as a brown bag lunch or "Fun Lunch" etc.

Designated Line: Any foodservice line which has been specified for particular food items or concepts – such as a pizza line, deli line, salad line etc.

Alternative entrée options: Any meal component which could also be considered an entrée for students - such as the salad bar, yogurt parfait, vegetarian/vegan or meatless options etc.

Reimbursable "Combo Meal" pairings: Any reimbursable components available independently on your foodservice lines which you have identified as a part of a promotional complete meal – For example you decided your beef taco, seasoned beans, frozen strawberries and 1% milk are part of a promotional meal called the, "Mi Amigo Meal!" etc.

Non-functional lunchroom equipment: Any items which are either broken, awaiting repair or are simply not used during meal service – such as empty or broken steam tables, coolers, registers etc.

Good Rapport: Communication is completed in a friendly and polite manner

All Points of Sale: Any location where a register/pin-pad is located for example: deli-line, snack window, a la carte line, hot line, kiosks/carts etc.

Focusing on Fruit

☐ At least two types of fruit are available daily

☐ Sliced or cut fruit is available daily

☐ Fruit options are not browning, bruised or otherwise damaged

☐ Daily fruit options are given creative, age-appropriate names

☐ Fruit is available at all points of sale (deli-line, snack windows, a la carte lines etc.)

☐ Daily fruit options are available in at least two different locations on each service line

☐ At least one daily fruit option is available near all registers (If there are concerns regarding edible peel, fruit can be bagged or wrapped)

☐ Whole fruit options are displayed in attractive bowls or baskets (instead of chaffing/hotel pans)

☐ A mixed variety of whole fruits are displayed together

☐ Daily fruit options are easily seen by students of average height for your school

☐ Daily fruit options are bundled into all grab and go meals available to students

☐ Daily fruit options are written legibly on menu boards in all service and dining areas

Promoting Vegetables & Salad

☐ At least two types of vegetable are available daily

☐ Vegetables are not wilted, browning, or otherwise damaged

☐ At least one vegetable option is available in all foodservice areas

☐ Individual salads or a salad bar is available to all students

☐ The salad bar is highly visible and located in a high traffic area

☐ Self-serve salad bar utensils are at the appropriate portion size or larger for all fruits and vegetable offered

☐ Self-serve salad bar utensils are smaller for croutons, dressing and other non-produce items

☐ Daily vegetable options are available in at least two different locations on each service line

☐ Daily vegetable options are easily seen by students of average height for your school

☐ A daily vegetable option is bundled into grab and go meals available to students

☐ A default vegetable choice is established by pre-plating a vegetable on some of the trays

☐ Available vegetable options have been given creative or descriptive names

☐ All vegetable names are printed/written on name-cards or product IDs and displayed next to each vegetable option daily

☐ All vegetable names are written and legible on menu boards

☐ All vegetable names are included on the published monthly school lunch menu

Moving More White Milk

☐ All beverage coolers have white milk available

☐ White milk is placed in front of other beverages in all coolers

☐ White milk crates are placed so that they are the first beverage option seen in all designated milk coolers

☐ White milk is available at all points of sale (deli-line, snack windows, a la carte lines etc.)

☐ White milk represents at least 1/3 of all visible milk in the lunchroom

☐ White milk is easily seen by students of average height for your school

☐ White milk is bundled into all grab and go meals available to students as the default beverage

☐ White milk is promoted on menu boards legibly

☐ White milk is replenished so all displays appear "full" continually throughout meal service and after each lunch period

Entrée of the Day

☐ A daily entrée option has been identified to promote as a "targeted entrée" in each service area and for each designated line (deli-line, snack windows, a la carte lines etc.)

☐ Daily targeted entrée options are highlighted on posters or signs

☐ Daily targeted entrée is easily seen by students of average height for your school

☐ Daily targeted entrées have been provided creative or descriptive names

☐ All targeted entrée names are printed/written on name-cards or product IDs and displayed next to each respective entrée daily

- ☐ All targeted entrée names are written and legible on menu boards
- ☐ All targeted entrée names are included on the published monthly school lunch menu
- ☐ All targeted entrees are replenished so as to appear "full" throughout meal service

Increasing Sales Reimbursable Meals

- ☐ A reimbursable meal can be created in any service area available to students (salad bars, snack windows, speed lines, speed windows, dedicated service lines etc.)
- ☐ Reimbursable "Combo Meal" pairings are available and promoted daily
- ☐ A reimbursable meal has been bundled into a grab and go meal available to students
- ☐ Grab and go reimbursable meals are available at a convenience line/speed window
- ☐ The convenience line offers only reimbursable grab and go meals with low-fat non-flavored milk fruit and/or vegetable.
- ☐ Grab and go reimbursable meals are easily seen by students of average height for your school
- ☐ The School offers universal free lunch
- ☐ A reimbursable combo meal pairing is available daily using alternative entrees (salad bar, fruit & yogurt parfait etc.)
- ☐ Reimbursable "Combo Meal" pairings have been provided creative or descriptive age-appropriate names (i.e. – The Hungry Kid Meal, The Athlete's Meal, Bobcat Meal etc.)
- ☐ Reimbursable "Combo Meal" pairing names are written/printed on name-cards, labels, or product IDs and displayed next to each respective meal daily
- ☐ All reimbursable "Combo Meal" names are written and legible on menu boards
- ☐ All reimbursable "Combo Meal" names are included on the published monthly school lunch menu
- ☐ Reimbursable "Combo Meal" pairings are promoted on signs or posters
- ☐ The named reimbursable "Combo Meal" is promoted during the school's morning announcements
- ☐ Students have the option to pre-order their lunch in the morning or earlier
- ☐ The cafeteria accepts cash as a form of payment

Creating School Synergies

Signage, Priming & Communication

- ☐ Posters displaying healthful foods are visible and readable within all service and dining areas
- ☐ Signage/posters/floor decals are available to direct students toward all service areas

- ☐ Signs promoting the lunchroom and featured menu items are placed in other areas of the school such as the main office, library or gymnasium.
- ☐ Menu boards featuring today's meal components are visible and readable within all service and dining areas
- ☐ A dedicated space/menu board is visible and readable from 5ft away within the service or dining area where students can see tomorrow's menu items
- ☐ Dining space is branded to reflect student body or school (i.e. – school lunchroom is named for school mascot or local hero/celebrity)
- ☐ All promotional signs and posters are rotated, updated or changed at least quarterly
- ☐ All creative and descriptive names are rotated, updated or changed at least quarterly
- ☐ A monthly menu is available and provided to all student families, teachers and administrators
- ☐ A monthly menu is visible and readable within the school building
- ☐ A weekly "Nutritional Report Card" is provided to parents detailing what thier student has purchased during the previous week.

Lunchroom Atmosphere

- ☐ Trash on floors, in, or near garbage cans is removed between each lunch period
- ☐ Cleaning supplies and utensils are returned to a cleaning closet or are not visible during service and dining
- ☐ Compost/recycling/tray return and garbage cans are tidied between lunch periods
- ☐ Compost/recycling/tray return and garbage cans are at least 5ft away from dining students
- ☐ Dining and service areas are clear of any non-functional equipment or tables during service
- ☐ Sneeze guards in all service areas are clean
- ☐ Obstacles and barriers to enter service and dining areas have been removed (i.e. – garbage cans, mop buckets, cones, lost & found etc.)
- ☐ Clutter is removed from service and dining areas promptly (i.e. – empty boxes, supply shipments, empty crates, pans, lost & found etc.)
- ☐ Students artwork is displayed in the service and/or dining areas
- ☐ All lights in the dining and service areas are currently functional and on
- ☐ Trays and cutlery are within arm's reach to the students of average height for your school
- ☐ Lunchroom equipment is decorated with decals/magnets/signage etc. wherever possible

- ☐ Teachers and administrators dine in the lunchroom with students
- ☐ Cafeteria monitors have good rapport with students and lunchroom staff
- ☐ The dining space is used for other learning activities beyond meal service (i.e. – home economics, culinary nutrition education activities, school activities etc.)
- ☐ Staff is encouraged to model healthful eating behaviors to students (i.e. – dining in the lunchroom with students, encouraging students to try new foods etc.)
- ☐ Staff smiles and greets students upon entering the service line continually throughout meal service
- ☐ Students who do not have a full reimbursable meal are politely prompted to select and consume a fruit or vegetable option by staff

Student Involvement

- ☐ Student groups are involved in the development of creative and descriptive names for menu items
- ☐ Student groups are involved in creation of artwork promoting menu items
- ☐ Student groups are involved in modeling healthful eating behaviors to others (i.e. – mentors, high school students eating in the middle school lunchroom occasionally etc.)
- ☐ Student surveys are used to inform menu development, dining space décor and promotional ideas
- ☐ Students, teachers and/or administrators announce daily meal deals or targeted items in daily announcements

Recognition & Support of School Food

- ☐ The school participates in other food program promotions such as: Farm to School, Chefs Move to Schools, Fuel Up to Play 60, Share our Strength etc.)
- ☐ The school has applied or been selected for the Healthier US School Challenge
- ☐ A local celebrity (Mayor, sports hero, media personality) is invited to share lunch with student 3 to 4 time a year

A la Carte

- ☐ Students must ask to purchase a la carte items from staff members
- ☐ Students must use cash to purchase a la carte items which are not reimbursable
- ☐ Half portions are available for at least two dessert options

---

_____ **Total Checked**	
Scoring Brackets	
70-100 – Smarter Lunchrooms Gold	
50-70 – Smarter Lunchrooms Silver	
30-50 – Smarter Lunchrooms Bronze	

It's not nutrition ...until it's eaten!

©The B.E.N. Center 2014

Point-of-View Annotation

TEXT	AUTHOR	SOURCE	TEXT TYPE
"How Smart Is It to Allow Students to Use Mobile Phones at School?"	Richard Murphy and Louis-Philippe Beland	www.theconversation.com	Research report

TIME ▸ 30 minutes

GROUPINGS ▸ Whole class, groups of four, individuals

STANDARDS MET ▸ See pages 306–307.

WHEN TO USE ▸ In our lessons so far, we have been inviting kids to write in their own "natural" voice. But skillful writers also know how to jump into someone else's shoes and see things from a different vantage point. When you want kids to revise their thinking and consider alternative reactions and interpretations of a text, point-of-view annotation is a useful strategy.

One skill of great readers, writers, and thinkers is to look at matters from different points of view—to see manifest destiny, for example, not just from the enthusiastic perspective of the miners, farmers, and ranchers moving west, but from the point of view of native peoples, the animals, and even the land itself.

In this lesson, we take up a hot-button issue for teens and teachers: What is the proper use (if any) of cell phones in school? Recently, Mayor Bill de Blasio overturned a long-running ban on cell phones in New York City schools. He made the argument that kids' phones could become a teaching tool in the classroom, not a disruption. On the other hand, a recent study (which your students will read about shortly) shoots down that belief, concluding that cell phone bans are associated with higher student test scores. Predictably, this study was lionized by a host of media outlets and trumpeted for days. However, like many social science research reports, this one's design and conclusions are highly disputable, and your kids may well identify significant flaws.

PREPARATION

1. Get your school's policy on cell phone use ready to project or hand out in Step 1. It may be in a student handbook, discipline code, or some other document, or only spoken (in which case you'll summarize it verbally).

2. Make a copy of "How Smart Is It to Allow Students to Use Mobile Phones at School?" for each student. Also, be ready to project the list of roles at Step 2.

3. Have a plan for creating groups of four at Step 2. If you have already established partners, you could join two existing pairs.

STEP 1 **Introduce the topic.** With the whole class, talk a bit about your school's policy on cell phone use by students. No need to take sides, just talk about what the deal is—maybe we use phones in class, maybe we have a BYOD plan in place, maybe we ban phones entirely from school, maybe you can turn yours on at 3:30, whatever the rules. This topic may provoke some gripes from kids—what a shock! We just want to acknowledge that cell phone use is a controversial issue these days and schools all around the country have different policies. And those policies are changing: 75 percent of schools that once banned cell phones have rescinded their bans in the past five years.

◀ **Steps & Teaching Language**

STEP 2 **Explain point-of-view annotation.** Have kids assemble in their groups of four. *You are going to annotate while you read this research report on cell phone use in schools. We have done this many times before. But this time, there is a wrinkle: you are going to read and annotate while pretending that you are* someone else. *Here are the four roles you can choose from* (project the list below). *Decide right now in your groups who is going to take each role. You have twenty seconds to each pick a different role, or I will assign them. Go!*

> *Roles*
> - A teacher
> - The principal
> - The parent of a student
> - A cell phone company executive

When kids have selected their roles, pass out the article and have them write their role right at the top of the page to remind them of their chosen point of view.

Reading from another person's perspective is hard and requires serious concentration. You will need to stop along the way and consciously think about how your person might be reacting to the text at that moment. And then, jot down words or phrases to label that thinking. By the time you are done, you should have stopped and annotated in your role at least five times.

STEP 3 **Students read and annotate in their roles.** Allow some reading time and be supportive as kids try out this unfamiliar activity. Some kids may choose to read straight through the text as they think about their roles, and then go back to insert their annotations. Just encourage them to keep working at it.

STEP 4 **Groups gather to share perspectives from different roles.** *All right, time's up! In your groups, go around the circle and hear some annotations from each perspective. Let's go in the same order, so the person who was playing the teacher will go first, then the principal, then the parent, and finally the cell phone executive. Take about one minute each to show some of your annotations, and tell what you thought the person would be thinking while reading.*

STEP 5 **Whole class discusses annotations.** Invite a couple of volunteers from each of the four perspectives to share what they were thinking from their role's point of view. *Point us to one place in the text where you stopped and wrote in that person's voice. What did you write? Why?* To get a breadth of response, it helps to prompt by asking, *Who else who was reading as a principal/cell phone exec/teacher/parent had a different annotation?*

STEP 6 **Write a new school policy on cell phones.** *Now that you have taken into account the opinions of many stakeholders in the cell phone debate and thought about the issue from their points of view, write a new or revised cell phone policy for our school. If you think it is perfect already, explain in detail why each aspect of the prevailing policy is correct.*

If possible, have kids use the same format that the school does in its official document: maybe it is written in paragraphs, in bullet points, or as a quasilegal document.

STEP 7 **Share the outcomes.** If it is politic and positive to do so, you can share this student input with school officials who might be enforcing or studying the policy.

STEP 8 **Collect all student writing.** Grab both the annotated articles and the revised phone policies. The articles will give you a notion of how well the kids can step into another reader's shoes (psychologists and business leaders tout empathy as necessary for happiness in life and for success in the twenty-first century). The revised phone policies will likely show kids blurting and whining less, and moving toward more nuanced and grown-up arguments.

Group size

◀ *Variation*

This is the first lesson where we have ramped up to groups of four. As you can see, the work is carefully structured and timed to help kids stay on task in this larger group setting. But if you still worry that your kids aren't ready for this, have them stick with pairs; they can still choose any two of the four reading roles. Adjust the rest of the steps accordingly.

Model point-of-view annotation

◀ *Tip*

At Step 2, if you feel that kids need more support to annotate as someone else, project a short piece of text and model how you would do it yourself. This is much like a standard think-aloud (see Lesson 19) except you are announcing that you are reading and annotating with someone else's eyes, and you make it very explicit as you go.

For example, if you were reading an article about mountain-climbing expeditions to Mount Everest, you could read as a climber, a Sherpa guide, an environmentalist, or an economic development officer for Nepal. If you read as a Sherpa, you might make notes like "These rich guys from America don't respect the mountain," or "They pay so much to climb here and we get paid so little," or "This is the only job in my village that can support a family."

Research Projects for Extended Writing ▶

Longer writing projects—reflecting the key genres required by the national standards—can be built on the work students have already done in this lesson. As kids continue to explore the topics of our reading selections, we expect that they will bring fresh background knowledge, recent thinking, and genuine curiosity to the task. When you use the lesson above with your own content, you can also use the assignments below as models for extending that content into longer writing projects.

Narrative: *Tell the history of an issue*

Research the turning points in cell phone use in schools. Share your findings in a narrative. Here's a starting point: In the early 1990s, most American schools banned *all* electronic devices (pagers, beepers, and newly common flip-phones), which were associated with drug dealers or gang members.

Informative/explanatory: *Describe a specific example*

The web is full of reports from schools where cell phones really seem to be improving students' learning, engagement, or test scores. Zoom in on a specific program that interests you, read their materials, and see if you can get an email or phone interview with teachers or students there. In a report, summarize the pluses and minuses in the program you researched. Use quotes, pictures, or comments from the program you've investigated.

Persuasive/argumentative: *Argue a side on a related educational issue*

Some people argue that using students' digital devices in the instructional program is completely inevitable and beneficial—and that those who still oppose this step are Luddites (look it up). As more schools drop their cell phone bans, it certainly looks like the fearful opponents are simply trying to block the path of history. But even amid this wave of new acceptance, is there still a serious and rational case to be made for keeping students' personal devices out of schools and the curriculum? There is lots of research and opinion published about the educational use of cell phones, especially smartphones. See what you can find, and write a manifesto in favor of continued bans.

How Smart Is It to Allow Students to Use Cell Phones at School?

Richard Murphy and Louis-Philippe Beland, www.theconversation.com

We conducted a study to find out what impact banning mobile phones has had on student test scores in subsequent years. We found that not only did student achievement improve, but also that low-achieving and at-risk students gained the most. We found the impact of banning phones for these students equivalent to an additional hour a week in school, or to increasing the school year by five days.

We studied mobile phone bans in England, as mobile phones are very popular there amongst teenagers. The research involved surveying schools in four cities in England (Birmingham, London, Leicester and Manchester) about their mobile phone policies since 2001 and combining it with student achievement data from externally marked national exams.

After schools banned mobile phones, test scores of students aged 16 increased by 6.4% of a standard deviation, which means that it added the equivalent of five days to the school year.

While our study was based in the UK, where, by 2012, 90.3% of teenagers owned a mobile phone, these results are likely to be significant even here in the US, where 73% of teenagers own a mobile phone.

The gains observed amongst students with lowest achievement when phones were banned were double those recorded among average students. Our results also indicate the ban having a greater impact on special education needs students and those eligible for free school meals.

Why did the ban work? Mobile phones provide students with access to texting, games, social media and the internet, potentially distracting them from instruction. Still, these findings do not discount the possibility that mobile phones and other forms of technology could be useful in schools if their use is properly structured. This is an ongoing debate in many countries today. Some advocate for a complete ban, while others promote the use of mobile phones as a teaching tool in classrooms.

Bill de Blasio, the mayor of New York, recently got rid of the ban on mobile phones with an argument that this would reduce inequalities. However, as our research shows, the exact opposite result is likely. Worse, allowing phones into schools would harm the lowest achieving and low-income students the most.

TIME FOR AN ARGUMENT

Most state and national standards call for students not just to persuade others in writing, but also to engage in formal arguments. This shift requires that, in addition to gathering abundant support for your position, you also anticipate and refute an opponent's objections in advance. So in these lessons, we focus kids on finding, weighing, assessing, and deploying specific text evidence in extended arguments.

LESSON 23

Do-It-Yourself Anticipation Guide

TIME ▶ Two 40-minute periods

GROUPINGS ▶ Whole class, pairs, individuals

STANDARDS MET ▶ See pages 306–307.

WHEN TO USE ▶ This is a great lesson to use when you want students to read closely for a purpose: creating a written document to be used with another class. Plus, this writing requires students to anticipate possible claims a reader might grapple with as the text unfolds.

TEXT	AUTHOR	SOURCE	TEXT TYPE
"The Perils of Adolescence"	Wray Herbert	Association for Psychological Science	Research report
"Teen Stress Rivals That of Adults"	Sophie Bethune	American Psychological Association	Research report

What is an anticipation guide? Remember that content-area reading methods class you were required to take in college? Maybe not, but if you stepped into the Wayback Machine (thank you, Mister Peabody and his faithful boy Sherman), we're certain that one of the strategy staples was the anticipation guide. Basically, it required you to study a text you were assigning to your students and come up with a series of debatable statements. You'd print these statements up, and have kids respond by agreeing or disagreeing with each statement *before reading* the article. This exercise would activate their background knowledge and opinions and spur some interesting prereading discussion—as well as subtly previewing the text. Then after reading the selection, students would respond to the same statements a second time, now basing their opinions on a much firmer knowledge base, thanks to the reading.

As we were thinking about this great but oft forgotten strategy, we noticed one inherent weakness: to synthesize the best debatable statements, it is the *teacher* who has to do the closest reading! What? So in this improved version, the students create an anticipation guide instead of the teacher.

This lesson breaks down classroom walls. Briefly, here's how it works: students in one of your classes create an "anticipation guide" about a short article you plan to assign. Then you bring their guides to a *different* class and use it to introduce the article to those kids. And it goes both ways: class #2 also prepares an anticipation guide for class #1. By writing anticipation guides for each other, students deepen their understanding of the subject matter while transforming key ideas into carefully crafted written statements. This lesson is written for two or more classes of the same subject. However, if you want to try this activity within the same class, no problem. We give those directions in the variation section. Sound complicated? The steps explain it all.

Day 1

1. Download and make copies of both articles, "The Perils of Adolescence" and "Teen Stress Rivals That of Adults," for each student. Make sure that each article is on a separate page. *Do not duplicate the articles back to back.*

2. Determine how to project the example anticipation guide based on the article "More Women Play Video Games Than Boys." This was an earlier read-aloud with which students should be familiar, Lesson 6 on page 49.

3. Duplicate the blank anticipation guide form so that each student will have two copies. *Do not* duplicate the forms back to back.

4. Decide how to pair students for Steps 2 and 5.

5. Consider appointing a student scribe for Steps 3 and 7.

Day 2

1. Decide ahead of time where you want students to stand and create response lines. Ideally, students will move to opposite sides of the room. Taping a big AGREE sign to one wall and a DISAGREE sign on the other will facilitate the activity.

Day 1

STEP 1 **Introduce the assignment.** *When you are going to read an article with a group, it is fun to share and compare background knowledge and opinions. An easy way to do this is by creating an anticipation guide, a set of debatable statements that get readers thinking and talking about issues a text will bring up. Let's take a look at an example for an article we've already read, "More Women Play Video Games Than Boys."*

STEP 2 **Pairs examine the anticipation guide.** *Move to sit with your partner and take a look at the projected example* (project the anticipation guide for the video games article). *What do you notice about this anticipation guide's statements? What makes them debatable? Intriguing? How do they invite users to share their opinions as well as hear what others have to say? Talk this over with your partner and make sure both of you jot down your ideas.*

As pairs work, monitor for on-task discussion, note taking, and careful study of the projected example.

STEP 3 **Develop a master list.** *It's time to put our ideas together. What are the characteristics of the debatable statements found in this anticipation guide? How are the statements worded to get people thinking and talking about gaming before they even read the article? Let's make a big list. And as the list grows, be sure to copy down any ideas you and your partner*

◀ **Steps** & **Teaching Language**

didn't think of. We'll jot your ideas down on the board. You'll need our complete list in just a moment! Enlist your student scribe to take notes at the board/computer so you can move about the room.

Students might mention items like these:

- Don't include the title.

- All statements should seem believable.

- Statements should make readers pause and think.

- Statements should provoke both agreement and disagreement.

- It's okay to have some false or misleading statements that seem true.

- Statements can focus on misconceptions so the reader is surprised by text information.

- Some statements might remain controversial after reading; there don't have to be correct answers.

- None of the statements use a direct quote from the text.

- Statements aren't just obviously true or false. They require you to form an opinion and back it up.

STEP 4 **Introduce the article and individual annotation.** Ultimately, two classes are going to try out each other's anticipation guides, so remember that at this step students in a given class should read *only* the article needed for anticipation guide creation. Beforehand, decide which article each class will read for this part of the lesson (either "The Perils of Adolescence" or "Teen Stress Rivals That of Adults").

Now we're going to read an article and work to create the ultimate anticipation guide for kids in another class. As you read this article, underline short passages that spur ideas for anticipation guide statements. Then, jot your ideas and possible statements in the margin. If you finish reading and annotating before I call time, reread the article and try to come up with a few more statements. Remember, we want to create the most intriguing anticipation guide possible—something that will get kids in the other class to want to read this article!

While the students work, make your way around the classroom to troubleshoot, encourage them, and applaud any particularly juicy bits they create for their guide.

STEP 5 **Partners compare anticipation guide statements.** *Get together with your partner and compare your statements for the article you both read. Notice which ones are similar and which ones are unique to one partner. After you've compared, each of you go back to your articles and put stars by your three best ideas. Between you, you'll have six. Remember: think about the characteristics of a good anticipation guide statement; don't forget to review the list we made earlier.* Project the master list while also encouraging students to refer to their earlier notes.

STEP 6 **Partners write anticipation statements.** Pass out one blank anticipation guide to each pair. *Here's the form. With your partner, work out the exact wording of your five best statement ideas. Remember to look back at your master list of what makes a good anticipation statement. Write each of your five final statements in a separate box on the form. When you're done, you should have one statement left over since you started with six.*

Project the blank form to clarify directions.

As students work, read over shoulders, gently encouraging statement revision when necessary. Do not hesitate to redirect students to their master list notes. You might also project the original example anticipation guide so that they can review how statements are worded.

STEP 7 **Partners share statements with the class.** *Before we regroup, pairs take a minute to rank your statements from one to five. One is your absolute best favorite statement while five is your least. The others are in between.* Move on to next step once ranking is complete.

Before continuing, enlist your student scribe to record ideas for the entire class to see. *When it's your pair's turn to share, I want you to give us your number one statement. If that one is already up on the board, give us your number two. If that one is up, give us your number three. If we get to you and all your statements are up there (highly unlikely if you've really worked to be creative), then read us your number one statement. Questions?* Instruct the scribe to put a check by a statement each time it is repeated as a number one.

Call on each pair for their best statement. Once all pairs have made a contribution, ask if any pair has an additional statement they think would work and would like to add.

STEP 8 **Class chooses the best five statements.** *We've got a lot of great statements up here, but we can use only five. Turn to your partner, look over our list, and choose the five statements you think would do the best job of getting the kids in the other class to think and discuss before they read the article.*

Give pairs a few minutes to discuss choices, and then negotiate the top five statements that will be used. You might want to step in to erase or to help the class rephrase statements for better wording or effect. At the end of this discussion, only five statements should remain on the board.

That was a hard decision, wasn't it? There were a lot of good statements to choose from and I'd really like to take a look at all of them, so make sure your and your partner's names are on the form and pass them in.

STEP 9 Class creates the final draft anticipation guides. After the "initial draft" anticipation guides are completely collected, pass out a new set of blank forms, one to each student.

On this new blank form, copy down our five final statements. Be sure to copy those statements neatly since they will be read by another class. Give students a couple of minutes to copy the statements.

Tomorrow you'll be responding to an anticipation guide created by another class while they'll be responding to yours! I'm collecting all the guides and articles so that there are no "spoilers." If anyone gets to read the other classes' article or anticipation guide, then the surprise is ruined.

Day 2

Steps & ▶
Teaching
Language

STEP 1 Students respond individually to the partner class's guide. Pass out the anticipation guides created by the other class. *Yesterday, while we created our anticipation guide, your partner class created one as well on a different article* (either "The Perils of Adolescence" or "Teen Stress Rivals That of Adults"). *Take a look at the five statements. For each one, mark* agree *or* disagree *on the left-hand side. Below each statement, jot down some notes that give specific reasons for why you agreed or disagreed.*

Monitor to make sure students are writing down their reasons, not just marking agree/disagree.

STEP 2 Students vote with their feet. *Grab your anticipation guide and stand up. When I read the first statement, move to the side of the room that matches your response. I've hung big AGREE and DISAGREE signs on the walls so you know where to stand. Any questions?*

Read the first statement and direct students to the wall that reflects their opinion. *Everyone on the correct side? Quickly, get with a partner and separate yourselves so that I can really see the pairs; no clumps allowed! And if your side has an uneven number, there will be one—only one—trio. Go, form those pairs!*

Monitor, enforcing the pair-only, no-clumps policy.

STEP 3 Pairs compare reasons. *Your pairs look great. Turn to your partner, greet them by name, and compare your reasons for responding as you did. Try to ask your partner some questions that would make him explain his position in more detail.*

Monitor conversations, listening in for some ideas that should be shared with the class. When you detect a conversation lull, move on to Step 4.

STEP 4 Pairs from each side share with the class. *Who had a partner with some interesting reasons for agreeing or disagreeing? I was walking around listening to your conversations, so I know there's a lot of good* *stuff out there that we should all hear. And remember to be a good audience as we carefully listen to other pairs' ideas. Remember to look toward whoever is speaking.* Allow for some wait time before cold calling. A stretch of uncomfortable silence will usually bring on some volunteers.

STEP 5 **Students continue voting.** After hearing a couple of responses from each side, it's time to move on to the next statement and repeat the instructions in Steps 2 through 4. If you notice students gravitating exclusively to friends as they line up, instruct them to actively engage with someone new. If momentum continues, you might discuss responses to all five statements. However, if you see energy flagging, it's okay to discuss responses to just the first three statements.

STEP 6 **Students read the article.** Pass out the article. *Okay, here's the moment you've been preparing for: reading the article. For the time being, put your anticipation guide face down. As you read, notice how the text connects with the discussion we just had about those guide statements. When you read, do not hesitate to do a little annotation. Mark down items that confirm what you thought, surprise you, or raise questions.* Share the following annotation symbols with students.

✓ = I thought so

! = surprise

? = question

Monitor individual student reading. As students finish up, move to the next step.

STEP 7 **Students respond again to the anticipation guide.** *Now that you've finished reading, flip the anticipation guide over. Reread each statement, and again mark AGREE or DISAGREE, this time in the column on the right side of the page.*

Once you're done, notice where your opinion changed and see if you can find the text evidence that led to this change. Mark the number of the guide statement by that part of the article.

STEP 8 **Pairs compare postreading responses.** *Move to sit with your partner. While you compare your postreading guide responses, also take a couple minutes to discuss the article information. What surprised you, what raised questions?*

Monitor pairs, keeping a lookout for those who saw some changes in their opinions after reading.

STEP 9 **Share response changes with the class.** *Who had a partner with a postreading change of opinion?* Once again allow for some wait time before resorting to calling on the students whose changes you noted. When you call on a student, remember to ask: *What in the article led you to change your opinion?*

STEP 10 **Compare articles.** Return the articles and first-draft anticipation guides used the previous day. *Remember that article we read yesterday? I'm returning it to you. Move back with your partner and take a couple of minutes to discuss the information presented in both articles. What conclusions can you draw from this information on navigating life at your age? What might you do differently or remember that might help you make more rewarding decisions and lead a less stressful life?*

Give pairs a few minutes to chat and then take some volunteers for a quick large-group discussion.

STEP 11 **Anticipation guide debrief.** You might have students write individual responses to these questions on an exit slip or discuss with their partner and then share with the class.

- Which required you to read the article more closely: reading an article and creating an anticipation guide, or responding to a guide and then reading the article? Why?
- How did completing and discussing the anticipation guide beforehand change what you noticed in the text?
- Which item on the anticipation guide created the most discussion/ thinking for you and your partner?

Shoptalk ▶ If students enjoy writing anticipation guides and testing them out on another class, this is an activity you could intersperse throughout the year with various pieces of text. Also, you'll develop quite a collection of guides that you might use with future classes!

Variation ▶ **Variation for One Class**

1. Divide the class in half, but make sure student pairs are retained.
2. Review the anticipation guide example as described.
3. Make sure half the pairs read "The Perils of Adolescence" while the other half read "Teen Stress Rivals That of Adults." Use the same annotation and anticipation guide development instructions, but emphasize that you need to keep everything *secret* from the other half of the class.
4. Rather than developing the final anticipation guide in front of anyone, have pairs for each article submit their best statement on an index card. Collect them, choose the ones you like, and prepare a five-statement anticipation guide for each article.
5. The following day, pairs in each half receive the anticipation guide for the article they have yet to read. During the response line parts, encourage the guide creator classroom half to lead the discussion.

Longer writing projects—reflecting the key genres required by the national standards—can be built on the work students have already done in this lesson. As kids continue to explore the topics of our reading selections, we expect that they will bring fresh background knowledge, recent thinking, and genuine curiosity to the task. When you use the lesson above with your own content, you can also use the assignments below as models for extending that content into longer writing projects.

Narrative: *Chart how the topic applies to your own life*

Create a one-day "stress journal" and use it to monitor yourself for a day or two. On the first page, make a list of events or situations that are often stressful to you. Some of these may come from the articles we read from the American Psychological Association, and others will come from your own self-knowledge, things that bug you. Then, on a day you choose, stop as many times as you can to note your stress level, what triggers it, and anything that makes your stress go down. Compare your experiences with other kids in the APA stress studies.

Informative/explanatory: *Gather and analyze your own data*

In social science, one thing researchers must do is *replicate* studies like the ones you just read—meaning, doing them over again to make sure the results are the same. While you don't have the support of a university sociology department or an international polling company, you can design and conduct a local sampling to see how your school community matches the national data. Look up the APA stress study, which shows the questions they used. Pick a few of them (maybe six to ten items), create and distribute your own survey to a selection of students in your school, tally the results, and report back with a comparison. Do kids at your school feel the same kinds of stress as teens elsewhere? Are there differences? What could explain them?

Persuasive/argumentative: *Argue your perspective to an audience of a different demographic*

Did you ever have a conversation with your parents when they were disapproving of your friends? Maybe it ended up with them saying something like, "If all your friends jumped off a bridge, would you jump too?" Their point being: you shouldn't blindly follow whatever your peers want to do. Turns out the jumping-off-the-bridge question has been used by parents forever. Look into that and what it means. (Yes, it is all over the web.) What don't adults understand (or what have they forgotten) about teenage peer groups? Use your research to write a persuasive piece aimed at educating parents.

ANTICIPATION GUIDE FOR "MORE WOMEN PLAY VIDEO GAMES THAN BOYS"

Before reading: Check agree or disagree for each statement. Under each statement, jot down your reasons for your opinion.

After reading: Based on the text information, mark how you would now respond to each statement. Notice where your opinions/assumptions have changed.

Before Reading		Statement	After Reading	
Agree	**Disagree**		**Agree**	**Disagree**
		1. Males play video games far more frequently than females.		
		2. Females are readily accepted into the online gaming community.		
		3. People are attracted to video games because of the violence		
		4. Video games may someday make movies and television obsolete.		
		5. Useful, everyday skills can be learned through recreational gaming.		

ANTICIPATION GUIDE FOR _____

Before reading: Check agree or disagree for each statement. Under each statement, jot down your reasons for your opinion.

After reading: Based on the text information, mark how you would now respond to each statement. Notice where your opinions/assumptions have changed.

Before Reading		Statement	After Reading	
Agree	**Disagree**		**Agree**	**Disagree**
		1.		
		2.		
		3.		
		4.		
		5.		

The Perils of Adolescence

Wray Herbert, Association for Psychological Science

Adolescence is a perilous time of life. It's a time of heightened risk taking—reckless driving, risky sex, excessive drug and alcohol use. For decades the prevalent view—the common wisdom of parenting manuals—was that teenagers feel invulnerable, immortal; they underestimate life's very real risks and dangers.

But scientists who study adolescent decision making now dispute this. Teenagers do indeed underestimate risk—sometimes—but at other times they overestimate how risky and harmful a situation is. So the actual risk taking cannot be simply explained by a diminished perception of risk.

So what does explain it? Well, one risk factor is almost certainly the influence of other people—especially other teenagers. When teens are with their friends, compared to when they are alone, they are much more likely to do things like use drugs, shoplift, and drive dangerously. And they spend a lot of time with their peers—far more than with their families. What's more, teenagers very much want to be accepted. They fear rejection. All of this would seem to implicate peer pressure and conformity in adolescent risk taking.

Yet surprisingly, the role of such social influence in adolescence is not well understood. That's why psychological scientist Lisa Knoll and colleagues, of the University College London's Institute of Cognitive Neuroscience, have been exploring social influence and risk perception in teenagers. Specifically, they wanted to see if social conformity varies depending on who is doing the influencing. Are teenagers' perceptions of risk influenced by others' perceptions? And if so, who are the most influential people in teenagers' lives, and does such social influence diminish over time?

Knoll and her colleagues studied the development of social influence on risk perception from late childhood into adulthood. They recruited volunteers who ranged from 8 to 59 years old, including children, young teens (12 to 14 years old), adolescents, young adults, and adults. All of these volunteers were asked to examine various risky scenarios having to do with health and safety—cycling without a helmet, for example, or crossing a street while texting.

The results were clear and provocative. People in every age group were influenced by others' perceptions, changing their own ratings to be more like those of others. Even mature adults demonstrated a need to conform, though social influence did diminish from childhood through adulthood.

But here's the real surprise: The scientists had predicted that teenagers would be more influenced by other teenagers rather than by adults. That was not the case: The older teenagers were influenced equally by adults and their same-age peers. Indeed, only the youngest teenagers were more strongly influenced by their peers. This suggests that the years between childhood and adolescence may be a crucial period in the development of risk perception. Young teens are challenging the experience and authority of adults and looking instead to the other teens whose opinion they value.

Teen Stress Rivals That of Adults

APA's *Stress in America*™ survey finds unhealthy behavior in teens, especially during the school year.

Sophie Bethune, American Psychological Association

If you think you're stressed out, imagine being a teenager in today's society. American teens say they experience stress in patterns similar to adults, and during the school year they report stress levels even higher than those reported by adults. These were the prime conclusions of APA's poll *Stress in America*™: *Are Teens Adopting Adults' Stress Habits?* The survey of adults and teens was conducted online on behalf of APA by Harris Interactive last August.

Teens reported that their stress levels during the school year far exceeded what they believe to be healthy (5.8 vs. 3.9 on a 10-point scale) and topped adults' average reported stress levels (5.8 for teens vs. 5.1 for adults). Even during the summer—from Aug. 3 to Aug. 31, 2013, when interviewing took place—teens reported their stress during the prior month at levels higher than what they believe is healthy (4.6 vs. 3.9 on a 10-point scale). Many teens also reported feeling overwhelmed (31 percent) and depressed or sad (30 percent) as a result of stress.

Too few managing stress

Few teens said their stress was on the decline—only 16 percent reported that their stress decreased in the past year—while approximately twice as many said their stress increased in the past year (31 percent) or believed their stress level will increase in the coming year (34 percent). Nearly half of teens (42 percent) reported they were not doing enough or were not sure if they were doing enough to manage their stress, and more than one in 10 (13 percent) said they never set aside time to manage stress.

Influence of stress on health behaviors

- **Stress and sleep:** On average, teens reported sleeping far less than the recommended amount—7.4 hours on school nights and 8.1 hours on non-school nights, compared with the 8.5 to 9.25 hours recommended by the National Sleep Foundation. Nearly one in five teens (18 percent) said that when they do not get enough sleep, they are more stressed and 36 percent of teens reported feeling tired because of stress in the past month.

- **Stress and exercise:** The survey found one in five teens (20 percent) reported exercising less than once a week or not at all. Teens who reported high stress during the past school year also said they spend an average of 3.2 hours online a day, compared with two hours among those reporting low stress levels during the past school year.

- **Stress and eating:** Of the 23 percent of teens who reported skipping a meal in the prior month due to stress, nearly one in four (39 percent) said they do this weekly or more.

Methodology

The Stress in America survey was conducted online by Harris Interactive Inc., on behalf of APA between Aug. 3 and 31, 2013, among 1,950 adults ages 18 or older and 1,018 teens, ages 13 to 17, who reside in the United States. This online survey was not based on a probability sample and therefore no estimates of theoretical sampling error could be calculated. To read the full methodology, including the weighting variables, visit Stress in America.

The Stress in America™ *survey is part of APA's Mind/Body Health campaign. Conducted annually since 2007, it seeks to examine the state of stress across the country and understand its impact. The results of the survey draw attention to the serious physical and emotional implications of stress and the inextricable link between the mind and body.*

Line Up for an Argument

TIME ▸ 45 minutes

GROUPINGS ▸ Whole class, pairs, individuals

STANDARDS MET ▸ See pages 306–307.

 Chapter 13's Text Set

WHEN TO USE ▸ This lesson gives students practice in defending a position on a controversial issue by having them argue with opponents, face to face.

TEXT	AUTHOR	SOURCE	TEXT TYPE
"The Benefits and Risks of Searching for Extraterrestrial Intelligence"	Roger Vector	WrapUp Media	Pro-con chart

Since the post-WWII "atomic age," outer space science fiction has been a prominent film and novel genre. And much earlier science fiction is now fact. Currently the Mars rovers Curiosity and Opportunity comb the red planet's surface while the twin unmanned Voyager spacecrafts speed toward the far edges of our solar system. The Kepler telescope has already discovered thousands of Earth-like planets, just in our own Milky Way galaxy. Simultaneously, technology research is inching toward spacecraft capable of even more distant missions. The goal? Possibly acquiring resources for use back on Earth, but also attempting to determine if we might encounter intelligent life out there. Here's the big question: If aliens do exist, should we attempt to make contact with them? This is a good issue to argue through *before* contact happens rather than after—and that's exactly what your class is going to do!

PREPARATION

1. Download and be ready to project the G-rated trailers of a couple of different alien movies, one that presents aliens as friendly allies and another that shows them as dangerous invaders. Our favorite pair are the trailers from the films *ET* and *Independence Day*.

2. Preview the Gathering Ideas for an Argument: Alien Movie Trailer Notes sheet and make one copy for each student. Also copy the article "Benefits and Risks of Searching for Extraterrestrial Intelligence" for each student.

3. Determine how pairs will form in Step 1.

4. You'll need a supply of 3×5-inch index cards for the class to use in Step 6.

5. Be sure there is an area in the room where the entire class can form two parallel lines in Step 7.

Steps & Teaching Language ▸

STEP 1 **Assign pair numbers.** *Move to sit with your partner. Now I need pairs to number off by twos.* Quickly point to pairs and help them count off so that you have an even number of pairs (not individual students) designated as ones and twos.

STEP 2 **Introduce the topic and videos.** *Currently the United States is participating in unmanned space exploration. We have two robotic probes exploring Mars while two other spacecraft are headed to the outer reaches of our solar system. How many of you have seen a science fiction* *movie that involves space aliens?* Take a show of hands or have students quickly compare movie notes with their partners. *How were the aliens depicted? Were they friendly or was their goal to destroy the human race?* Hear from a few volunteers.

We're going to take about five minutes to watch a couple of movie trailers from sci-fi alien films. In one movie, the aliens are depicted as friendly, while in the other, the aliens are dangerous. Pass out the Two-Column Video Notes sheet.

At the top of your sheet, mark down your pair number; you're either a one or a two. Before we start viewing, fold this sheet in half lengthwise so that just the Details About the Trailers column is showing. We'll use the top half for the first trailer and the bottom half for the second. Everybody follow? As you watch each trailer, remember to jot down some key details that you see or hear.

Show each preview. Allow a minute or two after each for students to jot down additional details they remember.

STEP 3   **Respond to the video details.** Ask students to open up their sheets so that they can now see the entire page.

Reread the details you recorded. In the second column, jot down your response to each trailer. Since film trailers are meant to intrigue you as well as manipulate your emotions, pay attention to your feelings as well.

Monitor the room as students jot their responses. *As you finish up, take a moment to reread your responses and put a star by the two most interesting ones you had for each trailer.*

STEP 4   **Pairs share their starred responses.** *Meet with your partner and compare your responses to the trailers. Start with the items you starred, but you can go ahead and compare your responses to other trailer details until I call time. Remember to take turns sharing.*

This discussion is a quick one. When most pairs have covered at least their starred items, call the class back together.

STEP 5   **Assign roles, and read individually.** *Since we're going to keep this discussion of aliens going a little longer, hang on to those sheets for later. Let's review our numbers one last time. Raise your hand if your pair is a number one. Number twos?* If there is any confusion, the numbers should be written at the top of the notes sheet, or you can reassign the correct number.

Pass out the two-column chart by Roger Vector. *Number one pairs, raise your hands. You will be arguing that connecting with intelligent alien life is a good idea, so circle **Pro**. Number two pairs, raise your hands. You will be arguing that connecting with alien life is a bad idea, so circle **Con**.*

Now take a few minutes to read your column silently. As you read, jot some notes and mark the reasons for your side that seem most powerful.

STEP 6 **Pairs prepare their arguments on index cards.** *Now it's time to get together with your partner and plan your side's arguments. At the top of this index card, write your name and pair number (one or two). Jot down the argument notes for your side on this card. You can use details from the handout, the film trailers, or your background knowledge. Be sure you and your partner each take your own notes because you'll be on your own a little later. Also, for the next step you can ONLY bring your index card with you; the Pros/Cons handout stays on your desk. Go!*

Roam the room, monitoring for sustained pair focus as well as checking that both partners are writing down sufficient argument details for their side.

STEP 7 **Sides form two lines.** Go to the spot in the room where you want the students to form lines. *In just a minute, we're going to form two parallel lines here. One line, here, will be the Pros; the other line, here, will be the Cons.* Indicate to students where they should stand. The two lines should be about three feet from each other. *Bring your index card and a pen, and find a spot on your side's line that is* not *next to your partner. Ready? Go!*

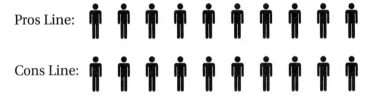

STEP 8 **Lines split into new shoulder partners.** *Now, turn to a person who is standing* next to you *(not across from you) in line, taking care that no one is left without a new "shoulder" partner. As soon as you know who your partner is, greet each other by name and start comparing notes. See if you can grab a new idea from your partner or together think of some additional argument points to add to your cards.*

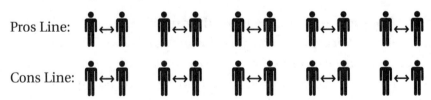

Give shoulder partners two minutes to compare notes.

STEP 9 **Lines move closer and face each other.** *Now, turn to face the opposite line, positioning yourself so that you're opposite one person on the other side. Introduce yourself to this new "face" partner.*

Pros Line:

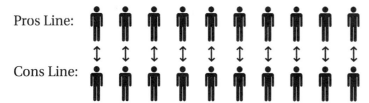

Cons Line:

STEP 10 **Face partners argue.** *Now it's time to argue. Position one, Pros, you've got ONE minute to argue why we should seek out extraterrestrial intelligence. Position two, Cons, your job is to listen carefully but not to talk. Everybody got that? The ONLY side that gets to talk is the Pros position. Go!* Use a stopwatch or a clock to time a minute.

Stop, time's up! Cons, now it is your turn to argue why we should not seek out extraterrestrial intelligence. The same rules apply in this round. Pros, your job is to listen carefully but not to talk. Go! Allow Cons to argue for a minute.

STEP 11 **Partners have an open discussion.** *In this round, you can talk with your face partner and have a Pros/Cons discussion. However, you must disagree politely. If you point out an opponent's weak argument, you must explain why in specific terms; then you need to listen to your partner's response without interrupting. Ask tough questions and do your best to convince your face partner to come over to your side. However, open discussion means listening 50 percent of the time. It doesn't mean interrupting or talking over the other person. Any questions? Go!*

Give face partners two to three minutes for open discussion. Monitor for talking about the topic as well as taking turns. If you see one partner failing to give equal floor time to her opponent, do not hesitate to intervene and coach.

STEP 12 **Drop advocacy and seek common ground.** *Wow, that was some heated discussion going on. However, now I want you all to take a deep breath and drop your positions. The final job for you and your face partner is to find a solution to this problem. Is it best to seek out alien life or choose to remain hidden from other intelligent extraterrestrial beings? Talk it over with your partner. Your solution might come down on one side of the issue, or you might come up with a solution that combines ideas from both sides. When you arrive at your answer, jot some notes on your index cards so that you remember it.*

Give face partners about two minutes to work and then call for their proposals. Everyone will be surprised at the number of different solutions there are to the problem.

Longer writing projects—reflecting the key genres required by the national standards—can be built on the work students have already done in this lesson. As kids continue to explore the topics of our reading selections, we expect that they will bring fresh background knowledge, recent thinking, and genuine curiosity to the task. When you use the lesson above with your own content, you can also use the assignments below as models for extending that content into longer writing projects.

Narrative: *Pitch some propaganda*

Often, a story can change someone's mind more effectively than a formal argument can. Choose a side of this issue to support, and then consider how a storyline about contact with aliens would sway others to your opinion. For example, is your alien friendly or ferocious? Use the items in the appropriate column in the Pro-Con chart to give you ideas for a "treatment" (also known as an outline) for your own alien contact movie. To start, you'll need some characters, a place, and an initial meeting. Then you need events or episodes, where things start going right—or wrong. Maybe your alien cures cancer his first day on earth, or maybe he eats Australia. Or both. It's your movie. Action!

Informative/explanatory: *Craft an introduction*

One big debate among alien hunters is this: If we find someone else, what should we say? What would be the just-right message to show us as friendly, intelligent, harmless, mighty, or whatever human traits we think would make us look like good galactic neighbors? There are already several pieces of Earth-made spacecraft that have been carrying such messages across space for years. Investigate these, study their messages, and read about other proposed messages to be attached to NASA craft. Then write a new, better message to possible life forms. *Research clue: Voyager, Pioneer.*

Persuasive/argumentative: *Argue the less-argued case*

The Pro-Con chart we just read lays out one of the loudest debates in modern-day science. If you dig into the issue, you'll find that many important public figures—physicist Stephen Hawking and inventor Elon Musk, to name two—have taken strong public positions against contacting aliens. In fact, some science leaders have started an international petition to prevent attempting any contact. In the face of such widespread opposition, is there still a realistic case to be made for actively seeking other life forms? Taking into account all the negatives, assemble the best evidence remaining and make the strongest possible case for phoning E.T.

GATHERING IDEAS FOR AN ARGUMENT: ALIEN MOVIE TRAILER NOTES

Details About the Trailers (important narration, dialogue, and images)	Your Response to the Trailers (your own thoughts and questions)
Trailer 1:	**Trailer 2:**
Trailer 1:	**Trailer 2:**

The Benefits and Risks of Searching for Extraterrestrial Intelligence (SETI)

Roger Vector, WrapUp Media

The current controversy over whether or not to seek direct contact with alien life forms (if any exist) has polarized the scientific community. Drawing on the many vigorous debates under way, here are some of the main arguments made by the two sides.

PRO ↑

This search fulfills the human urge to explore.

We will find out if we are alone or have company in the universe.

Any advanced civilization that has survived for this long will have evolved beyond war and destruction.

No one will "drop by," and even messages would take scores or hundreds of years to be exchanged.

We might gain scientific knowledge that could accelerate our development.

We could find solutions for hunger, cancer, climate change, pollution.

Awareness of now-unknown dangers in the universe (e.g., Darth Vader/Kylo Ren types) will help us defend ourselves.

Contact enables the development of allies we can count on in a crisis or galactic conflict.

Space exploration could create an appreciation of new perspectives, beliefs, and cultural practices.

We might develop a pathway for finding new planets for human expansion—or for escape, if Earth dies.

When interstellar travel is feasible, trade in goods, ideas, tourism.

We have already been sending TV and radio signals for seventy years. There's no new risk here.

↓ CON

Respect the unknown. Don't "howl in the jungle" if you don't know what's out there.

Aliens might harm us intentionally through warfare, slavery, or exploitation.

Aliens might harm us inadvertently by bringing us dangerous diseases, microbes, or harmful creatures.

Contact with a more advanced civilization might resemble contact between Europeans and native peoples around the world.

We have not yet heard from other ETIs. Maybe in this galaxy, it is smart to keep quiet and lie low.

Some top scientists and tech leaders (Steven Hawking, Elon Musk, Neil deGrasse Tyson) have petitioned against active SETI.

This decision should not be made by one country or science agency. It should be a worldwide choice.

Other life forms could be so different as to be unmanageable.

Active SETI programs would be very costly; other needs should prevail.

The signals we have sent to date are weak and insignificant. Active SETI means powerful, direct beaming to specific Earth-like planets.

LESSON 25   Argument Notes

TEXT	AUTHOR	SOURCE	TEXT TYPE
Excerpts from *The Cure for Dreaming*	Cat Winters	Harry Abrams Publishers	Letter to the editor

The Cure for Dreaming is a recent young adult novel that takes place in 1900 Portland, Oregon. The main character, Olivia, is caught between her father's traditional (and *very* limited) view of women and her own desire to attend college and—gasp—vote! When Olivia is deemed too headstrong for her own good, her father hires a traveling hypnotist to do some "therapy" on her to tame her desire for gender equality. Great read.

Early in the novel, before her "therapy," Olivia anonymously responds to a letter to the editor that denounces the suffragist movement; these complementary letters are the text for this lesson. Though, thankfully, women have been "franchised" since 1920, letters to the editor are still a popular means of expressing opinion, whether online or in print. Their examination is a great way for students to develop and hone their own skills at argument.

PREPARATION

1. Duplicate *The Cure for Dreaming* excerpts back-to-back, one copy for each student.
2. Make two copies of the blank Argument Notes template for each student (you can duplicate them back to back on a single sheet so that each student gets just one piece of paper).
3. For initial modeling, you will also need to project the Argument Notes sheet on a whiteboard or use a document camera. Later in the lesson, a doc camera will make it easier for students to share their work with the rest of the class.
4. Decide how pairs will be formed in Step 3.
5. Decide who will serve as student scribe in Step 4.

STEP 1   **Introduce the topic.** If you have already used the *Age of Brass* image found in Lesson 16, then your students will need only a quick review of the women's suffrage movement in the United States. However, if you haven't, here's a quick intro you can share with students:

> *How many of you know someone who has the right to vote but didn't vote in a recent election? What kept them from voting? Hear some responses. While some people didn't vote because work, family, or other serious obligations kept them away from the polls, a lot of you said in one way or another that some people you know didn't vote because they just weren't interested. For a variety of reasons the desire just wasn't there.*

TIME ▶ 45 minutes

GROUPINGS ▶ Whole class, pairs, individuals

STANDARDS MET ▶ See pages 306–307.

 USED IN   Chapter 13's Text Set

WHEN TO USE ▶ When your students are getting ready to write longer argument pieces or "position papers" in which they have to take a stand, this lesson shows them how to dig useful evidence out of source materials and then organize it.

download

◀ **Steps & Teaching Language**

Did you know that before 1920, women did not have the right to vote? Prior to ratification of the Nineteenth Amendment, women's voting rights were determined in each state. In some states, particularly in the West, women had full voting rights. Elsewhere voting rights ranged from none whatsoever to being able to vote only in school board elections, municipal elections, or presidential elections. And just because you could vote in one election, it didn't mean you could vote in another. What do you think of that? Check in with your partner and see what they think.

STEP 2 **Distribute the text and explain annotation directions.** *Today we're going to take a look at a couple of letters to the editor on the topic of whether or not women should have the right to vote. Although the letters are fictional excerpts taken from the novel* The Cure for Dreaming, *they are rooted in the historical facts and opinions of 1900. Remember, women did not get the right to vote until 1920! We're going to take a look at one letter at a time. First we're going to read the letter from the fictional Judge Percival R. Acklen.*

As you read his letter, I want you to do a little bit of annotation. Judge Acklen's claim is that women should not get the right to vote. When you notice him giving a specific reason, an assertion, related to this claim, underline it and put an A *by your underline in the margin. Then, if the judge supports that assertion by giving specific facts or examples— underline that part twice and put an* S *(for support) by it in the margin.*

Monitor individual work, giving students a few minutes to read and annotate. When most are done, move on to Step 3.

STEP 3 **Partners quickly share.** *Since everyone is finished, turn to your partner and quickly share your annotations. Pay particular attention to places where your annotations differ and see if you can agree on one interpretation. Remember to discuss whether a specific assertion has real evidence to back it up, or the writer is just attempting to support the assertion with more opinion.*

STEP 4 **Distribute the Argument Notes form and model note taking.** *Now that everyone has a form, write down Judge Acklen's claim on the line at the top: Women should not get the right to vote.*

While it's easy to make a claim, a claim's strength depends on the underlying support. When you read or listen to a person's argument, you have to tease out the presence and validity of a writer's or speaker's assertions and support in order to determine if the original claim is convincing. Before we take a look at the counterclaim, let's dissect Judge Acklen's arguments carefully. What is Judge Acklen's first supporting assertion?

Give students a minute to confer with their partners and then take a few answers. Remember to have students point to the actual text evidence as they share. They will probably come up with something along the lines of "Women's brains aren't made for voting." While you are leading this text examination, be sure that your student scribe is taking down notes at the doc cam or on the whiteboard and that the rest of the class is copying these example notes on their individual Argument Notes forms.

If women's brains aren't made for voting, what evidence does Acklen use to support this? Students will cite details such as "scientific research proves women were created for domestic duties, not higher-order thinking."

Continue in this manner, dissecting Acklen's assertions and support, as you also model the note taking that students should be recording on their sheets.

Finish by asking this question: *How solid are Acklen's supporting details? Does he give real scientific evidence, or is he just attempting to use his own prejudices and beliefs as legitimate evidence?*

STEP 5 **Individuals read the letter from "A Responsible Woman."** *Go ahead and read the second letter. Use the same annotation system as earlier. Underline an* assertion *once and put an* A *by it in the margin. Then, if that assertion is supported with specific facts or examples, underline the* support *twice and put an* S *by it in the margin.*

Monitor individual work, giving students a few minutes to read and annotate. When most are done, move on to Step 6.

STEP 6 **Pairs share their annotations and fill out Argument Notes together.** *Turn your Argument Notes sheet to the blank side. Now, working with your partner, use your annotations to delineate the assertions and support from the "Responsible Woman." Be sure to discuss whether she does a better job supporting her claim—women should be allowed to vote—than the judge did. As you discuss the assertions and support, each partner should record them on her Argument Notes form.*

As you monitor partner work, encourage students to use text evidence and direct quotes or accurate paraphrasing. Remind pairs that both partners should be taking accurate notes on the form.

STEP 7 **Pairs share Argument Notes sheets with the class.** Move through the letter and call up different groups to display their sheets via the doc cam as they explain one of the "Responsible Woman's" assertions and support.

End by having pairs compare the two writers' notes and decide which one is actually more persuasive because of the assertions and the evidence.

The Argument Notes handout is an excellent tool for examining existing arguments, but it is equally effective when students are researching and writing their own argument pieces.

Research Projects for Extended Writing ▶

Longer writing projects—reflecting the key genres required by the national standards—can be built on the work students have already done in this lesson. As kids continue to explore the topics of our reading selections, we expect that they will bring fresh background knowledge, recent thinking, and genuine curiosity to the task. When you use the lesson above with your own content, you can also use the assignments below as models for extending that content into longer writing projects.

Narrative: *Tell the story of a famous debate*

History is filled with legendary debates. Some have taken place in politics (like presidential debates), some among scientists (whether to bring back extinct species), and some behind closed doors (whether to drop atomic bombs in WWII). Find a famous debate that intrigues you, and read several different accounts about it. Then write your own one-page summary of the event and its significance. If one side is viewed as having won, what can you say about the quality of its support? *Research clue: famous debates.*

Informative/explanatory: *Study and summarize a local controversy*

Newspapers offer a wealth of argument writing online—not just in opinion columns, but in the comments that readers can now post right under many articles. A *New York Times* article about Amazon.com provoked a lot of arguing among readers: it gathered 5,842 responses! Using your community online newspaper, read and evaluate the arguments of people who wrote in response to a local controversy, possibly about an issue concerning the community or school. Find one that uses strong arguments and thorough supports. Make a poster or infographic, using arrows and captions pointing out the most effective sections.

Persuasive/argumentative: *Support or disprove a related assertion*

We tend to feel that arguments are usually won by the strength of their supports: the strongest facts, data, research, and/or expert testimony carry the day. But is that all that determines the "winner" in an argument? Some high school debaters will tell you (and author Harvey can attest) that it is sometimes easier to take the negative side. Maybe it's not as hard to knock something down as it is to build it up. Write your thinking about this: is it easier to support your own assertion or to counter someone else's previous claim? If possible, show some examples of the "negative advantage" (if it exists)—and get quotes from expert arguers.

LETTER TO THE EDITOR

From Judge Percival R. Acklen

As nearly everyone knows, in June of this year, the men of Oregon voted down a referendum that would have given the women of this great state of ours the right to vote. As this upcoming Tuesday's presidential election draws nearer, irate females have taken to the steps of the courthouse in downtown Portland to complain about their lack of a voice in American politics—and to bemoan their jealousies over their voting sisters in neighboring Idaho.

What these unbridled women lack is a thorough knowledge of the female brain. Two of my closest friends, Drs. Cornelius Piper and Mortimer Yves, two fine gentlemen educated at East Coast universities, both support the staggering wealth of scientific research that proves women were created for domestic duties alone, not higher thinking. A body built for childbearing and mothering is clearly a body meant to stay in the home. If females muddle their minds with politics and other matters confusing to a woman's head, they will abandon their wifely and motherly duties and inevitably trigger the downfall of American society.

Moreover, we would never allow an unqualified, undereducated, ignorant citizen to run our country as president. Why, therefore, would we allow such a person to vote for president?

Women of Oregon, you preside over our children and our homes. Rejoice in your noble position upon this earth. Return to your children and husbands, and stop concerning yourselves with masculine matters beyond your understanding. Silence in a woman is feminine, honorable, and, above all else, natural. Save your voices for sweet words of support for your hardworking husbands and gentle lullabies for your babes—not for American politics.

(Excerpt from Cat Winters, *The Cure for Dreaming*)

LETTER TO THE EDITOR

From "A Responsible Woman"

To Judge Acklen:

You state that women were made for domestic duties alone. Have you ever stopped to observe the responsibilities involved with domestic duties?

What better person to understand the administration of a country than an individual who spends her days mediating quarrels, balancing household budgets, organizing and executing three complex meals, and ensuring all rooms, appliances, deliveries, clothing, guests, family members, and pets are tended to and functioning the way they ought to be? I do not know of any other job in the world that so closely resembles the presidency itself.

Moreover, females are raised to become rational, industrious, fair, and compassionate human beings. Males are taught to sow their wild oats and run free while they're able. Which gender is truly the most prepared to make decisions about the management of a country? Do you want a responsible individual or a rambunctious one choosing the fate of our government?

You insinuate that women's minds are easily muddled, yet you entrust us with the rearing of your children, America's future. Mothers are our first teachers. Mothers are the voices of reason who instill the nation's values in our youth. Mothers are the ones who raise the politicians for whom they are not allowed to vote. Why would you let an easily muddled creature take on such important duties? Why not hire men to bring up your sons and daughters?

I can already hear you arguing that women's bodies were designed for childbearing, but this is not true, sir. Our bodies may have been built for birthing children and nourishing them during their first meals, but it is our minds that are doing the largest share of the work. On a daily basis, we women prove that our brains are sharp and quick, yet you are too blind to see our intelligence.

Furthermore, you have no need to fear that we would forgo our domestic duties if we were to become voting citizens, for we have been trained all our lives to balance a multitude of tasks. We do not let our homes fall into ruin simply because we have been given one more item to accomplish. Worry more about the males who have only one job and no household chores. Their minds are more likely to stray than ours.

Do you call your own mother "undereducated" and "ignorant," Judge Acklen? Was her mind in too much of a muddle to keep your childhood household intact? Was she so easily confused that she was unable to raise a boy who would one day become a judge? I think not. Your mother was undoubtedly a quick-witted, accountable individual who would probably make a far better president than the pampered male you gentlemen vote into office this Tuesday.

(Excerpt from Cat Winters, *The Cure for Dreaming*)

ARGUMENT NOTES

Claim _____

Assertions (arguments/reasons)	Support (facts/statistics/examples)

Supporting an Argument

TEXT	AUTHOR	SOURCE	TEXT TYPE
"The Cost of a Decline in Unions"	Nicholas Kristof	*New York Times*	Opinion

TIME ▶ 40 minutes

GROUPINGS ▶ Whole class, pairs, individuals

STANDARDS MET ▶ See pages 306–307.

 USED IN Chapter 13's Text Set

WHEN TO USE ▶ When students are ready to focus on anticipating and discrediting an opponents' position on an issue, this lesson shows exactly how to prepare such refutations—and disarm skeptical readers in the process.

Throughout this chapter, we've had kids practice making and supporting arguments. Anyone who has been teaching for more than ten minutes has a pretty good idea what *persuasive* means—clearly taking a position and then supporting that position with lots of solid evidence, reasons, or facts. Depending on the topic at hand, the evidence might come from different places. If you are supporting your interpretation of a novel or play, the evidence might be quotes or passages from within that text. If you are writing about issues in history, social policy, science, and other fields, your evidence is likely to come from statistics, data, research, expert testimony, and other carefully vetted sources.

Argumentative writing, which the Common Core strongly promotes, essentially takes persuasive reasoning one step further by anticipating and countering the likely objections of an adversary. In other words, argumentative writers habitually think of ways people may disagree with them or doubt their sources, and then knock down these objections along the way, before a reader ever arrives.

In this lesson, we look at how a veteran professional opinion writer moves beyond persuasion to making a complete argument—and we help kids pull back the curtain and see how it is done.

PREPARATION

1. Make a copy of "The Cost of a Decline in Unions" for every student.
2. Decide how pairs will be formed at Step 4.
3. Be ready to project "Three Tasks of Making an Argument" in Step 5.
4. Be ready to project the text at Step 9.

Steps & Teaching Language ▶

STEP 1 Activate background knowledge. *Who knows an adult who is a union member? Maybe a parent, neighbor, older sibling? Or maybe a grandparent? Do you know what union they are or were in?* (Your further comments depend on the response.) *As recently as 1975, 40 percent of American workers were in labor unions. These days, the participation is down to 14 percent overall, and only 7 percent in private companies. So, if we could time travel and poll a class of kids from back then, we'd have maybe ten or twelve hands go up, but now we have only a few. So, for lots of reasons you'll learn about, union membership in America has declined rapidly in the past few decades. We're about to read an article in* *which the author, Nicholas Kristof, thinks this is a very bad thing. Plenty of other people disagree with him.*

STEP 2 **Introduce the author.** *Nicholas Kristof has what some people consider the best job in journalism. He has a twice-a-week opinion column in the* New York Times. *He is free to cover and write about virtually any topic he wants: world affairs, politics, culture, social issues, travel, you name it. He got this job by being a reliable, fair, and balanced reporter for many years. But he is also a very passionate advocate for what he believes in, and his columns are highly persuasive—even argumentative. Today, we're going to learn from him how to construct a powerful argument.*

STEP 3 **Students read silently.** Distribute the text. *Let's just read this through silently. Keep your pencil in hand, and when you run across something in the column that surprises you, or interests you, or provokes a question, underline it so we can come back to it later. Don't worry about the paragraph numbers for now. Happy reading, everyone.*

This is one of the longest pieces we have provided—our selections usually feature just *one* page of text. But this elaborate argument bears no editing. Since reading rates inevitably vary (and do not always correlate with the quality of comprehension), you'll likely have to coach early finishers to reread, going back to add underlines while the slower readers catch up. Alternatively, read the article aloud to set a steady pace for all.

STEP 4 **Pairs share first impressions.** *Get with your partner and talk for a minute. Did Kristof convince you that the decline in unions is a bad thing? Why or why not? What did you notice or wonder about his writing? Talk about items you underlined.* After some talk time, invite a few pairs to share their reactions.

STEP 5 **Discuss argument tasks.** *When writers make a full argument, they need to do three things.* Project the tasks and read them aloud as students follow along.

Three Tasks of Making an Argument

1. State a clear claim/position/opinion/point of view.
2. Offer assertions/reasons that are supported with evidence, facts, statistics, research, expert testimony, and/or logical explanations.
3. Anticipate and answer the objections of someone who might disagree.

Kristof has already accomplished the first task in his title, right? It says the decline in unions is a loss, that it's costing us all. But where is the evidence? How, specifically, does he support that case? And how does he counter or defuse an opponent's possible objections in advance?

STEP 6 **Students read a second time with annotation.** *Let's go back through the article and do a little detective work. Let's mark specific places where the author:*

—*Supports his position*

—*Answers possible objections*

Use the letters S *and* A *to mark those spots and write some key words in the margin to label what specific supports or answers you found.*

If it will help to give kids a quota, you can say something like: *When I read this, I saw many pieces of support and several places where Kristof anticipates a reader's objection and answers it. So you should easily find a half dozen places to mark with an* S *or an* A.

Allow reading time. Decide if you want this work to be silent, or if kids can talk quietly with their partners as they go through the article.

STEP 7 **Debrief supports.** Project the text (one page at a time) and have volunteers call out and locate argument supports they found. The numbering of the paragraphs should help with this—and almost *every* paragraph has some support in it: expert testimony, statistics, and research citations. If kids don't mention it explicitly, you can point out that an abundance of evidence makes for a stronger argument.

STEP 8 **Debrief answers.** Project the text again, and ask for kids to call out and locate answers to objections they found. The first three paragraphs are all horror stories about unions. So one way Kristof defuses the opposition is by saying, "I used to think the same thing as you, but I changed my mind when I heard all the evidence." Several times, he cozies up to potential adversaries in this way: "Just like you, I am shocked by the terrible things unions have done, but corporations are even worse."

STEP 9 **Let students try out the same technique on another text.** Use "Choking the Oceans with Plastic" (see Lesson 15) or another opinion piece of your choice, and subject it to the same cycle of reading, annotation, and discussion. This should strongly reinforce kids' understanding of the distinction between persuading and arguing, and support them in writing their own complete arguments.

Research Projects for Extended Writing ▶ Longer writing projects—reflecting the key genres required by the national standards—can be built on the work students have already done in this lesson. As kids continue to explore the topics of our reading selections, we expect that they will bring fresh background knowledge, recent thinking, and genuine curiosity to the task. When you use the lesson above with your own content, you can also use the assignments below as models for extending that content into longer writing projects.

Narrative: *Tell another's related story*

Find an adult who has been in a labor union for many years and who is willing to let you interview him or her about that experience. Your goal in the interview will be to gather enough information to write a narrative about this person's experience in the union—perhaps a piece that tells the story of his or her involvement with the union, or one that focuses on a particular situation or event related to his or her union membership. Before the interview, find out what union(s) your interviewee joined. Next, do research on the union—its background, operation, and goals in recent times. Look for information in national or local publications (were there any strikes, lockouts, contracts, or disputes that made the news?). Make a list of questions for your subject, and conduct the interview. You might hold the interview through email (this will give you a clear written record and time for thoughtful follow-up questions). Or, go "live" and talk in person or via Skype, FaceTime, Google Hangouts, whatever (listen hard and take notes!).

Informative/explanatory: *Research and report on related extremism*

Why did unionization sometimes spark violence, and who has been mostly to blame—workers, company owners, or both? The labor movement in America traces back to industrialization and urbanization in the nineteenth century. Workers wanted better pay, safer working conditions, and the ability to seek bargaining rights. Companies wanted an inexpensive work force, a good return on their investment, and profit for their stockholders. Sometimes these differences escalated into disputes that became violent. The history of unions in the United States is filled with strong arguments. Either investigate the phenomenon called "union busting" (practices that corporations used to resist the emerging worker movement) or study pro-management/corporate sources to learn about extremism among workers and union leaders.

Persuasive/argumentative: *Flip an argument*

Take Kristof's prounion conclusion and turn it upside down, writing your own column about why the decline of unions in the United States is a *good* thing. You can even use some of Kristof's own supports, but you'll also need to read further to find more negative information about labor unions. (Look in probusiness publications like *The Wall Street Journal*, *Fortune*, and the like.) Try to follow Kristof's own model, offering both supports and answering the objections of prounion readers.

The New York Times

The Cost of a Decline in Unions

By Nicholas Kristof

1 Like many Americans, I've been wary of labor unions.

2 Full-time union stagehands at Carnegie Hall earning more than $400,000 a year? A union hailing its defense of a New York teacher who smelled of alcohol and passed out in class, with even the principal unable to rouse her? A police union in New York City that has a tantrum and goes on virtual strike?

3 More broadly, I disdained unions as bringing corruption, nepotism and rigid work rules to the labor market, impeding the economic growth that ultimately makes a country strong.

4 I was wrong.

5 The abuses are real. But, as unions wane in American life, it's also increasingly clear that they were doing a lot of good in sustaining middle class life—especially the private-sector unions that are now dwindling.

6 Most studies suggest that about one-fifth of the increase in economic inequality in America among men in recent decades is the result of the decline in unions. It may be more: A study in the American Sociological Review, using the broadest methodology, estimates that the decline of unions may account for one-third of the rise of inequality among men.

7 "To understand the rising inequality, you have to understand the devastation in the labor movement," says Jake Rosenfeld, a labor expert at the University of Washington and the author of "What Unions No Longer Do."

8 Take construction workers. A full-time construction worker earns about $10,000 less per year now than in 1973, in today's dollars, according to Rosenfeld. One reason is probably that the proportion who are unionized has fallen in that period from more than 40 percent to just 14 percent.

9 "All the focus on labor's flaws can distract us from the bigger picture," Rosenfeld writes. "For generations now the labor movement has stood as the most prominent and effective voice for economic justice."

10 I'm as appalled as anyone by silly work rules and $400,000 stagehands, or teachers' unions shielding the incompetent. But unions also lobby for programs like universal prekindergarten that help create broad-based prosperity. They are pushing for a higher national minimum wage, even though that would directly benefit mostly nonunionized workers.

11 I've also changed my mind because, in recent years, the worst abuses by far haven't been in the union shop but in the corporate suite. One of the things you learn as a journalist is that when there's no accountability, we humans are capable of tremendous avarice and venality. That's true of union bosses—and of corporate tycoons. Unions, even flawed ones, can provide checks and balances for flawed corporations.

12   Many Americans think unions drag down the economy over all, but scholars disagree. American auto unions are often mentioned, but Germany's car workers have a strong union, and so do Toyota's in Japan and Kia's in South Korea.

13   In Germany, the average autoworker earns about $67 per hour in salary and benefits, compared with $34 in the United States. Yet Germany's car companies in 2010 produced more than twice as many vehicles as American companies did, and they were highly profitable. It's too glib to say that the problem in the American sector was just unions.

14   Or look at American history. The peak years for unions were the 1940s and '50s, which were also some of the fastest-growing years for the United States ever—and with broadly shared prosperity. Historically, the periods when union membership were highest were those when inequality was least.

15   Richard B. Freeman, a Harvard labor expert, notes that unions sometimes bring important benefits to industry: They can improve morale, reduce turnover and provide a channel to suggest productivity improvements.

16   Experts disagree about how this all balances out, but it's clear that it's not a major drag. "If you're looking for big negatives, everybody knows they don't exist," Professor Freeman said.

17   Joseph Stiglitz notes in his book "The Price of Inequality" that when unions were strong in America, productivity and real hourly compensation moved together in manufacturing. But after 1980 (and especially after 2000) the link seemed to break and real wages stagnated.

18   It may be that as unions weakened, executives sometimes grabbed the gains from productivity. Perhaps that helps explain why chief executives at big companies earned, on average, 20 times as much as the typical worker in 1965, and 296 times as much in 2013, according to the Economic Policy Institute.

19   Lawrence F. Katz, a Harvard labor economist, raises concerns about some aspects of public-sector unions, but he says that in the private sector (where only 7 percent of workers are now unionized): "I think we've gone too far in de-unionization."

20   He's right. This isn't something you often hear a columnist say, but I'll say it again: I was wrong. At least in the private sector, we should strengthen unions, not try to eviscerate them.

CHAPTER 9

WRITING FOR UNDERSTANDING

In this section, we ask kids to read nonfiction texts even more closely, locating the core evidence of the author's purpose, and then writing about it succinctly.

LESSON 27

Prereading Predictions

TIME ▸ 40 minutes

GROUPINGS ▸ Whole class, pairs, individuals

STANDARDS MET ▸ See pages 306–307.

WHEN TO USE ▸ This lesson reinforces a key strategy for understanding content-area text: predicting or anticipating the subject matter before reading. This exercise helps kids enter the text thinking, actively looking for confirmation or contradiction of their ideas, and prepares them to write cogently.

TEXT	SOURCE	TEXT TYPE
Sample U.S. Naturalization Civics and History Test	U.S. Citizenship and Immigration Services, Department of Homeland Security	Test

Our longtime colleague and reading educator Marilyn Bizar has the best-ever explanation of why we must activate kids' background knowledge as they approach complex readings. "They have to enter the text thinking," Marilyn says, "demanding clarity and insisting on meaning." We love that: we are raising readers who allow the text no excuses for failing to reveal itself.

In this lesson, we are leading kids toward a "patriotic text" (much favored by the Common Core writers) that has no special interest for most teenagers. Initially. But if we give them a quick summary of the text and then ask them to create their own version before ever seeing the model, we can evoke surprising energy and effort. Predicting and guessing what a text will be about, even on the basis of a few slender clues, is one of the best ways we know to enhance student buy-in.

PREPARATION

1. Because immigration is such a polarizing issue these days, teaching this lesson requires some delicacy, diplomacy, and good sense. If you teach it, do so *only* if you feel well-informed about the immigration issues in your community. If things are mishandled, there are aspects that might make undocumented kids feel uncomfortable (though we know they are tremendously interested in this topic), and there are steps where a prejudiced student could blurt out stereotyped ideas.

   On the other hand, we are a nation of immigrants, and many families have inspiring, often heroic stories about making it to the United States and becoming citizens. The two of us think that immigration is an area where the United States still works better than many other nations. We should never be afraid to celebrate how immigration has built and benefited our country. Sure, it can be a tough conversation, but that's democracy.

   In general, we all lose if loudmouths place this topic off limits. But locally, in your school, if things are just too tense and volatile, by all means choose another lesson.

2. Determine how groups of three will be formed at Step 4.

3. Determine how to project the sample question at Step 4.

4. Select a student scribe to chart or project the immigration test questions that students suggest during Step 7. If you use Edmodo, TodaysMeet, or a similar digital platform, kids can send their suggested test questions directly into a projected class feed, and no scribe is needed.

5. Make a copy of the immigration test for each student (Step 8).

STEP 1 **Introduce the topic.** *In a few minutes we are going to read a sample of the civics and history test that's given to people seeking to become new American citizens.*

This test is one of several requirements for becoming a U.S. citizen, including a five-year waiting period, learning to read and write English, showing good moral character, and proving yourself to be "attached to the principles of the Constitution of the United States, and well disposed to the good order and happiness of the United States."

STEP 2 **Invite students to share relevant experiences.** *Has anyone heard of this test? Do you know anyone who has taken the test? What do you imagine it might be like?*

Invite any students with relevant information to share. Obviously, be careful not to single out or embarrass any students who may be uncomfortable about their family's immigration status.

STEP 3 **Students write their own test questions.** *Before we see the official sample test, let's think about what kinds of questions might be included. If you were designing a test for people to become your fellow Americans, what topics would you cover? What questions would you ask? What kinds of knowledge about our country would be most important for a new citizen to have? On your own, jot down a couple of questions you think would be critical for determining whether an applicant would make a good citizen.* Give students a couple of minutes to think and write on their own.

STEP 4 **Student trios discuss ideas.** *Now move into your groups of three. I'm going to give you five minutes in your groups to discuss your ideas and develop several specific questions you think should be included on a test for would-be Americans. The questions can only be factual items about U.S. history and government. Also, you need to keep these within the format of the actual exam. The civics test has ten questions, and all of them can be answered by a word, a name, or a phrase that the applicant provides after the question. Like this:*

Sample Naturalization Question: Who was the Father of Our Country?

Answer: George Washington

◄ **Steps & Teaching Language**

All questions must follow this format. There are no matching, fill-in-the-blank, multiple choice, or essay questions. And, as always, we want school-appropriate suggestions only. Write each question out in full and then provide the correct answer (look it up to be sure). Write as many as you can in the time we have.

Leave this sample projected for kids' reference as they create their own questions.

STEP 5 **Monitor and assist groups.** Circulate and clarify instructions as needed. You'll probably need to remind students of the test question format and constraints. Allow more time if kids are being productive; call them back when the generation of test questions dwindles.

STEP 6 **Instructions for sharing test questions.** Have your student scribe ready to chart/type in suggested questions as they are volunteered by different teams.

Okay, let's hear some of the naturalization questions you came up with. Let's take one from each group and we'll keep going around until we run out of unique questions. When you volunteer a question, read it aloud and give us a chance to answer it. Then be ready to tell us the correct answer and why you think it is important for new Americans to understand. Okay? Let's go.

STEP 7 **Groups suggest test questions.** As groups volunteer questions, let class members guess at the correct answers. Make it playfully competitive if you like, keeping score or awarding points.

After the correct answer has been revealed, ask teams to explain why their question is important. Be sure that answers come from different members each time.

Before moving on to additional questions, ask whether other groups had created a similar item, perhaps asking the same question in different words. Such overlap might imply significance, or at least some consensus, about what's important to know about America.

Enjoy these questions and answers as long as engagement is strong.

STEP 8 **Students read and discuss an actual test sample.** Hand out the test. *Now let's have a look at a real naturalization civics test. Go ahead and take it as if you were an applicant.* Monitor as students take the test, playing a little proctor role if they are talking too much.

STEP 9 **Give answers while letting students self-grade and reflect on scores.** *Six out of ten is passing. Write for one minute about each of these questions:*

—How do you feel about your score? Why?

—Do you think the test was fair? Why or why not?

—Do you think the test is a good measure of what Americans should know about their country?

STEP 10 **Groups prepare for whole-class discussion.** *Rejoin your group and compare how you responded to the test questions we just read.* Give groups a few minutes to discuss and then invite them to share their thoughts and feelings about the test with the whole class. As time permits, you may also choose to expand upon initial comments by inviting kids to respond to any of these additional questions: *What can you say about the official test? What kind of knowledge do naturalization officials want citizenship applicants to demonstrate? How do these questions compare to the ones we developed earlier? Are some of our questions better? Which ones? What makes them superior? If you were designing a brand-new "perfect" citizenship test from scratch, what would you do differently from the existing exam's format and questions?*

Longer writing projects—reflecting the key genres required by the national standards—can be built on the work students have already done in this lesson. As kids continue to explore the topics of our reading selections, we expect that they will bring fresh background knowledge, recent thinking, and genuine curiosity to the task. When you use the lesson above with your own content, you can also use the assignments below as models for extending that content into longer writing projects.

◀ ***Research Projects for Extended Writing***

Narrative: *Trace an individual's journey through a system*

Interview someone who has immigrated to America and achieved citizenship. (If you anticipate students having trouble finding such folks in your community, check around with school employees to find willing relatives or friends.) Get the whole story of their naturalization process, from the time they first moved here until their naturalization ceremony. Write the story, including recollections or quotes from your informant. Create a timeline of significant events from their journey to accompany your story.

Informative/explanatory: *Compare policies*

Research the citizenship rules for another country that interests you. In a short article, compare the rules. What would it take for you to become a citizen of that country? How does its naturalization process compare to that of the United States?

Persuasive/argumentative: *Research and take a side on a policy*

Many countries, including the United States, have immigration quotas or limits on the number of people they will accept from each country each year. Find out how the current system works in the United States. In your opinion, do the quotas make sense? Are they fair? Are refugees from war or oppression provided for? Write an essay in which you defend the national quota system—or argue for specific changes in it.

Sample U.S. Naturalization Civics and History Test

U.S. Citizenship and Immigration Services,
Department of Homeland Security

There are 100 civics (history and government) questions and answers for the naturalization test. The civics test is an oral test and the USCIS officer will ask the applicant up to ten of the 100 civics questions. An applicant must answer six out of ten questions to correctly pass the civics portion of the naturalization test.

Below is a set of ten questions from the item bank.

1. The idea of self-government is in the first three words of the Constitution. What are these words?

2. How many amendments does the Constitution have?

3. What are two rights in the Declaration of Independence?

4. What stops one branch of government from becoming too powerful?

5. Who was president during World War I?

6. Who is the chief justice of the United States now?

7. When was the Constitution written?

8. During the Cold War what was the main concern of the United States?

9. The Federalist Papers supported the passage of the U.S. Constitution. Name one of the writers.

10. What territory did the U.S. buy from France in 1803?

Sample Test Questions with Answers

U.S. Citizenship and Immigration Services,
Department of Homeland Security

1. The idea of self-government is in the first three words of the Constitution. What are these words? (We the people)

2. How many amendments does the Constitution have? (27)

3. What are two rights in the Declaration of Independence? (life, liberty, the pursuit of happiness)

4. What stops one branch of government from becoming too powerful? (separation of powers, checks and balances)

5. Who was president during World War I? (Woodrow Wilson)

6. Who is the chief justice of the United States now? (John Roberts)

7. When was the Constitution written? (1787)

8. During the Cold War what was the main concern of the United States? (communism)

9. The Federalist Papers supported the passage of the U.S. Constitution. Name one of the writers. (James Madison, Alexander Hamilton, John Jay, Publius)

10. What territory did the U.S. buy from France in 1803? (Louisiana)

Reread and Write with Questions in Mind

TIME ▶ 30 minutes

GROUPINGS ▶ Whole class, pairs, individuals

STANDARDS MET ▶ See pages 306–307.

 USED IN Chapter 12's Text Set

WHEN TO USE ▶ When kids need practice at second readings of data-heavy text, this lesson turns the "drudgery" of rereading into a detective story kids can pursue.

TEXT	AUTHOR	SOURCE	TEXT TYPE
"Time Off: Vacation Days Around the World"	Roger Vector	WrapUp Media	Data sheet

One fundamental principle of most state and national reading standards is that kids need to *reread texts* to achieve deeper understanding. (Well, what else is new?) And that's probably good advice for us adults too; even we veteran comprehenders can succumb to superficial or sloppy first readings. But in too many "core aligned" curricula, rereading is implemented mainly through teacher coercion: "Read it again! Read it again!" Much as we endorse the value of second visits to enhance understanding, we cringe at the mechanical, forced-march rereadings we see in so many sample lessons and units these days.

Here's a different approach: as teachers, let's make it *our* responsibility to make rereading not an obedience ritual, but an *adventure* for students. Hey, at the family dinner table, when we go back for second and third helpings, we do so because the food is delicious and we want more. Let's make second helpings of text just as tasty as that. We should set up each return to text as a puzzle, a mystery, a quest, a detective story. To do that, we tap kids' curiosity, make the rereads sociable, not solitary, and focus on debatable details.

PREPARATION

1. Download and make a copy of "Time Off: Vacation Days Around the World" for each student.
2. Download and be ready to project task instructions in Step 1, 5, and 6.
3. Decide how to form pairs for Step 3.
4. Appoint a student scribe to create the list in Step 4 so that you will be free to circulate and orchestrate the discussion.
5. Have index cards, one for each student, ready for Step 6. Have writing materials or devices ready for Step 8.

download

Steps & Teaching Language ▶

STEP 1 **Introduce the reading and annotation.** *Who knows what a "fact sheet" is?* Take a few volunteers. *Usually a fact sheet is just what it says—a listing of facts or statistics without a visible author to guide you through it. But fact sheets do not always include only pure facts, or all the facts. Often, these documents are put out by organizations seeking to change your mind or sell you something. So you have to read between* *the lines, bringing your past experience and your critical reading skills to bear, as you do with any piece of text.*

In a minute we are going to read an interesting fact sheet about vacation days in different countries. Pass out "Time Off: Vacation Days Around the World" to each student. *While reading, please stop anytime you have a question or wonder about something in the text. You might find yourself having thoughts like these* (project the following list):

Some Ways Readers Wonder About and React to Text

- What???
- How can that be true?
- Where did they get this information?
- I am puzzled.
- What does this sentence mean?
- This doesn't make sense.
- Whoa, no way. I can't believe this.

When you notice yourself thinking like this, stop and place a question mark in the margin and briefly jot down what your question or wonder is.

Leave this list projected to support kids as they work. If your students will need a "quota" to guide them, say something like: *For me, this fact sheet raised lots of questions; I expect you to have several annotations by the time you are done reading it.*

STEP 2 **Students read and annotate.** Give kids a few minutes to read the fact sheet using their question mark annotations. Circulate and assist.

STEP 3 **Partners share questions.** *Okay, now get with your partner and discuss the questions each of you had.* Give students one or two minutes to compare their questions.

STEP 4 **Whole class shares and lists questions.** Activate your student scribe and invite each pair to suggest one of the questions they marked on their fact sheets. As you go around the room, require subsequent pairs to mention a new question each time until fresh questions are exhausted. That way you'll capture the whole range of puzzles and curiosities about the topic—and your student scribe should end up creating a fairly long list. (Why doesn't the U.S. guarantee vacation by law? Why do many poorer countries have better vacation policies than we do? Do people in those countries actually get that much vacation, or are those numbers just government propaganda? And so on.)

STEP 5 **Students reread with annotation.** Almost every time we teach this lesson, many kids ask why Americans don't take all the vacation they have earned. They'll say things like, "Well, when I get a job, you better believe I am taking all my vacation days!" and "These people are dumb to skip their vacations." If your kids don't happen to bring up this puzzling phenomenon, you can focus them on it now.

So let's zoom in on the last part of the chart, about how Americans so often fail to take their earned vacation days. The fact sheet gives many different reasons, especially since the survey allowed people to mark several answers. Now we are going to reread this section with a specific question in mind. Read the following questions aloud as you project them:

Rereading with a Question in Mind

What really makes Americans leave unused vacation days on the table? Is it mainly because:

Employers make it feel risky or disloyal to take days off?

OR

Workers love and enjoy their jobs and don't want/need vacations?

OR

Some of both?

As you reread, you will probably find parts of the fact sheet that help you understand the data better, or help you determine what workers' thinking really is. Mark this important evidence with a star.

STEP 6 **Quick card write.** Pass out index cards. *Now that you have read the fact sheet closely and annotated the last section of the data especially carefully, let's do a quick write: What are the most important reasons why many Americans don't take their full vacations? Reread the text as necessary to find information to back up your ideas. Use your star annotations to help you relocate important evidence. We'll write for three minutes on this.* Project the topic on screen to help students get started.

Quick Write Topic

What are the most important reasons why many Americans don't take their full vacations?

Explain your thinking.

Use your star annotations to help you locate important evidence.

Give students a few minutes to write independently.

STEP 7 **Whole class shares.** Invite kids to read aloud sections of their writing. You can orchestrate a variety of responses by asking: *Who wrote about employers pressuring employees? Who wrote about people taking pride in their jobs? Who had another take on the subject?*

STEP 8 Collect student writing. Gather kids' writings (including annotated texts) and review them later for engagement, quality of thinking, and ideas for future minilessons.

◄ **Variations**

Obviously at Step 4, we left behind a whole raft of questions kids brought up so we could focus more deeply on just one. But that scribed list of questions raised by the fact sheet can be a goldmine of further discussion and short writing projects for individual kids. One way we do this is called a *mini-inquiry*, based on Smokey and Stephanie Harvey's Book *Comprehension and Collaboration* (2015).

Have each student choose one of those initial questions, something that really has some magnetism, that provokes some real curiosity for them. Then give kids five minutes to chase down information or answers, using whatever resources are available in the room: computers, mobile devices, books, magazines, people to interview (or phone). Have kids make notes on which sources they consult and what information they gather. Allow five minutes for a quick sharing of findings. This is a great way to demonstrate that kids' questions really do matter in our class, and to have students practice the art of "finding out"—which is to say, doing research.

◄ **Research Projects for Extended Writing**

Longer writing projects—reflecting the key genres required by the national standards—can be built on the work students have already done in this lesson. As kids continue to explore the topics of our reading selections, we expect that they will bring fresh background knowledge, recent thinking, and genuine curiosity to the task. When you use the lesson above with your own content, you can also use the assignments below as models for extending that content into longer writing projects.

Narrative: *Write to understand a point of view that puzzles you*

Reread the explanations for why people don't use their vacation time. Choose the reason you find hardest to understand. Then talk with some employed adults in school, in your neighborhood, or in your family. Ask them if they consider that reason to be valid or have worked with anyone who thinks it is. Use follow-up questions to try to learn more about what might make this reason seem valid to employed adults. Then, write a scene in which an adult decides to not use vacation time for the reason you've identified. Your piece should aim to help readers understand the character's decision, even if they might not agree with it.

Informative/explanatory: *Compare situations*

Look further into the research on worker benefits around the world. Pick one other country you are interested in and compare its policies on vacations, sick days, parental leave, health care, disability coverage, unionization, and child care to those in the United States. Try to get information that reflects actual services, not just political or government claims.

Persuasive/argumentative: *Speculate about a phenomenon*

People sometimes speak about "American exceptionalism." This is the belief that America is not just different from every other country on Earth but absolutely unique and, some say, inherently better than all other countries. Do you see evidence in this data that supports the idea that the United States is different and/or better than other countries? What does this data show us about our national character, values, or fears? Explain your findings in a brief essay.

Time Off: Vacation Days Around the World

Roger Vector, WrapUp Media

Days of paid vacation guaranteed by law:

Russia: 28

Switzerland: 28

Brazil: 25

France: 25

Sweden: 25

Cuba: 22

Kuwait: 22

Republic of the Congo: 22

Afghanistan: 20

Australia: 20

Iraq: 20

China: 5

Mexico: 5

United States: 0

Additional paid public holidays:

India and Columbia (tied for most): 18

United States: 10

Mexico (least): 7

Days of vacation earned by average U.S. worker:

About 74% of U.S. workers receive some paid vacation days, at the discretion of their employer. Typically, the rates are

10 days after one year of service

14 days after 5 years

17 days after 10 years

19 days after 20 years

Days of vacation taken by average U.S. worker:

1980: 21

2014: 16

Average number of unused vacation days per worker in 2014:

4.9

Total number of unused vacation days in 2014:

429,000,000

Value to employers of these "free" work days:

$53 billion

U.S. workers' reasons for skipping some or all of their vacation days:

40%: I have too much work to do

37%: It's not easy to use vacation days at my job

35%: Nobody else can do my work

33%: I can't afford to take vacation

28%: I want to show my dedication

22%: I don't want to be seen as replaceable

20%: I don't need the time off

17%: I enjoy my job

(Survey takers could check several responses)

Summarize in 140 Characters

TEXT	SOURCE	TEXT TYPE
"America's Changing Labor Force"	U.S. Census Bureau	Infographic

TIME ▶ 30 minutes

GROUPINGS ▶ Whole class, individuals

STANDARDS MET ▶ See pages 306–307.

WHEN TO USE ▶ It is vital that students be able to write accurate summaries of all types of subject matter. Here we capitalize on kids' love of social media to practice the disciplines of concision and accuracy.

Do you realize that today's teenagers actually spend part of every day summarizing their thoughts into concise writing? We didn't either—until we realized that our students are texting all day long, editing their messages down to the minimum keystrokes to get the word out fast. Some are even meeting Twitter's exacting standard of 140 characters, which we use in this lesson.

But hey, if texting is something kids love to do, let's capitalize on it and bring it into the curriculum! We can do this with kids' real phones, with tablets or laptops, with pretend texts posted on Edmodo, TodaysMeet, Google Classroom, or even on paper (but good luck counting spaces)—as long as we impose the 140-character limit. You can't use actual Twitter unless every student has an account, which is highly unlikely.

PREPARATION

1. Make a copy of the "America's Changing Labor Force" infographic for each student.

2. Decide how kids will create their 140-character summaries so they can be shared—using tablets, laptops, or an online classroom platform. Obviously you'll want to use a program (like Word or Twitter itself) that has a character counter built in. If possible, project these writings.

Steps & Teaching Language ▶

STEP 1 **Students read and annotate text.** *Today I've brought you an infographic from the U.S. Census Bureau about men and women in the workforce. This is based on the 2010 census, so we will have to wait until 2020 to get the next round of information about this.*

While you are reading, please stop and annotate the text for important or interesting information. When you run across some fact or detail that jumps out at you, put a star in the margin and write a few words to help you remember why it seems significant. Allow students a few minutes to read and think about the data and graphics. Help kids to accumulate three or four annotations on their pages.

STEP 2 **Introduce the rules of tweeting.** *I'll bet almost everyone in here texts. Right? Does anybody use Twitter?* (If kids raise hands, ask them to explain how it works, especially the 140-character limit.)

So when you are texting, you generally keep your message short so people can read it fast and respond. But when you are tweeting, you have an actual limit of 140 characters, spaces included. If you write 141 characters, it won't send. So you have to be brief, clear, and organized.

Today, you guys are going to tweet this infographic, meaning you are going to write a concise summary of the most important ideas you found in these charts. What's the big picture, the takeaway, the main message of this text? What can we say about the workers in the United States after having studied this data?

You have to do this in less than 140 characters, spaces included. And here's one last challenge. See if you can hit 140 characters right on the nose for a "perfect" tweet. Enjoy.

STEP 3 **Students compose tweets.** Circulate and confer as kids work. Writing the tweets should take no more than five minutes.

STEP 4 **Whole class shares.** This sharing can be done on the screen if you are using a digital platform. You can just scroll through tweets while kids silently read them. Otherwise, kids can read theirs aloud off their devices or their papers. As always, we are looking to discover the whole range of kids' thinking, so we prompt the discussion with cues like these: *Who was tweeting a different set of highlights? Who tweeted about something we haven't mentioned yet?* Since kids tend to love trivial competition, be sure to ask: *Did anyone have exactly 140 characters in your summary? Read it for us!*

STEP 5 **Collect all tweets.** If you are doing this digitally, just have the kids text or email their tweets to you. As always, you can study these products as barometers of individual engagement, examples of kids' thinking in action, and clues for future lessons you might teach.

At Step 2, if you have kids who've never tried Twitter (it has become more of a grown-up thing these days), model it yourself. Whether you are texting or tweeting, it's a process of whittling down an idea you want to share to the most economical number of words or characters. Twitter just adds the absolute 140-character limit.

◀ *Tips*

Let's say I want to tweet about the school's upcoming musical. The information I'd want to get across might read something like this:

Tonight at P.T. Barnum High School, our fall musical opens in the auditorium at 7:30 PM. The play is Hairspray and it features a full orchestra, comedy hijinks, great dance numbers, and hilarious songs from a cast headed by Mindy Washington and Charlie Rivera. Tickets are still available at the box office. Don't miss it!

But this message has 324 characters! How can I be more concise, and summarize the information in a much shorter space? Then show kids how—by editing out unnecessary words, using abbreviations, and omitting redundant elements—you would whittle this down to 140 characters without losing meaning or accuracy.

> "Hairspray" opens at Barnum H. S. 7:30 tonight! Music, dancing, plenty of laughs. Mindy Washington & Charlie Rivera star. Tix at box office.

This one happens to weigh in at exactly 140 characters. Just saying.

Research Projects for Extended Writing ▶ Longer writing projects—reflecting the key genres required by the national standards—can be built on the work students have already done in this lesson. As kids continue to explore the topics of our reading selections, we expect that they will bring fresh background knowledge, recent thinking, and genuine curiosity to the task. When you use the lesson above with your own content, you can also use the assignments below as models for extending that content into longer writing projects.

Narrative: *Research and write narrative nonfiction*

An author named Studs Terkel wrote several very popular books in which he simply interviewed workers about their jobs. Many times, these people's stories completely contradicted assumptions people had about certain occupations. Interview two or three women in the workforce (these could be relatives, neighbors, family friends, or school employees) and ask them to tell the story of their jobs or their career, starting with their earliest employment. Record the interviews as you go. Later, use the information you gathered about their work life to write a narrative nonfiction account that either reflects or contradicts the official data we have on women's changing roles.

Informative/explanatory: *Compare national data to local data*

Research the most common industries and occupations for males and females in your town. In a brief essay, compare your town's data to the data in the infographics you read with the class. *Research clue: city-data.com.*

Persuasive/argumentative: *Take a position on a related social issue*

Some economists, politicians, and women's advocates tend to see the steadily increasing levels of women in the workforce as a triumph of choice for females. Recent surveys reveal that 60 percent of U.S. children live in households where both parents work at least part time. Other economists, family researchers, and assorted think tanks argue that having both parents employed is a culturally destructive phenomenon. In other words, some are making the case for old-fashioned one-earner/one-caregiver families. Look into this debate and take a position.

HOW DO WE KNOW?

America's Changing Labor Force

The Equal Employment Opportunity (EEO) Tabulation, based on the American Community Survey (ACS), provides statistics on the demographics of the workforce by occupation. The U.S. Census Bureau has produced this tabulation after every census since the 1970s. However, for the first time, this tabulation uses five years of statistics from the American Community Survey (2006-2010). They serve as the primary benchmark for assessing the diversity of the labor force and monitoring compliance with civil rights laws. This infographic focuses on men and women in the civilian labor force and what we can learn from the EEO tabulations over the past five decades.

Composition of the Labor Force by Sex

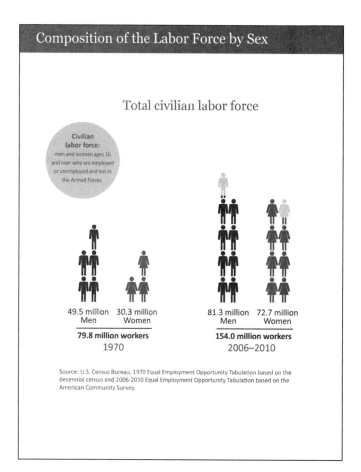

Total civilian labor force

Civilian labor force: men and women ages 16 and over who are employed or unemployed and not in the Armed Forces.

49.5 million Men	30.3 million Women	81.3 million Men	72.7 million Women
79.8 million workers		**154.0 million workers**	
1970		2006–2010	

Source: U.S. Census Bureau, 1970 Equal Employment Opportunity Tabulation based on the decennial census and 2006-2010 Equal Employment Opportunity Tabulation based on the American Community Survey.

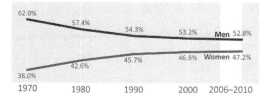

Women's representation in the labor force has increased

Source: U.S. Census Bureau, 1970, 1980, 1990, and 2000 Equal Employment Opportunity tabulations based on the decennial census and 2006-2010 Equal Employment Opportunity Tabulation based on the American Community Survey.

Women's share of the labor force has increased since the first Equal Employment Opportunity Tabulation. The largest increase was between 1970 and 1980, increasing by 4.6 percentage points. Between 1980 and 1990, women's share of the labor force increased by 3.1 percentage points. The pace of growth slowed to 1.1 percentage points between 1990 and 2000 and 0.4 percentage points between 2000 and 2006-2010.

Occupations

Change in Women's Representation in Select Occupations Since 1970

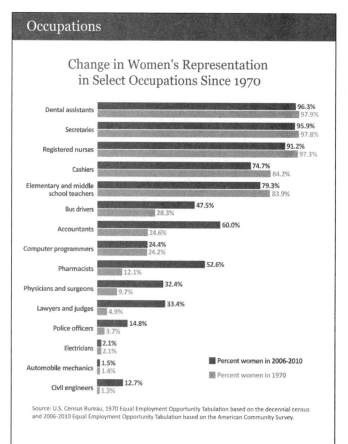

Source: U.S. Census Bureau, 1970 Equal Employment Opportunity Tabulation based on the decennial census and 2006-2010 Equal Employment Opportunity Tabulation based on the American Community Survey.

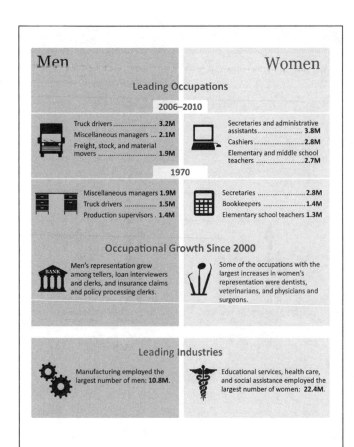

Men   Women

Leading Occupations

2006–2010

Men
Truck drivers **3.2M**
Miscellaneous managers ... **2.1M**
Freight, stock, and material
movers **1.9M**

Women
Secretaries and administrative
assistants **3.8M**
Cashiers **2.8M**
Elementary and middle school
teachers **2.7M**

1970

Men
Miscellaneous managers **1.9M**
Truck drivers **1.5M**
Production supervisors . **1.4M**

Women
Secretaries **2.8M**
Bookkeepers **1.4M**
Elementary school teachers **1.3M**

Occupational Growth Since 2000

Men's representation grew among tellers, loan interviewers and clerks, and insurance claims and policy processing clerks.

Some of the occupations with the largest increases in women's representation were dentists, veterinarians, and physicians and surgeons.

Leading Industries

Manufacturing employed the largest number of men: **10.8M**.

Educational services, health care, and social assistance employed the largest number of women: **22.4M**.

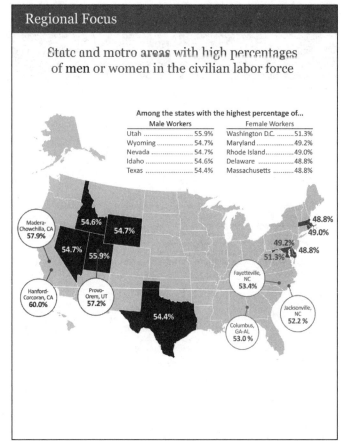

State and metro areas with high percentages of **men** or **women** in the civilian labor force

Among the states with the highest percentage of...

Male Workers		Female Workers	
Utah	55.9%	Washington D.C.	51.3%
Wyoming	54.7%	Maryland	49.2%
Nevada	54.7%	Rhode Island...............	49.0%
Idaho	54.6%	Delaware	48.8%
Texas	54.4%	Massachusetts	48.8%

Madera-Chowchilla, CA **57.9%**

Hanford-Corcoran, CA **60.0%**

Provo-Orem, UT **57.2%**

54.6%

54.7%

54.7%

55.9%

54.4%

48.8%
49.0%
49.2%
51.3%
48.8%

Fayetteville, NC **53.4%**

Jacksonville, NC **52.2 %**

Columbus, GA-AL **53.0 %**

May be photocopied for classroom use. *Texts and Lessons for Content-Area Writing* by Nancy Steineke and Harvey "Smokey" Daniels, © 2016 (Portsmouth, NH: Heinemann).

Charting the Author's Purpose

TEXT	AUTHOR	SOURCE	TEXT TYPE
"Measles: A Dangerous Illness"	Roald Dahl	www.roalddahl.com/charity	Opinion

In this lesson, we tackle the mother of all end-of-chapter (and standardized test) questions: What is the author's purpose? This query usually evokes an oversimplification. In the real world, most writers—scientists, journalists, bloggers, historians—are juggling many intentions as they work. These "author's purposes" are multiple and intertwined, both overt and implicit. To truly grasp what an author is trying to achieve requires close reading and defensible inferences. In this lesson, we invite kids to respect and explore this complexity. Then, they can apply these insights to their own reports and essays.

The text used here is one of a kind. Have you ever read (or taught or seen the movies based on) *Charlie and the Chocolate Factory, The BFG, James and the Giant Peach,* or *Matilda*? If so, you might be as big a fan of Roald Dahl, the late British children's author, as we are. If you've read his autobiography *Boy,* or any of his adult writings (*Kiss Kiss, Switch Bitch*), you know that there is another, less jolly side to the man who entertained millions of young readers so joyfully. The piece kids will read in this lesson may shed some light on a man whose stories contain both joy and heartbreak.

PREPARATION

1. Before you teach this lesson, casually interview a few students to see if they know and remember books by Roald Dahl. In most U.S. elementary and middle schools, his work is highly popular with young readers. If you get blank looks, adapt Step 1 accordingly, introducing Dahl instead of simply reminding kids about him.

2. Make a copy of the article, "Measles: A Dangerous Illness," for each student to read in Step 2. Leave side two of the handout blank for writing.

3. Decide how kids will form partners at Step 3 and be ready to project the discussion questions at that point.

4. Download the blank chart handout for Step 7. Make copies for all students and be ready to project it. Determine how to appoint a student scribe for Step 7.

5. Think about how to schedule the extension if you decide to use it.

STEP 1 **Introduce the author.** (Adapt this step to your preinterview on the kids' background knowledge about Dahl.) *Have any of you read any books by the British children's author Roald Dahl? Books like* Charlie and the Chocolate Factory, The BFG, James and the Giant Peach, Matilda,

TIME ▸ 30 minutes without extension

GROUPING ▸ Whole class, pairs, individuals

STANDARDS MET ▸ See pages 306–307.

WHEN TO USE ▸ We are always asking kids to identify the "author's purpose" in readings we assign. But real-life authors have multiple purposes, and students need explicit lessons in how to identify, weigh, and write about the complex aims of nonfiction writers.

◂ Steps & Teaching Language

or Boy? *He also wrote the story behind* Willie Wonka and the Chocolate Factory. *Can anyone say something about Dahl as an author? What kinds of characters or stories he created? What his writing sounds like?*

Take answers from a few volunteers.

Dahl passed away in 1990, but he left behind lots of writing, and not just children's books. Today we are going to read one of his more unusual short pieces.

STEP 2 **Students read the article.** Distribute the article copies. *Just to get you set on the time period, Dahl wrote this in 1986. Let's read.* Allow reading time. Encourage early finishers to reread.

STEP 3 **Set up partner writing.** *Wow, huh? Let's do a one-minute pen pal note to your partner (as in Lesson 20). Turn your articles over to the blank side and write about any of these topics.* Project the topics. *We'll exchange notes in one minute.*

> ### Idea Starters for Pen Pal Notes
> How did you react to this piece of writing?
>
> What images did it conjure up for you?
>
> What feelings?
>
> Personal connections?
>
> Questions?

STEP 4 **Partners exchange and discuss notes.** After a minute or two of writing time, have kids swap notes and read their partner's ideas. Then allow about two minutes of pair talk. Encourage students to look back at the article during the discussion to reference what they noticed.

STEP 5 **Volunteers share responses to the story.** Reconvening the whole group, try to get the widest range of reactions: *Who thought of something else? Who had a different take on the article?*

STEP 6 **Pairs reread, seeking purposes.** *Now, you guys have done plenty of worksheets in English and other subjects that ask, "What is the author's purpose?" Right? Now we are going to dig a little deeper into Dahl's purpose—or purposes—for writing this.*

Let's reread the piece in pairs and try to identify some purposes Dahl might have had in mind. Sit side by side and read it silently from the top. Whenever either of you notices a goal, an intention, or a purpose that Dahl expresses, stop and talk about it. What is the writer trying to make us readers feel, think, or do?

Make some notes in the margin so you can tell us what you found later.

If kids need a quota, you can say something like this: *When I read this, I found about a half dozen goals he seemed to be working on. When we get back together, our goal will be to make a list of all the reasons Dahl might have had for writing this piece.*

Allow at least five minutes, monitoring and supporting kids as they seek and jot notes about Dahl's purposes.

STEP 7 **Explain and begin creating a purpose/evidence chart.** Pass out a blank chart to each student while signaling that kids need to refocus their attention on you so that they can hear the instructions. *You can see this chart has two columns—one for the purposes we think Dahl had in writing this piece, and the other for evidence, meaning places in the text where we can show him working on that particular purpose. We'll come back to the right-hand column in a minute; for now, our goal is to fill up the left one.*

Have students write down everything that is said in the next few minutes. They will be using their charts with partners shortly.

Okay, who can tell us one reason why you thought Dahl wrote this article? What was one of his aims? Expect to hear purposes like these:

To get information out

To encourage vaccinations

To warn other parents

To honor his daughter's memory

To cope with his grief

To save other children from death

To make me sad while reading this

To shock the reader

Don't be too bugged if kids list purposes like "to make money," or "to get famous"—all writers have these intentions in the background somewhere.

Have your scribe jot down all ideas kids suggest; if they are unsupportable, it will be obvious soon enough when no evidence can be found. Keep going until all unique purposes have been listed in the left-hand column.

STEP 8 **Model finding evidence of purpose.** Go back to the first purpose listed at the top left of the chart. Ask volunteers to point out some locations in the text where this particular purpose is evident. Jot that information in the "Evidence" column, reducing it to key words and phrases to save space. For many of Dahl's purposes, there are multiple spots where you can see that intention at work.

STEP 9 **Students complete the chart.** Now it's time for the kids to take over and fill out the rest of the chart. *Okay, now go back to your partners and fill out the rest of the chart, finding and noting the evidence for each purpose we came up with. If you cannot find anything, note that too!*

STEP 10 **Reconvene and review.** Back in the whole group, invite pairs to share the evidence they found for different author purposes. A good way to start this: *What's one purpose on our list that you found lots of evidence for, so you felt really sure that Dahl was working on that goal? What's another one that had lots of evidence? How about one where the evidence was thin? Did anyone find any evidence for that? If not, then we can't be sure.*

Is there any purpose we listed where you thought Dahl was working on it subconsciously, but not intentionally? Which one? What made you think that?

If kids have dug deeply into the story, this discussion can run long, so cut it off while conversation is still lively.

Extension ▶
(on a following day)

STEP 11 **Students examine their own "author purposes."** Have students bring in a paper they wrote previously for any class, and take it through the purpose/evidence note-taking process just as they did in Steps 8–11. This means kids will be charting their own (perhaps previously unconscious) purposes. While "following the assignment" or "getting a good grade" may be the first purpose that comes to mind, as kids dig through their own work they often find they had other goals, too. For example, once they connected with the material, kids may have wanted their writing to have an authentic voice or to be clear, original, or surprising.

This activity may evoke some comparisons between Dahl's enormous passion for his topic, and the less galvanizing motivations for writing school papers. A great conversation to have: How can we find more energy and commitment for the writing we do in school? How can we make assigned topics our own? How can teachers help students to pick more engaging and sustainable topics?

Variation ▶

If you are a Dahl fan (and have a few extra minutes), you can kick off this lesson with a short read-aloud from one of his books. One favorite is the short story "The Landlady," from the collection *Kiss Kiss*. It gives kids a taste of how clever and creepy Dahl can be. Thanks to Donalyn Miller for reminding us of this delectable delight.

Longer writing projects—reflecting the key genres required by the national standards—can be built on the work students have already done in this lesson. As kids continue to explore the topics of our reading selections, we expect that they will bring fresh background knowledge, recent thinking, and genuine curiosity to the task. When you use the lesson above with your own content, you can also use the assignments below as models for extending that content into longer writing projects.

Narrative: *Recount an illness or injury of your own*

Roald Dahl's story about his daughter is a very sad one, with the unhappiest possible ending. But most of us survive our childhood illnesses—and they often leave strong memories. Tell the story of an illness or an injury that you had as a youngster, from the first day through to your recovery, as best you remember it. If you can interview older family members (mother, father, siblings) or anyone else who took care of you, that will probably give you more information to work with. (Obviously, you may decide not to use this topic if kids in your room have had or are battling life-threatening illnesses.)

Informative/explanatory: *Analyze a related public health issue*

To protect everyone from contagious and deadly illnesses, we have to achieve "herd immunity." Investigate this term and explain what it means. Try to answer some of these questions: What percentage of people in a population need to be vaccinated in order to achieve herd immunity? At what point does herd immunity fail? To put it another way, how many people need to abstain from vaccinating their children to put everyone else at risk? (You could also work with a classmate who is doing the related persuasive topic below.)

Persuasive/argumentative: *Research and take a side on a current raging controversy*

As you may know, there has been a steady controversy over vaccinations and immunizations in recent years. Some parents and activists believe that commonly given vaccinations might actually *cause* illnesses, or conditions such as autism. While the scientific community and authorities like the Centers for Disease Control flatly state that there are no such dangers, many "anti-vaxxers" are persistent. Investigate the cases for and against vaccination. Then, write a persuasive letter to new parents arguing either for or against vaccinating their young children.

IDENTIFYING AN AUTHOR'S PURPOSES IN A TEXT

Purpose	Evidence of this purpose

MEASLES: A Dangerous Illness

Roald Dahl

Olivia, my eldest daughter, caught measles when she was seven years old. As the illness took its usual course I can remember reading to her often in bed and not feeling particularly alarmed about it. Then one morning, when she was well on the road to recovery, I was sitting on her bed showing her how to fashion little animals out of colored pipe-cleaners, and when it came to her turn to make one herself, I noticed that her fingers and her mind were not working together and she couldn't do anything.

"Are you feeling all right?" I asked her.

"I feel all sleepy," she said.

In an hour, she was unconscious. In twelve hours she was dead.

The measles had turned into a terrible thing called measles encephalitis and there was nothing the doctors could do to save her. That was twenty-four years ago in 1962, but even now, if a child with measles happens to develop the same deadly reaction from measles as Olivia did, there would still be nothing the doctors could do to help her.

On the other hand, there is today something that parents can do to make sure that this sort of tragedy does not happen to a child of theirs. They can insist that their child is immunized against measles. I was unable to do that for Olivia in 1962 because in those days a reliable measles vaccine had not been discovered. Today a good and safe vaccine is available to every family and all you have to do is to ask your doctor to administer it.

It is not yet generally accepted that measles can be a dangerous illness. Believe me, it is. In my opinion parents who now refuse to have their children immunized are putting the lives of those children at risk. In America, where measles immunization is compulsory, measles like smallpox, has been virtually wiped out.

Here in Britain, because so many parents refuse, either out of obstinacy or ignorance or fear, to allow their children to be immunized, we still have a hundred thousand cases of measles every year. Out of those, more than 10,000 will suffer side effects of one kind or another. About 20 will die.

LET THAT SINK IN.

Every year around 20 children will die in Britain from measles. It really is almost a crime to allow your child to go unimmunized.

I dedicated two of my books to Olivia, the first was *James and the Giant Peach*. That was when she was still alive. The second was *The BFG,* dedicated to her memory after she had died from measles. You will see her name at the beginning of each of these books. And I know how happy she would be if only she could know that her death had helped to save a good deal of illness and death among other children.

CLOSER WRITING ABOUT CONTENT

This final set of lessons offers students the opportunity to read more closely as they begin to think like writers. In this section, students are asked to pay particular attention to how writers structure their use of fact and detail in order to grab the reader's attention, hold it throughout the piece, and in the end give the reader something to think about—and hopefully act upon.

LESSON 31

TIME ▶ 40 minutes

GROUPINGS ▶ Whole class, pairs, individuals

STANDARDS MET ▶ See pages 306–307.

WHEN TO USE ▶ This lesson is a great way to let students practice incorporating data or statistics from content-area sources into their own writing.

Writing from Data

TEXT	AUTHOR	SOURCE	TEXT TYPE
"Breadwinner Moms" (two excerpts)	Wendy Wang, Kim Parker, and Paul Taylor	Pew Charitable Trust	Research report

As students move ahead in school, it's vital they learn how to accurately study and use numerical and statistical data in their own writing. A good first step is summarizing the data found in various charts, tables, and other graphics. Sometimes this information is striking enough to stand on its own; more often, though, you have to also explain it to the reader.

Women in the American workforce, looked at over a span of fifty-plus years: what a great topic. And, depending on how old you are, a great chance to be shocked by how little your kids know about the good old days. I mean, didn't everyone's moms *always* go to work?

> **PREPARATION**
>
> 1. Decide how pairs will be formed for Step 1.
> 2. Download and be ready to project the pair discussion questions at Step 1.
> 3. Make copies of the two "Breadwinner Moms" excerpts for each student, to use in Steps 3 and 6.
> 4. Download and be ready to project Table 1 and the accompanying paragraph at Step 5.
> 5. Download "How to Revise Drafts with a Partner" for projection at Step 8.

Steps & Teaching Language ▶

STEP 1 **Partners discuss the topic.** *We all know that in general, women's roles in the family and the workplace have changed in the last couple of generations, right? Especially since 1960 (before your parents were born, maybe), there has been a shift toward more women working outside the home. Discuss with your partner what you know (or guess) about these developments.*

What do you know about women in the workforce?

- What percentage of women do you think worked outside the home in 1960? Why do you choose this number?

- What percentage do today? What makes you choose this number?

- What have been some benefits of more women working?

- What aspects of women working might raise concerns?

- How have these changes affected your own family (grandparents, parents, cousins)?

Allow about three minutes for discussion. Circulate and eavesdrop on the kids' guesses so you will have a sense of the range and can call on some pairs later if needed.

STEP 2 **Partners share background knowledge with the class.** *Who can tell us some of your estimates or predictions on those numbers? And what was your reasoning? How about benefits and costs—what did you mention? Any connections with your own families?*

STEP 3 **Students read the first excerpt.** Pass out Excerpt 1 from the Pew report. *In a minute, we are going to read parts of a report about this topic from the Pew Charitable Trust, a highly respected research organization that tracks many aspects of American life. Keep your guesses and predictions in mind, and when you run across information that answers your questions or gives you some interesting examples, put a check in the margin, right beside it.* Give students time to read and annotate, checking in with anyone who seems to need help.

STEP 4 **Students share initial responses.** Invite a few students to share their first reactions. *Look over your checkmarks. Did any of the workforce percentages surprise you? Were they higher or lower than you expected? If you made a pretty good estimate, what was your thinking? How about the benefits and downsides of more women working—did those concerns match your expectations? Did you find that your own family history matched these changes?*

STEP 5 **Point out the summarization.** *Look at the first paragraph that accompanies the first table:*

> A record 40% of all households with children under the age of 18 include mothers who are either the sole or primary source of income for the family, according to a new Pew Research Center analysis of data from the U.S. Census Bureau. The share was just 11% in 1960. These "breadwinner moms" are made up of two very different groups: 5.1 million (37%) are married mothers who have a higher income than their husbands, and 8.6 million (63%) are single mothers.

Read it over again and talk with your partner. What is the content of this section? What is it doing? Allow a minute of talk time. *Who can tell us? Yes, the paragraph summarizes or restates the content of the table in a few sentences. Many times, these kinds of articles have charts, tables, and graphs filled with numbers and trends—but then the authors also translate the charts into sentences that help people "see" all the information in the graphic.*

Before moving on, be sure to note the additional information in the summary: *The paragraph goes on to add some additional information that is not in the chart—that's where you found more specifics and examples to help you check your predictions and estimates.*

STEP 6 **Students read additional tables.** Hand out the second excerpt with the three tables. *Now here are three more tables from that same report. Read these and think about them as you go. In a minute, you will choose just one to write about, so look for the one that interests you most.* Allow about three minutes, or longer if kids seem absorbed.

STEP 7 **Individuals write about their chosen table.** *Now it's your chance to do a job that real researchers do—translating some numerical data into sentences that help people understand the information. Using Table 1 and its accompanying paragraph as a model, write a paragraph that explains the information in the table you have chosen—2, 3, or 4. Be sure you include all the data that is present.*

For now you are working individually, but you'll get with your partner and help each other revise. Ready? Write away! Circulate and assist. Sit down and confer with any kids who are struggling with their table. Allow at least five minutes of writing time.

STEP 8 **Students revise drafts with a partner.** *Sit down with your buddy, with both of your drafts and the tables you chose to summarize. The person who is wearing the coolest shoes today is Author 1 and shares first. Here's the sequence* (project steps as you explain):

How to Revise Drafts with a Partner

1. Both partners reread Author 1's chosen table.

2. Author 1 reads draft paragraph aloud while buddy listens to make sure that all information is included and is accurate.

3. After reading aloud, listening buddy offers suggestions for including additional table information or clarifying parts of Author 1's table explanation. Author jots down the buddy's suggestion on his draft.

4. Switch roles and repeat Step 5. Now Author 2 reads aloud while buddy listens and helps.

5. After both of you have read aloud as authors and also been a listening buddy, be sure to thank each other for the conversation and the help.

STEP 9 **Authors make revisions and prepare to share.** *Okay, take a minute to enter any changes or additions to your paragraph. As you revise, be sure you can follow your changes well enough to read your draft smoothly and with expression when we share in a few minutes.* Allow just a couple of minutes for this. Many of the written changes will have been inserted during partner work. Encourage kids to actually read their text aloud (several times, if possible) for practice.

STEP 10 **Volunteers read paragraphs aloud.** Get as many students to read as possible. *Who has a paragraph for Table 2? Who wrote about Table 2 in a different way? How about Table 3, who had a partner that did a nice job with that one? Another? And Table 4, who'd like to share?*

STEP 11 **Collect student work.** This lesson yields some short but hopefully concentrated writing.

◀ **Tip**

A logical next step would be lessons in extracting *individual* facts from a graphic display and working them into a prose text. And after that, how to grab a quote from an interview or article and stitch it into your own text.

◀ **Research Projects for Extended Writing**

Longer writing projects—reflecting the key genres required by the national standards—can be built on the work students have already done in this lesson. As kids continue to explore the topics of our reading selections, we expect that they will bring fresh background knowledge, recent thinking, and genuine curiosity to the task. When you use the lesson above with your own content, you can also use the assignments below as models for extending that content into longer writing projects.

Narrative: *Interview a working woman*

Make a list of the women in your life who work and choose one who would be receptive to being interviewed, either in person or via phone, Skype, or email. Develop a list of questions that will help your subject tell her work story. Write up your research in the form of a question-answer interview modeled after the "haunted house" text in Lesson 2. Or write about one significant work memory/ experience using the style of a personal narrative or memoir.

Informative/explanatory: *Compare parental job benefits offered U.S. workers versus those of other wealthy, industrialized countries*

Many countries offer parents significant benefits that enhance their abilities to work and raise a family. For example, Japanese women receive fifty-eight weeks of maternity leave, twenty-six of which are paid. Fathers are entitled to the same amount of time off. On the other hand, the United States has no national parental leave policy. What other differences can you find between parental job benefits in the United States and in other countries? Research parental benefits for U.S. parents as well as for parents in another country that has significantly different benefits. Share your findings in the form of an informative two-column chart.

Persuasive/argumentative: *Argue for or against additional work benefits*

While lack of uniform parental leave is one benefit that separates U.S. workers from those in other wealthy industrialized nations, American workers lack other benefits as well. Research worker benefits in the United States compared to other countries and then argue whether the absence of these benefits improves the overall U.S. economy or hinders it.

Breadwinner Moms, Excerpt 1

Mothers Are the Sole or Primary Provider in Four-in-Ten Households with Children; Public Conflicted About the Growing Trend

Wendy Wang, Kim Parker, and Paul Taylor, Pew Charitable Trust

A record 40% of all households with children under the age of 18 include mothers who are either the sole or primary source of income for the family, according to a new Pew Research Center analysis of data from the U.S. Census Bureau. The share was just 11% in 1960. These "breadwinner moms" are made up of two very different groups: 5.1 million (37%) are married mothers who have a higher income than their husbands, and 8.6 million (63%) are single mothers.

The income gap between the two groups is quite large. The median total family income of married mothers who earn more than their husbands was nearly $80,000 in 2011, well above the national median of $57,100 for all families with children, and nearly four times the $23,000 median for families led by a single mother.

The groups differ in other ways as well. Compared with all mothers with children under age 18, married mothers who out-earn their husbands are slightly older, disproportionally white and college educated. Single mothers, by contrast, are younger, more likely to be black or Hispanic, and less likely to have a college degree.

The growth of both groups of mothers is tied to women's increasing presence in the

Table 1

Mother as the Sole or Primary Provider: 1960-2011

% based on households with children under age 18

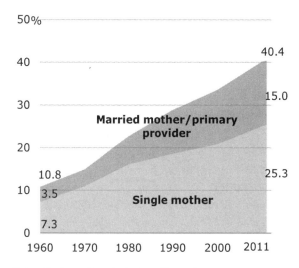

Note: Single mothers include mothers who are never married, divorced, widowed, separated, or married but the spouse is not in the household.

Source: Pew Research Center analysis of the Decennial Census and American Community Surveys (ACS) Integrated Public Use Microdata Sample (IPUMS) files

PEW RESEARCH CENTER

workplace. Women make up almost half (47%) of the U.S. labor force today, and the employment rate of married mothers with children has increased from 37% in 1968 to 65% in 2011.

Breadwinner Moms, Excerpt 2

Mothers Are the Sole or Primary Provider in Four-in-Ten Households with Children; Public Conflicted About the Growing Trend

Wendy Wang, Kim Parker, and Paul Taylor, Pew Charitable Trust

Table 2

Employment Arrangements among Couples, 1960-2011

% of married couples with children under age 18

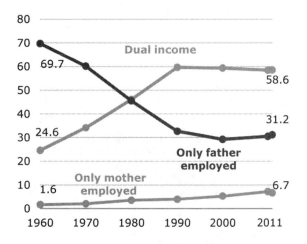

Source: Pew Research Center analysis of the Decennial Census and American Community Surveys (ACS) Integrated Public Use Microdata Sample (IPUMS) files

PEW RESEARCH CENTER

Table 3

Women, Work and Families

% saying the increasing number of women working for pay outside the home has made it easier/harder for ...

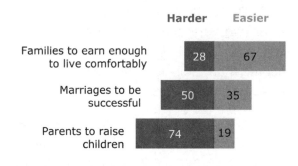

Note: "Hasn't made much difference" and "Don't know/Refused" responses not shown.

Source: Pew Research Center survey, conducted April 25-28, 2013, N=1,003.

PEW RESEARCH CENTER

Table 4

The Public Differs in Role of Fathers and Mothers

% saying children are ...

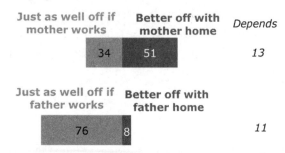

Note: The questions were asked separately for mothers and fathers. Responses of "Just as well if mother/father works" and "Depends" are not shown.

Source: Pew Research Center survey, conducted April 25-28, 2013, N=1,003.

PEW RESEARCH CENTER

See/Think/Wonder: Digging Deeper into an Image

TEXT	SOURCE	TEXT TYPE
Women's Suffrage Map, 1919	www.flatworldknowledge.com	Political map

TIME ▶ 20 minutes

GROUPINGS ▶ Whole class, pairs, individuals

STANDARDS MET ▶ See pages 306–307.

WHEN TO USE ▶ Content-area textbooks are filled with charts, graphs, maps, and infographics. Use this lesson to help kids examine and discuss the information in these graphics in a deeper, thought-provoking way.

In several previous lessons, we've had kids study an image, photograph, or artwork. Much of this work has focused on supporting students to notice, capture, and think about all the details in a historical or contemporary image. In this last iteration, we use a hybrid image: a U.S. map that combines historical information from different time periods and uses categories most adult Americans have never heard of. So with this lesson, we are zooming in on students' ability to seek deeper meaning from a genuinely complex text. To aid in this, we introduce a "think sheet," called a See/Think/Wonder Chart, that helps students explore an image more thoughtfully, capturing multiple levels of thinking along the way.

The subject matter of the map—women's suffrage—reframes the usual conversation. It turns out that "getting women the right to vote"—which Susan B. Anthony worked on for fifty years (pages 37 and 238)—has meant different things in different places at different times. The map's date of 1919 obviously reflects the year before the Nineteenth Amendment was finally ratified, August 18, 1920. Thus, it shows us certain circumstances that might have remained the same or changed very slowly without the following year's legislation and ratification.

PREPARATION

1. Download and make a copy of the See/Think/Wonder chart for each kid at Step 2.

2. Download the Women's Suffrage map and be ready to project it at Step 3. If you make student copies as well, printing in color will work best to delineate state suffrage status.

3. Determine how pairs will form at Step 3 (or just begin the lesson with kids sitting with partners).

STEP 1 **Introduce the lesson.** Invite kids to jump in and answer these two questions: *Does anyone know when women got the right to vote in America? Right, it was 1920, just about a hundred years ago. And how did that right become established? Yes, by an amendment to the Constitution that required a two-thirds vote of both houses of Congress and approval by three-fourths of state legislatures. Not an easy thing to achieve, gaining that very high level of approval from all around the country, wouldn't you say? That's one reason our Constitution so rarely gets changed—so no*

◀ **Steps &
Teaching
Language**

small group of crackpots can come along and easily throw out the rules all the rest of us live by.

STEP 2 **Introduce the map and explain how to use the See/Think/Wonder sheets.** *You might wonder, what was the situation for women's voting rights before the amendment, say in 1919? Could some women already vote? Where? If so, how long had they had the right to vote, or suffrage?*

In a minute, I will show you a map that paints exactly that picture: What were the conditions for female citizens in 1919, the year before the Constitution was amended? What needed to be changed?

To examine this map, we're going to use a See/Think/Wonder chart. (Distribute the forms.) *You're going to look at the map in three ways, using this sheet to jot down your thoughts on each. Here are some questions to consider as you make notes in each column:*

See: *What do you see? Notice? What jumps out? What did you already know? Does anything surprise you? What are your personal responses? How do you connect with this?*

Think: *What new learning are you having? What fresh understanding? What inferences are you making? How are you making sense of things like the key listing different kinds of suffrage? How would you summarize the information on this map? What does it tell us about the United States?*

Wonder: *What questions do you have? What's puzzling or confusing about the different labels? About the different states? About the meaning of the map as a whole? What one question would you most want to investigate or learn more about right now?*

Your responses will probably come up in random order, so it's okay to jump around between columns.

STEP 3 **Students study the map.** Project the map and pass out color copies if you choose to duplicate.

Sit with your partner while you do this. It's fine to talk with each other as you make sense of the map, but be sure you both make your own notes for our discussion later. Allow a good chunk of work time, at least five minutes, and keep an eye on how the different columns on kids' See/Think/Wonder sheets fill up. You may need to coach students who get "stuck" in one column to diversify their note taking.

STEP 4 **Debrief kids' "see" responses.** Take the thinking in order. First ask kids to share what they "saw," drawing from their think-sheet notes. Keep probing: *Who saw something different? Something else someone noticed or jotted down?*

STEP 5 **Debrief thinking.** Next, move on to the second column, asking for different kinds of thinking. Press for inferences: *Did you talk about* *why the states were so different? Did you draw any conclusions about policies in different regions of the country? What does this map say about our country?*

STEP 6 **Debrief what kids wonder.** Finally, probe kids' questions. *Who can share something you wondered about the map? Or about the women's suffrage issue? What parts did you find confusing or puzzling? Who has a specific question they would like to ask or investigate in the future?*

Longer writing projects—reflecting the key genres required by the national standards—can be built on the work students have already done in this lesson. As kids continue to explore the topics of our reading selections, we expect that they will bring fresh background knowledge, recent thinking, and genuine curiosity to the task. When you use the lesson above with your own content, you can also use the assignments below as models for extending that content into longer writing projects.

◀ *Research Projects for Extended Writing*

Narrative: *Present an alternative history*

Some historians write books about how the world would be different if Hitler had never been born or if the atomic bomb had been a dud. What would have happened after 1920 if the constitutional amendment had failed? Make up a fact-based story, a plausible "alternate history." What course would the women's suffrage movement have taken in 1920 and beyond? Who would be its new leaders and opponents? What tactics would they use? Who would be allies—and opponents? Was suffrage inevitable, or could it have been delayed for decades?

Informative/expository: *Investigate a government claim*

Investigate the history of women's suffrage in other countries around the world. You may find that some countries *still* do not allow women to vote, or that they lie about it. We've learned to ask the question, "What does suffrage mean, specifically?" Can females vote only in local or school elections, or do they exercise the same full privileges as men in their society? To limit your topic, pick three to five countries, perhaps one from each continent, to get a sense of the diversity.

Persuasive/argumentative: *Research an anomaly*

The map shows some interesting and not necessarily predictable regional patterns. Look more deeply into historical patterns of voting eligibility in New England, the South, and the West. Why would the West have been so "generous" with voting rights, and other regions more resistant? Why the solid block of states refusing women the vote from Pennsylvania to Alabama, but not through Mississippi or Louisiana? Why is New York State an outlier in its region? Why, of all western states, didn't New Mexico offer women's suffrage? Pick one of these historical anomalies and research the reasons for its suffrage rules in 1919. Then, in the voice of a state legislator, write a short speech or letter to the editor that defends your state's suffrage laws as well as refutes those who believe differently. Depending on the state, refutation might support women's suffrage—or not!

SEE	THINK	WONDER

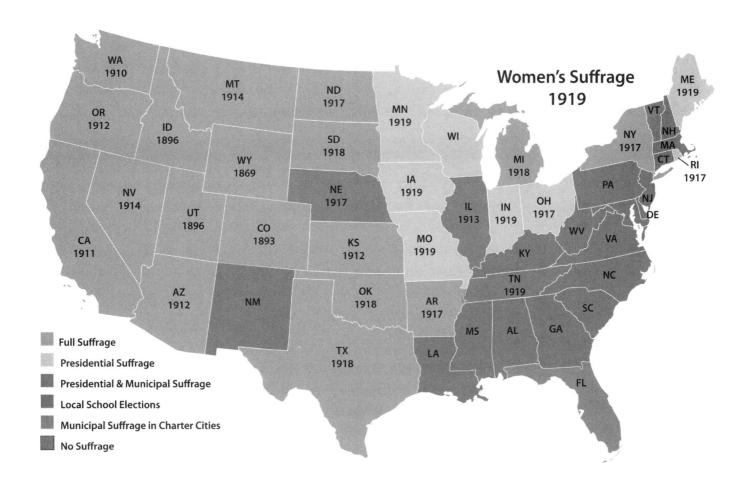

Women's Suffrage 1919

WA 1910
OR 1912
MT 1914
ID 1896
ND 1917
MN 1919
WI
ME 1919
VT
NH
NY 1917
MA
CT
RI 1917
SD 1918
IA 1919
MI 1918
NV 1914
UT 1896
WY 1869
NE 1917
IL 1913
IN 1919
OH 1917
PA
NJ
DE
CA 1911
CO 1893
KS 1912
MO 1919
KY
WV
VA
AZ 1912
NM
OK 1918
AR 1917
TN 1919
NC
MS
AL
GA
SC
TX 1918
LA
FL

Legend:
- Full Suffrage
- Presidential Suffrage
- Presidential & Municipal Suffrage
- Local School Elections
- Municipal Suffrage in Charter Cities
- No Suffrage

Write an Opening

TIME ▶ 40 minutes

GROUPINGS ▶ Whole class, pairs, individuals

STANDARDS MET ▶ See pages 306–307.

WHEN TO USE ▶ When students must write in more traditional, prescriptive styles (test writing, standard five-paragraph essays), coming up with an interesting start is often a roadblock. This lesson shows students how to approach an opening paragraph that captures the topic—and the reader.

TEXT	AUTHOR	SOURCE	TEXT TYPE
"Is It Safe? Young Teens Look to Older Kids, Not Adults, for Advice in Risky Situations"	Sarah D. Sparks	*Inside School Research* (*Education Week* blog)	Research summary

If you ever taught elementary school, you might remember a reading lesson called a "cloze" procedure. That's when kids are given a reading passage with a few words omitted, and then must guess the best word for each blank space, based on their background knowledge and the content of the selection. For the next three lessons, we are offering your kids a chance to write or predict *whole missing sections* from articles they read. This first one draws young writers' attention to the importance of creating a "hook" for readers, a beginning that draws the reader in while giving an accurate, though perhaps perplexing or fragmentary, preview of what's to come.

Our topic is how teens seek help when making high-risk decisions. Maybe parents (or even teachers) would love to believe that young people will ask their guidance in a pinch, but this study shows they are just as likely to ask an older peer.

PREPARATION

1. Make a copy of the body of the article "Is It Safe?" minus the opening (as we have set it up here in the book and online) for each student to use in Step 5. Also download that opening and be ready to project it for the final step of this lesson.

2. Decide how pairs will form at Step 1.

3. Appoint a student scribe to make the list at Step 2, so you can focus on moderating the contributions.

4. At Step 5, be ready to project the annotation codes.

Steps & Teaching Language ▶

STEP 1 **Pairs discuss risk taking.** *You guys, teenagers, are famous for engaging in so-called risky behavior. I am going to ask you to think about two questions related to that. Here's the first one: Can you list some situations where someone your age might do something dangerous? One category might be texting while driving—see what other ones you can think of. Work with your partner to make a list.* Assure them they will not be handing this in, if that concern seems present.

STEP 2 **Make a whole-class list.** *Let's see what we've got. Who thought of some risky behaviors that teenagers might try?* While a student scribe is recording on a whiteboard/chart paper/computer with LCD, elicit list items; expect things like drag racing, scaling heights, playing contact sports, tagging or vandalism, using drugs or alcohol, sexual experimentation, ignoring parent or legal curfews, not wearing a seat belt, riding with a drunk driver, running with a "bad" crowd, gang activity, trespassing, fooling with guns, self-harm, suicide, petty or serious crime. When you've listed at least ten items, move on to Step 3.

STEP 3 **Pairs discuss the second question.** *Okay, talk about this and be ready to vote on it in sixty seconds: Who do you think teens trust most for advice about risky behavior—another kid or an adult?* Tally the result and jot it down on the chart to assist kids with their upcoming reading.

STEP 4 **Preview Steps 5–7.** *Now that we have thought a bit about the risks that teens sometimes take, and whom they look to for advice, let's read a recent research report on this topic. Here's the catch: I have removed the opening section of the article—what journalists call the lead—which happened to be five sentences and ninety-two words long.*

This means that you will be jumping into the middle of this research report without knowing how the author started it off. So picking up the thread may be a little harder than usual. I'll help you with that.

But here's the fun part: after you have read the rest of the article, you and your partner get to create your own great opening to the piece. We will read these aloud before we see the author's real opening. Finally, we'll vote on which openings were best, yours or the author's. There may not be cash prizes, but applause and admiring looks will definitely be awarded!

STEP 5 **Set up the reading.** *This is a challenging article even when its opening section is intact! So it will be important to annotate the text as you go. While you are reading, be sure to stop when you come upon some information that helps you understand whom teens turn to for advice about risky behavior. You can mark the text with these codes.*

> ### Annotation Codes
>
> **A** – evidence that teens rely more on **A**dults for advice
>
> **T** – evidence that teens rely more on other **T**eens for advice
>
> **B** – evidence that teenagers rely on **B**oth peers and adults for advice

Project the codes for kids to see while reading.

Okay? Happy reading, everyone. Allow ample time for reading.

STEP 6 **Kids share impressions.** Invite conversation about the study findings.

STEP 7 **Individuals write new openings.** *Working alone for about three minutes, you are going to write the best opening you can think of for this article, which you have studied so closely. Remember, an opening gives the reader an idea of what the piece will be about, so you'll need to consider what you noticed as you read. Openings also reflect the tone or voice* *of the rest of a text, so consider how the author would sound when writing about this and try to match that in your own writing. Finally, keep in mind that openings often try to grab a reader's attention. You'll recall that the author's "real" opening was just five sentences (and ninety-two words) long. So that's your limit; come up with just a few sentences that really get people interested in reading this whole article.*

Allow three or more minutes of writing time, depending on what you observe about kids' progress with the task.

STEP 8 **Partners combine their openings.** *Now turn to your partner and share what you each wrote. Talk about what would be both an interesting and an accurate way to begin this article. Draw on the best parts of each of your openings and then co-create one that does the job best. Be ready to read your coauthored opening aloud (and with expression) in five minutes.*

Allow five or more minutes of writing time, as you observe pairs at work. If kids need more time, and they are seriously polishing their leads, allow it. Encourage out-loud reading practice.

STEP 9 **Volunteers read openings aloud.** Try to get a range of different approaches—puzzling, amusing, using a quote, asking the reader a question, telling a quick anecdote, and so on. Invite discussion about the kind of opening for a nonfiction article that makes people really want to grab it and read it.

STEP 10 **Reveal the original opening.** Project the text and invite discussion about the effectiveness of the author's lead. Don't sanctify it. If the reader doesn't happen to know the "jump off a bridge" reference, it isn't nearly as effective. It is entirely possible that one or more students may have come up with a better one for their own audience. If you want to make this a lighthearted contest, you can have the class vote for their favorite replacement openings.

Research Projects for Extended Writing ▶ Longer writing projects—reflecting the key genres required by the national standards—can be built on the work students have already done in this lesson. As kids continue to explore the topics of our reading selections, we expect that they will bring fresh background knowledge, recent thinking, and genuine curiosity to the task. When you use the lesson above with your own content, you can also use the assignments below as models for extending that content into longer writing projects.

Narrative: *Compare research findings to your own experience*

Tell the story of a time that you took some kind of a risk in your life. Choose something you are comfortable writing about. This could have happened recently or earlier in your childhood. If someone was guiding you or influencing you, who were they and how did they affect your choices? Pay special attention to the opening of your story, using one of the techniques we discussed to hook your readers.

Informative/explanatory: *Organize specific examples into a continuum*

So-called risky teen behavior can range from simply playing soccer or football (because of injury risks) all the way to engaging in serious crime. Using the list we created in Step 2, research other behaviors to create a "continuum of teen risk." This might be a chart or infographic that displays risks running from sociably acceptable, adult-approved behaviors (swimming across a lake, playing hockey) up through increasingly dangerous (and often illegal) behaviors like drunk driving and shoplifting. Write an introductory paragraph as a lead for the visual.

Persuasive/argumentative: *Consider a less-widespread belief*

Many sociologists, psychologists, and educators work hard to document the dangers of teen risk taking and to prevent it. But other developmental experts believe that risk taking is wired into the teenage brain, and that the attraction to risk should be channeled, not suppressed. Maybe, they speculate, the best life is not the most risk-free life. Dig into this topic, gather evidence, and take a position. Is most teenage risk taking simply negative, or are some aspects of it healthy enough to be expressed, even encouraged, by adults? What are some ways we could offer "safe risk taking"?

Is It Safe? Young Teens Look to Older Kids, Not Adults, for Advice on Risky Situations

Sarah D. Sparks, *Inside School Research* (*Education Week* blog)

[The five-sentence, 92-word opening section is omitted.]

. . . Researchers led by Lisa Joanna Knoll, a psychologist at the Institute of Cognitive Neuroscience at University College London, in the United Kingdom, asked 563 visitors to the London Science Museum to rate the riskiness of common activities such as walking down a dark alley or crossing the street against a light. After one round of risk assessment on a 1 to 10 scale, the guests were shown a randomly generated "rating" labeled as being given by an adult or teenager, and later asked to rate the activities again.

In general, all groups tended to alter their risk assessments based on those of others, but the older they got, the more they stuck to their original ratings. Moreover, children under age 11, and teenagers and young adults ages 15 and older, both were more likely to change their response in reaction to an adult's perception of how risky an activity was. Of all age groups, only young adolescents ages 12 to 14 were more likely to favor another teenager's view of risk over an adult's view, but throughout adolescence peer and adult influence ran neck and neck.

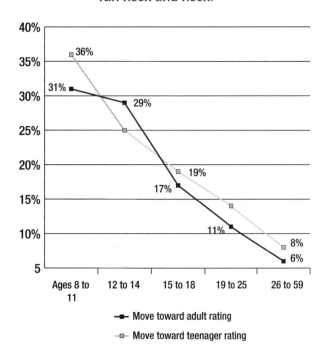

"We cannot say whether teenagers want to show off or feel safer in a group," Knoll told me. "We can only speculate that adolescents seek to conform to the same-aged influence group, not because they trust the ratings of *teenagers* more than they trust the ratings of *adults*, but because they want to be accepted by their peer group (in this case the *teenage* group)."

What's Behind Peer Pressure?

The findings are in line with emerging evidence suggesting adolescence may be as rapid and critical a period of development in social skills as the toddler years are in cognitive development. Teenagers' seeming obsession with peers—so often bemoaned by adults—may be critical to students' developing healthy adult relationships.

Knoll said she was surprised that teenagers responded strongly to a totally imaginary peer, even when it was made clear that no one else would know how they rated a situation. Previous brain-imaging research found that teenagers showed stronger risk-and-reward responses to a game when they thought their play might be viewed by peers, even when no one was in the room.

Moreover, prior studies have shown that teenagers regularly overestimate how often other teenagers are engaging in risky behaviors. "Adolescence is the time when individuals begin to explore their independence, they start to spend more time with their peers than children do and social influence tends to change," Knoll said.

Knoll's findings give further evidence that traditional "scared straight" style programs may be the wrong approach for teenagers, but, "this social influence effect works in both directions," she said. "Our young teenage participants lowered their risk rating when other *teenagers* judged the risk as less risky and increased their risk ratings when other *teenagers* judged the risk as more risky, respectively."

Is It Safe? Young Teens Look to Older Kids, Not Adults, for Advice on Risky Situations

Sarah D. Sparks, *Education Week* blog, *Inside School Research*

Opening section:

If all of your friends jumped off that bridge, would you do it too? Well, it depends on how old you are, according to a new study in *Psychological Science*.

If you are in elementary school, the answer is probably "No way!" And if you are about to graduate from high school, the answer may well be, "What does Dad say?" But at the start of adolescence, students may just shrug; of all age groups, they are most likely to jump on the assumption that other teenagers must know what they are doing.

LESSON 34 What's Next? Predict the Next Section

TEXT	AUTHOR	SOURCE	TEXT TYPE
"Why Is Turnout So Low in U.S. Elections?"	Eric Black	*Minnesota Post*	News analysis

TIME ▶ 45 minutes

GROUPINGS ▶ Whole class, pairs, individuals

STANDARDS MET ▶ See pages 306–307.

WHEN TO USE ▶ This lesson encourages students to think like writers and notice how information is organized in order to raise questions and lead the reader from one point to the next.

Many times students read just to get the reading done. Though we want students to be quick, fluent, skillful readers, to read with comprehension often means they must slow down so that they can really think about the text: How does this information mesh with what I already know? What information is new? How am I responding, personally, to this information? Based on what I've already read, what will be the focus of the next section?

It is this last question that this lesson refines: Students comprehend and remember better when they are actively predicting what comes next.

PREPARATION

1. Decide whether you will project the article "Why Is Turnout So Low in U.S. Elections?" or provide a copy of the article to each student. A key feature of this lesson is preventing students from reading ahead; you want them to focus on their predictions before moving to the next page. If you choose to duplicate this longer article, we recommend copying each page on a separate piece of paper rather than running the article back to back. However, instead of using up all that paper, you might choose to project one page of the article at a time while the kids listen and record their predictions on a sheet of paper.

2. Practice reading the article aloud. Whether you duplicate or project, you'll be reading this piece aloud so that students can move through the sections at the same pace.

3. Determine how students will form pairs in Step 3.

STEP 1 **Introduce the topic.** *How many eligible voters do you think actually vote in a presidential election?* Take some numbers. *In a typical presidential election, about 60 percent vote. What about a midterm election? There is no president running, but every seat in the House is up for grabs as well as a third of the Senate. Since all laws emanate from Congress, in some ways these elections might be even more important than a presidential election. How many people vote in these elections?* Take a few volunteers. *The turnout for midterm elections seldom reaches 50 percent; it usually hovers between 35 and 45 percent.*

How many of you know someone who didn't vote in a recent election? What kept them from voting? Hear some responses.

◀ **Steps** & **Teaching Language**

STEP 2 **Distribute/project page one of the text.** *In our quick conversation just now, you mentioned several different reasons why people you know didn't vote, and it seemed like a common reason was apathy, just not being interested in or invested enough to take the time to vote. Let's see if this article, "Why Is Turnout So Low in U.S. Elections?," proves our assumption that people just don't care enough to vote.*

So that we all can think together on this article, I'm going to read aloud as you follow along.

Read aloud the first page. Then stop and allow students to write their individual responses to the prompts at the bottom of the page: What questions does the author want the reader to ask? What elements do you think contribute to low voter turnout?

STEP 3 **Pairs share and then contribute to whole-class discussion.** *Take a minute with your partner to compare questions and thoughts you jotted down about low voter turnout.* Circulate and eavesdrop for a minute or two, noting interesting comments that you would like pairs to share with the whole class.

Now let's hear some of your ideas. Call on a few pairs; encourage volunteers to share ideas/questions that have not been mentioned. Move to the next page.

STEP 4 **Distribute/project subsequent pages of the text, one at a time.** Pairs share and then contribute to the whole class. For each page, read it aloud, stop to allow students to individually respond in writing to the prompt, let pairs share, and then encourage a brief whole-class discussion.

STEP 5 **Discuss final responses.** *How did your initial thoughts and predictions compare with the voting research in this article?* Hear responses.

What do you think the U.S. needs to do to get more people to vote? Turn to your partner and talk about this for a minute. Hear responses.

Research Projects for Extended Writing ▶ Longer writing projects—reflecting the key genres required by the national standards—can be built on the work students have already done in this lesson. As kids continue to explore the topics of our reading selections, we expect that they will bring fresh background knowledge, recent thinking, and genuine curiosity to the task. When you use the lesson above with your own content, you can also use the assignments below as models for extending that content into longer writing projects.

Narrative: *Interview and tell the story of a voter*

Interview some adults you know who are regular voters. Ask them about registration requirements, how they prepare to vote in an election, and which elections stand out in their memories. Then choose one of your interview subjects and write a short profile that focuses on this voter's election participation history.

Informative/explanatory: *Compare local findings to national data*

Expand on the idea from Step 1 of the lesson, where you talked about some adults who don't vote. Create your own survey about voting habits and give it to a selection of adults you know. Include questions about how often people vote in presidential, congressional (so called "off-year"), and local elections. For those who don't usually vote, ask them to jot down why or select from a list of reasons (examples: I just don't care, I can't get off work, all candidates are the same, too busy). As an alternative, do your study with interviews instead of paper questionnaires. Sometimes what people blurt out about an issue like this is more powerful than any choice they might circle on a form. Display your survey data in the form of a chart or infographic with one or two paragraphs of further explanation accompanying it. Use "Breadwinner Moms" text and images in Lesson 31 as a writing model.

Persuasive/argumentative: *Research and evaluate both sides of a debate*

There's a very active debate about "voter suppression" in the United States. In recent years, a number of states have made it even more difficult for people to vote by restricting voting hours, making registration more complex, or demanding harder-to-get forms of identification. Proponents of such measures say this will prevent voter fraud, which means people voting illegally. Opponents say voter fraud is virtually unknown in the United States, and that the new regulations are mainly designed to reduce voting in certain segments of the population. Look into these claims and explain which side has the strongest evidence.

MinnPost

Why Is Turnout So Low in U.S. Elections?

Eric Black, *Minnesota Post*

Every close race in the country depends on whose supporters show up at the polls and are allowed to vote. This, technically, is true of close elections all over the democratic world. But turnout issues in the United States are especially fraught with weirdness because of our general pattern of lower voter participation, and even more so during a non-presidential election when turnout falls even lower. There is no other developed democracy in the world that, when it holds an election in which all of the seats in the lower house of the national legislature are on the ballot, has a turnout of less than half of its eligible voters. In the United States, it happens every midterm election.

Those who study comparative democracy assure me that it's wrong to assume that this terrible-awful turnout merely reflects a higher level of apathy in the United States. There are many differences in rules and systems that help explain the gap and these have been discussed for years by those political scientists who specialize in comparing political systems around the world.

Most of us are not parties to that conversation—including me until I started asking—but I was quite impressed with the list of structural, legal and procedural elements of U.S. elections that seem to contribute to our poor turnouts.

What questions does the author want the reader to ask? What elements do you think contribute to low voter turnout?

Requiring registration

Most scholars who seek to solve the riddle of low U.S. voter participation start with this explanation. Personally, I was shocked that the United States' voting system is rare among world democracies in that it requires voters to register to vote. In most of the rest of the democratic world, there's no separate step called registration. It happens automatically; registering citizens to vote is the responsibility of the government. In general, the governments know the names, ages and addresses of most of its citizens and—except in the United States—provide the appropriate polling place with a list of those qualified to vote. The voter just has to show up.

In the United States, the responsibility is on the citizen to get registered. Scholars who rely on this explanation typically say that it makes voting a two-step process. A significant number of potential voters don't take that first step. You can criticize them for not taking that step if you like. In most instances, it's not that hard. But there are undoubtedly many who would vote if they were registered.

While many U.S. jurisdictions are making it easier to, for example, register to vote while getting a driver's license or even offering "same-day registration," many Americans don't live in these places.

There are also many who have registered, or at least think they have, and find out on Election Day that there's a problem. Sometimes it can be fixed on the spot, or the vote can be cast provisionally. But sometimes it can't, and another vote goes down the drain.

If requiring voters to register is so unusual, why do we do it? It started in the early 19th century—when immigrants were flooding into U.S. cities—in part to ensure that non-citizens wouldn't vote, but also to suppress the participation of those who were entitled to vote.

What do you think is another big reason people don't vote? Jot it down along with any real-life info or examples you can recall from your background knowledge.

Holding elections on Tuesday

No one else does that. Most democracies vote on weekends, or have more than one day to vote, or get a day off work to vote. But in America it's Tuesday. When pollsters ask non-voters why they haven't voted, two of the common answers have been "too busy" or "schedule conflicts."

If you're wondering whether this is in the U.S. Constitution: Nope. Not even slightly. The Framers had nothing to say on the subject. Each state was on its own in the early days and there was no national Election Day. But in 1845 Congress established the first Tuesday after the first Monday in November as a nationwide date for federal elections.

Why Tuesday? Made sense at the time. Most Americans still lived on farms. For them, it could take all day to get to the county seat to vote. Many Americans observed a Sabbath ban on travel. Tuesday voting would give the (white, male) farmers the Sabbath day off, Monday to get to the county seat, Tuesday to vote and Wednesday to get back home. Made some sense in 1845. Makes little sense now.

A few states have worked to solve this timing problem. Minnesota law guarantees every citizen time off from their jobs to vote without penalties or reductions in their pay, personal leave or vacation time. In 2000, Oregon switched to a system of exclusively voting by mail. It had a voter-participation rate of about 80 percent that year. There has been a bill introduced in recent Congresses to establish weekend voting, your choice of Saturday or Sunday. But it's never gotten far.

What do you think is a third big reason people don't vote? Jot it down along with any real-life info or examples you can recall from your background knowledge.

Felon disfranchisement

A lot of countries, and a lot of the states of the United States, do not let felons vote from prison but eventually restore the right to vote after the felons have been released. This is often on a sliding scale that depends, for example, on the felony of which they were convicted. But the United States is the only one of 31 democracies that allows for felons to be barred for life from voting.

Four U.S. states permanently bar ex-felons from voting, no matter how long they have been out of prison. That doesn't happen anywhere else in the democratic world. Then there are a range of policies that reduce the likelihood of former inmates getting their franchise back. In many states, they have to apply for the restoration after they are released. In some (Florida, for example), they can't make that application until five years after they are out of prison. In Iowa, an inmate must apply and prove he or she has repaid all court fees and made restitution to victims.

A study by The Sentencing Project heading into the 2012 presidential election found a startling level of racial and regional disparities. More than three million convicts and ex-cons who had not regained their right to vote were concentrated in six contiguous Southern states—Alabama, Florida, Kentucky, Mississippi, Tennessee and Virginia. Because of felon disfranchisement, 23 percent of blacks in Florida, 22 percent in Kentucky and 20 percent in Virginia were barred from voting. Since the United States locks up far more inmates than any other democracy, the impact on the electorate, or at least the potential electorate, is considerable.

Look back over your predictions. Which ones were accurate? What information about why people don't vote was new or surprising? Might there still be other reasons people don't vote that were not mentioned in this article?

LESSON 35

Write a Closing

TIME ▶ 40 minutes

GROUPINGS ▶ Whole class, pairs, individuals

STANDARDS MET ▶ See pages 306–307.

WHEN TO USE ▶ When students must write in more traditional, prescriptive styles (test writing, standard five-paragraph essays), the hardest part is coming up with an original concluding paragraph that doesn't just parrot the introduction. This lesson shows students how to write endings that leave the reader with something to think about.

TEXT	AUTHOR	SOURCE	TEXT TYPE
"On Women's Right to Vote"	Susan B. Anthony	www.nationalcenter.org	Speech

Writing a closing is probably one of the most difficult tasks of composing nonfiction. Students are often instructed to double down on their thesis statement and revisit key points while putting it all in fresh language. Newsflash: even if students manage to rephrase things they have already said, the writing still comes across as formulaic, stiff, and boring. Also, if you take a look at any real-world writing, versus the school-only genre of "Writing-Test Writing," you see that no published authors ever use such mechanical conclusions if they can possibly avoid them.

In real nonfiction writing, authors usually are attempting to raise awareness, to move the reader, to persuade. Therefore, the best way to end a piece is not with a recap, but with some suggestions, solutions, or demands. And, of course, this is exactly what Susan B. Anthony does in her speech about women's suffrage. But, rather than just having kids examine the closing of her speech, this lesson asks them to study her first few paragraphs and then construct their own original conclusion.

PREPARATION

1. Make a copy of the speech "On Women's Right to Vote" for each student. Be sure you do not include the final paragraph. Instead, download that paragraph and be ready to project it in the final step of this lesson.

2. Review the speech and directions. There is challenging language throughout the speech. Also, in paragraph 4, you will need to offer students some context as to why Anthony demands remedies to gender inequality above other inequalities facing people in 1872.

3. Download and be ready to project the annotation instructions for Step 3 and the question prompts that will lead pairs into their own conclusion writing in Step 6.

4. Determine how students will form pairs in Step 4.

Steps & Teaching Language ▶

STEP 1 **Introduce the topic.** *Ever hear the phrase "civil disobedience"?*

What does it mean? Hear a few suggestions, and build off these.

Civil disobedience refers to purposely breaking a law that the protester feels is unjust.

Henry David Thoreau participated in civil disobedience when he refused to pay a tax that he knew would go to support the United States' War with Mexico. As a consequence, he was arrested and held in jail (until his aunt went behind his back and paid the taxes he owed).

Another person who participated in civil disobedience was Susan B. Anthony. Anybody know what she was arrested for? Take some volunteers and build on their answers. *Anthony was arrested for voting in the 1872 presidential election.*

You are probably wondering, how can that be? Was she interfering with other people's rights? Creating a scene? No, in 1872 a woman's right to vote was a state decision, as we just saw in Lesson 32. Depending on where you lived, a woman might be able to vote only in some elections or not at all—rarely were they offered complete suffrage.

After voting, Anthony was arrested, charged, tried, and fined $100, which would be a fine of about $2,000 today; not cheap. Like Thoreau, she planned to go to jail, but her attorney friend, Henry Rogers Seldon, paid the fine.

STEP 2 **Distribute the speech (minus the last paragraph) and read it aloud.** *Before you is the speech Anthony gave after her conviction. If you guessed that this speech argues for women's voting rights, you would be correct. In a moment you'll be reading the document on your own, but for now, follow along as I read it aloud. This speech contains some unfamiliar words. I'm going to stop along the way and explain them, so stay tuned.*

Read the speech aloud, stopping to give a contextual definition for words/phrases such as *disfranchisement, posterity, odious aristocracy, oligarchy, ordains,* and *sovereigns. Were there any other word choices that stumped you? Let's take a look at those for a second.* Clear up any lingering confusion.

You may also wish to explain the context of paragraph 4. As mentioned in Step 8, Anthony put women's suffrage on hold while she fought with other abolitionists for an end to slavery. Unfortunately, when the Fifteenth Amendment was ratified in 1870—prohibiting the federal and state governments from denying a citizen the right to vote based on that citizen's "race, color, or previous condition of servitude"—it *completely* disregarded women's suffrage. To this end, Anthony felt betrayed by the very men (white and black) whom she had supported in the abolitionist movement.

And it isn't just voting Anthony is referring to in paragraph 4. "The hateful oligarchy of sex" also refers to the fact that in most states married women had absolutely no property rights: their husband owned everything. At this point in history, a man, whether rich or poor, black or white, educated or not, had complete control over his wife's property and could do with it as he pleased. Married women of *any* color were subjugated to a husband's whims. In the end, neither of the issues Anthony highlighted in her speech were resolved any time soon. The "Married Women's Property Act"—modeled after language used in the New York state law passed in

1848—was not present in all states until 1900. And women did not have complete suffrage in all states until 1920, almost fifty years after Anthony first gave this speech!

STEP 3 **Students reread individually and annotate.** *As you read on your own, I want you to do some annotation.* Project or write these instructions on the board as you explain.

> ### Annotating Anthony's Speech
>
> 1. Underline specific assertions and the supports that back up her claim: Women should have the same voting rights as men.
> 2. Circle parts that raise questions or confuse you and jot down the question you need to ask.

Now I'm going to give you some time to read. Since this speech was written over one hundred years ago, you'll find the language different. Take your time. Don't forget to follow the annotation instructions.

As students read, monitor for following the directions and individual on-task work. When a few students finish before the pack, instruct them to reread and see what else they notice or understand as they move through the speech again.

STEP 4 **Pairs share and help answer each other's questions.** *Now turn to your partner. Take turns pointing out something Susan B. Anthony uses to support her claim that all women should have the right to vote. Also, see if you can answer each other's questions. When you come across something that still confuses you or seems unsettled, put a star by it.*

Monitor for on-task pair discussion work. Observe text confusion points and decide whether to intervene in a pair or save a clarification point for the large-group share.

STEP 5 **Whole class shares.** *What were some of the ways Susan B. Anthony attempted to persuade her audiences that women should have the right to vote?* Hear from a number of pairs. Prompt with questions like: *Did anyone say something similar? Who noticed some different support?*

STEP 6 **Pairs write a conclusion.** Project the following prompts, read them aloud, and leave them projected throughout the writing.

> ### Writing Susan B. Anthony's Conclusion
>
> Anthony's conclusion begins with this phrase:
>
> > "The only question left to be settled now is":
>
> - Based on her speech, what is the only question?
> - How is she going to settle it?
> - What will be her specific ideas for solving the problem?
> - What will she suggest that those in office do?

- How will she grab listeners emotionally so that they join her fight?

With your partner, use the answers to these questions in your conclusion for Anthony's speech. Your ideas should offer solutions and create a call to action. As you work, make sure both of you are writing down notes as you discuss ideas.

When you start drafting the conclusion, see if you can imitate Anthony's style so that your ending fits in with the rest of the speech. Again, both partners are recording the draft. The conclusion should be about six sentences long.

Monitor for focused pair work, and nudge with guiding questions or a text reference if a pair gets stuck. If a pair is finished, have them quietly read their draft aloud to you. Then remind them to polish the product and practice reading it aloud with conviction. After all, this is a high-stakes public speech!

STEP 7 **Pairs share conclusions with the class.** *Now we're going to hear your conclusions. As you listen, notice the language that best captures Anthony's speech. Also note which conclusions do the best job naming specific action steps or solutions. Finally, see who best reads in a way that conveys conviction and enthusiasm. The energy of a good performance can be just as persuasive as the words themselves.*

Call on pairs at random (everyone should have something) to stand up and read their conclusions aloud. Pairs can share the reading or assign the task to one partner; however, both members should stand up together during the reading. If you have time, hear all of the conclusions since they are only about six sentences long.

After the performances, debrief and discuss what makes an ending memorable and persuasive.

STEP 8 **Project and discuss the original conclusion.** Project the conclusion and read it aloud to the class. As with the main part of the speech, you will probably have to explain some language so that kids fully comprehend her final words. Also, giving some additional background information before reading Anthony's conclusion will help students understand the historical context framing it.

First, remind students that in 1872 the terms *black* or *African American* had not yet come into use. Referring to African Americans as Negroes was considered respectful. Second, prior to the conclusion of the Civil War, Anthony had deferred her goal of women's suffrage and instead devoted her energies to the abolitionist movement, working alongside one of her closest friends: Frederick Douglass. Third, Anthony's final line—**"Hence, every discrimination against women in the constitutions and laws of the several states is today null and void, precisely as is every** one against Negroes"—might require a modern translation. Use this one or develop your own wording.

> *Every discrimination women face due to inconsistent state laws should be considered invalid and unenforceable just as any law that discriminates against Negroes is considered invalid and unenforceable [because of the Thirteenth Amendment].*

The Thirteenth Amendment abolished slavery and overruled all state laws related to slavery. Anthony was not only speaking out in favor of women's voting rights, she was speaking out against *any* laws that resulted in reducing the civil rights of any U.S. citizen. Seventeen years later in 1890, Anthony and her fellow women were still second-class citizens in the eyes of the law. Furthermore, once reconstruction was "officially over," some states began legislating "Jim Crow" laws that legalized discrimination and segregation. Still alive, Anthony saw her vision of universal equality ever more difficult to achieve. She died in 1906, fourteen years before the Nineteenth Amendment was ratified, giving women full voting rights.

Once students fully understand her words, lead a final discussion of how well her conclusion works.

What do you think? What works? What doesn't? What did she do that we didn't think of? What parts of our classes' conclusions would you like to donate to Susan B.?

Research Projects for Extended Writing ▶ Longer writing projects—reflecting the key genres required by the national standards—can be built on the work students have already done in this lesson. As kids continue to explore the topics of our reading selections, we expect that they will bring fresh background knowledge, recent thinking, and genuine curiosity to the task. When you use the lesson above with your own content, you can also use the assignments below as models for extending that content into longer writing projects.

Narrative: *Experiment with endings*

To begin, write a one-page story about some memorable experience in your life. It might have been an adventure, an accident or injury, a trip, a change, a discovery. (It may be easiest to write this if you choose a story you've often shared with other people.) Write it up to where the story would end, and then stop. Now write three endings—different ways you could close the story. They should all be true, but take different angles. One might simply finish off the narrative; in another, you might look back on the event from the future; or, you might tell the reader what the "moral of the story" is. For still another conclusion, you could let someone else speak at the end. Let some readers sample your alternative endings and tell you which one they like best.

Informative/explanatory: *Trace an aspect of today's life back to a historical event*

In these recent lessons, we've read a good deal about women's rights, employment, and status throughout American history. But what's happened since women got the right to vote in 1920? The most important recent legislation in terms of women's rights is Title IX of the Civil Rights Act, implemented in 1972. You may have heard of Title IX in terms of guaranteeing girls' equal participation in school sports teams—there is even a company making women's athletic wear under the name "Title 9 Sports." But *sports were never even mentioned* in this law, which had far higher and wider purposes. Investigate the history and aims of Title IX and write a summary of its key provisions.

Persuasive/argumentative: *Defend your interpretation of the text*

Reread the last two paragraphs of Susan B. Anthony's 1872 speech. Some historical scholars wonder why Anthony included the racially incendiary comment "an oligarchy of race, where the Saxon rules the African, might be endured." On the surface, this sounds as if Anthony is saying that women's rights trump the abolition of slavery. But Anthony was a long-time abolitionist, and slavery had already ended with the ratification of the Thirteenth Amendment in 1865. Five years later, the Fifteenth Amendment gave voting rights to African American men—yet excluded all women (white and black). So what might have been the true intent of her controversial words? What was the effect she was trying to have on her audience? Look for any additional evidence in the speech or online. Then write your best interpretation of that critical line about how slavery "might be endured." Was it a slip of the tongue, a bit of over-the-top rhetoric, a refocus of women's issues, an indication of underlying racism, or something else?

On Women's Right to Vote

Susan B. Anthony
www.nationalcenter.org

This speech was given by Susan B. Anthony after her arrest for casting an illegal vote in the presidential election of 1872. She was tried and then fined $100 but refused to pay.

1 Friends and Fellow Citizens: I stand before you tonight under indictment for the alleged crime of having voted at the last presidential election, without having a lawful right to vote. It shall be my work this evening to prove to you that in thus voting, I not only committed no crime, but, instead, simply exercised my citizen's rights, guaranteed to me and all United States citizens by the National Constitution, beyond the power of any State to deny.

2 The preamble of the Federal Constitution says:
"We, the people of the United States, in order to form a more perfect union, establish justice, insure domestic tranquility, provide for the common defense, promote the general welfare, and secure the blessings of liberty to ourselves and our posterity, do ordain and establish this Constitution for the United States of America."

3 It was we, the people; not we, the white male citizens; nor yet we, the male citizens; but we, the whole people, who formed the Union. And we formed it, not to give the blessings of liberty, but to secure them; not to the half of ourselves and the half of our posterity, but to the whole people—women as well as men. And it is a downright mockery to talk to women of their enjoyment of the blessings of liberty while they are denied the use of the only means of securing them provided by this democratic-republican government—the ballot.

4 For any State to make sex a qualification that must ever result in the disfranchisement of one entire half of the people is to pass a bill of attainder, or an ex post facto law, and is therefore a violation of the supreme law of the land. By it the blessings of liberty are forever withheld from women and their female posterity. To them this government has no just powers derived from the consent of the governed. To them this government is not a democracy. It is not a republic. It is an odious aristocracy; a hateful oligarchy of sex; the most hateful aristocracy ever established on the face of the globe: an oligarchy of wealth, where the right govern the poor; an oligarchy of learning, where the educated govern the ignorant; or even an oligarchy of race, where the Saxon rules the African, might be endured. But this oligarchy of sex, which makes father, brothers, husband, sons, the oligarchs over the mother and sisters, the wife and daughters of every household—which ordains all men sovereigns, all women subjects, carries dissension, discord and rebellion into every home of the nation.

On Women's Right to Vote

Susan B. Anthony
www.nationalcenter.org

Conclusion

The only question left to be settled now is:

Are women persons? And I hardly believe any of our opponents will have the hardihood to say they are not. Being persons, then, women are citizens; and no state has a right to make any law, or to enforce any old law, that shall abridge their privileges or immunities. Hence, every discrimination against women in the constitutions and laws of the several states is today null and void, precisely as is every one against Negroes.

INTRODUCTION TO THE TEXT SETS

In this final section of the book, we offer three extended lessons in reading, writing, and discussion. The topics are:

Chapter 11: Paul Robeson, an Overlooked American

Chapter 12: Edible Insects

Chapter 13: Military Animals

Each text set:

Begins with a fascinating topic. Some subjects (like the consumption of insects and use of war dolphins) evoke kids' curiosity immediately, while the Robeson lesson reels kids in as its puzzling protagonist is revealed. Between the three lessons, many key concepts from science and social studies arise, as do connections to English language arts and mathematics.

Is built upon a collection of two to six related readings from a variety of sources and genres: articles, photographs, transcripts, graphics, biographies, government documents, and international reports. These selections vary in difficulty, but all are incorporated into lessons that provide a high degree of engagement, support, structure, and sociability.

Provides step-by-step plans for one to three class periods of writing experience in an essential mode: narrative, informative/explanatory, or persuasive/argumentative.

Includes a *mentor text* that serves as an example or model of what the target genre of writing looks like. Each selected mentor text comes from earlier in the book (and thus may have already been read by students). This time through, students will use the piece to look closely at the author's craft, style, voice, and construction strategies—and adapt those techniques to a piece of their own writing.

Gives students opportunities to alternate between individual work, partner and group collaboration, and developing and sharing ideas in the whole class.

Is presented in a combination of *explanation* (numbered steps set in roman type) and *direct teacher talk* (set in *italics*)—the kind of language we actually use with kids. You can try our wording or make up your own.

Provides all necessary projectable materials, downloadable from our website (http://hein.pub/textsandlessonscaw).

Invites students to do significant research and build knowledge. Additional possibilities for extended inquiry are provided.

Addresses state and national standards for writing. The chart on pages 306–307 shows key correlations.

Is highly adaptable. The underlying structure and teaching language can be applied to countless other topics and texts. Make these lessons your own. Revise, replace, build on, expand, or toss out the articles we have chosen. Find images to go with an article, or articles to go with other images. Add videos and primary sources; collect interviews and surveys; scour websites and Twitter handles. Once you get started tweaking and reinventing these lessons, it becomes pleasantly addictive. Enjoy!

Writing Focus: Nonfiction Narrative

Texts Used ▶

TEXT	AUTHOR/SOURCE	TEXT TYPE	
Paul Robeson, 1942, Leads Oakland, CA, Shipyard Workers in Singing the National Anthem	National Archives	Photograph	
Paul Robeson in Othello	National Archives	Photograph	
Paul Robeson, 1943	Charles H. Alston, National Archives	Editorial drawing	
"Paul Robeson"	Anne Leigh, WrapUp Media	Biography	
"The Many Faces of Paul Robeson"	National Archives	Biography	
"What Paul Robeson Said"	Gilbert King, www .smithsonian.com	Feature story	
"Testimony of Paul Robeson Before the House Committee on Un-American Activities"	84th Congress, House Committee on Un-American Activities	Testimony transcript	
MENTOR TEXT	**AUTHOR/SOURCE**	**TEXT TYPE**	**WHERE TO FIND IT**
"Here's How You Sell a Haunted House"	Gwynne Watkins, www.vulture.com	Interview	Lesson 2, page 30

TIME ▶

Reading/Discussion One or two class periods, depending on number of articles read

Writing One or two class periods, depending on whether students revise and how you choose to have students share their pieces

GROUPINGS ▶

Reading/Discussion Individuals, pairs, whole class

Writing Individuals, pairs, whole class

STANDARDS MET ▶ See pages 306–307.

LESSONS USED ▶ The following lessons were used in the construction of this text set:

- Lesson 2: Interviewing an Expert and a Classmate
- Lesson 3: Analyzing People with Identity Webs

WHEN TO USE ▶ This lesson's "faction" interviews combine all the elements of narrative but are written within the parameters of researched facts. This format can be used any time students engage in research about an issue, person, or topic. While we modeled interviewing a person, students can also summarize their research as they interview an architecturally significant building, a radioactive atomic particle, or an endangered species.

Why This Topic?

As we researched topics for this book, we started to notice one specific category: important people who—for various reasons—have been forgotten. As you might have noticed, we think Susan B. Anthony is one of those people.

Another heroic, yet forgotten person in U.S. history is Paul Robeson. When you begin to look at his record, it is absolutely astounding: son of a former slave, Rutgers University valedictorian, graduate of Columbia Law School, professional football player, movie and Broadway star, recording artist, international celebrity. An African American, Paul Robeson managed all of these accomplishments in the age of Jim Crow. Yet when given the choice—to retain his lucrative, multifaceted career or stand publicly by his beliefs—he chose the latter. Every day our students encounter the same dilemma: Should they "play it safe," or should they speak up when they witness an injustice? We're hoping that the story of Paul Robeson gives students a model for being an upstander, not a bystander, when they encounter issues of injustice.

1. Download and determine how you will project the photographs of Paul Robeson listed in the text set. You might also do an image search for additional photographs. Be sure to search "Paul Robeson album covers," and you'll see what a prolific recording artist he was, making well over fifty records.

2. Be ready to project either the Katniss Everdeen identity web (from Lesson 3) or, if you've already worked through this lesson with students, a student-generated identity web for Susan B. Anthony.

3. Make enough copies of the two biographical summary articles for half the class; in the lesson, pairs will "jigsaw" this reading, meaning that some students will read one of the articles while the rest of the kids read the other text. Then, the students will share what they've learned with one another. If possible, duplicate the two bios on different color paper. This will simplify the jigsawing (*Do you want to read the blue article or the green one?*) as well as make it easier for you to monitor who's reading what.

4. Duplicate the support articles you would like students to read. If you are looking for longer, complex text, you might choose "What Paul Robeson Said." If you would like students to interact with a primary document, you might have them read "Testimony of Paul Robeson Before the House Committee on Un-American Activities." And of course, you can certainly have students read both articles.

5. Since this lesson focuses on identity web note taking, you will need a sheet of unlined paper for each student.

6. Determine how pairs will be formed in Step 3.

7. A selection of different color pens (one for each student) is an option in Step 7.

1. Each student will need a hard copy of the mentor text: "Here's How You Sell a Haunted House," originally used in Lesson 2. If students still have their copies from the original lesson, there is no need to make copies again.

2. Determine how you will select a student scribe for Step 2.

3. Determine how to form pairs in Step 4.

4. Decide how writing will be shared: public read-aloud (which will take a bit longer) or gallery walk. If you do choose to do a gallery walk, be sure to have a supply of sticky notes on hand so that kids can comment as they view.

STEP 1 **Review the identity web concept.** Project an identity web from Lesson 3, either the Katniss Everdeen example or a Susan B. Anthony student sample. *An identity web is a graphic way to map the many different aspects of a person. Look at the sample and see how many categories of information you can find.* Expect kids to notice birth, childhood, race, religion, family, hometown, jobs, hobbies, favorites, turning points, attitudes, beliefs, accomplishments, and so on. You can list these on the

◄ **Reading/ Discussion Steps**

whiteboard or screen or, if you've already worked with identity webs with this class, put up the list made earlier and just add any new items.

STEP 2 **Begin a Paul Robeson identity web.** Write Paul Robeson's name on the board. Pass out blank sheets of paper. *There are lots of different details that make up a person's identity. Today we're going to examine some details from the life of a famous person that you may never have heard of: Paul Robeson. Write his name in the center of your paper.*

STEP 3 **Project images as partners discuss.** *I'm going to show you some different photos and drawings of Paul Robeson. As I project the images, I want you to look closely and see what you can find out about him. Then add those details to the identity webs we just started.* Show images one at a time, giving students enough time to study the visual and jot down what they discover. Before moving to the next image, give partners a moment to look and talk together, comparing notes.

STEP 4 **Students develop questions.** *Look over your Paul Robeson identity web. What questions would you need to have answered to know more about Robeson and really understand his importance? Jot those questions on your web.* After a few minutes of individual work, allow pairs to compare and trade questions. You might take a couple of minutes for whole-class question sharing.

STEP 5 **Students read and add to their webs.** Pass out one copy of "Paul Robeson" and "The Many Faces of Paul Robeson" to each pair. *I'm passing out two different articles on Paul Robeson to each pair. You and your partner will each read only one, but you'll have to read it really carefully because your partner will be depending on you to share the information. Go ahead and turn to your partner and decide which article each of you will read and then write your name at the top of your article.*

Everybody know which article you're reading? As you read, please underline any information that seems important or that answers one of the questions you jotted on the web.

Then, after finishing the article, reread the parts you underlined and add information to your web. However, instead of giving each new detail its own branch, work to connect details of Robeson's life and try to show those relationships on the web. In other words, see if you can cluster related information together.

As students work individually, monitor for careful reading, following directions, and attempting to make information connections.

STEP 6 **Pairs compare articles and webs.** *Now get together with your partner and talk about what you learned about Paul Robeson. Work to find out how the information in your articles was similar, but also search for ways the information differed. Compare your webs and discuss how this new information can be categorized and connected.*

After pairs compare and share, take a few minutes to talk about new web details pairs decided were important to include. Also, prompt students to talk about how the details are connected—what kinds of patterns are they starting to notice in Robeson's life?

STEP 7 **Pairs brainstorm additional questions.** *I often notice that the more I find out about someone, the more questions I have. Now that you've looked at images and done some reading on Paul Robeson, what are some new questions you have about him? What are you wondering about? Remember, this man was TOTALLY famous in the 1930s and '40s, but he is mostly forgotten today. Turn back to your partner and talk about this. What questions would you like to ask Paul Robeson himself that would explain this puzzle? Jot down your questions on your identity web near the details that made you think of the question.* To keep the types of web entries distinct, you can have students use different color pens for this or start their question notes with a *Q.*

Give pairs a chance to think, talk, and write down additional questions. Monitor for progress. When conversation begins to wind down, call the class back together and ask pairs to share their best, most thought-provoking questions.

STEP 8 **Students continue their research.** At this point, you can distribute either or both of the remaining articles we've included in this text set, or you can open Paul Robeson up to a larger-scale inquiry where students can research using available e-devices. Either way, remember to emphasize that research means looking for answers to questions posed but also discovering new questions to be answered. Continue to use the structure set out earlier in the lesson: students research individually and then, when they have enough information, they share with their partners.

STEP 9 **Students share with the class.** *What are some of the most important things you found out about Paul Robeson? Who has some lingering questions about him? Why do you think he's pretty much forgotten today despite all his accomplishments?*

At this point, students have had the opportunity to use identity web note taking much more extensively than in Lesson 3. Also, they've had the chance to practice an important habit of mind: curiosity. This writing extension takes their notes a step further and shows them how to use research for creating a faction interview, a *fact*-based, yet *fictional* "conversation" with Paul Robeson. In addition to their annotated texts and identity webs, each student will also need a copy of "Here's How You Sell a Haunted House."

◀ Writing Steps: "Faction" Interview

STEP 1 **Students review interview questions.** Students will need to look at the "haunted house" article used in Lesson 2. Before starting the instructions, either pass out a new copy of the article or have students retrieve the article from their binders/folders.

A while ago we read the interview "Here's How You Sell a Haunted House," and you marked your two favorite questions. Take a moment to reread those parts of the interview. This time I want you to notice how the author made the answer interesting.

Give students a chance to look over the interview, then ask them to share their observations with their partner.

STEP 2 **Create a master list.** *What did the author do to make the interview answers interesting? Will a student scribe please step up to take notes as we put together an interview technique master list? As we create the list, remember to copy it down since you'll need to refer to it later. Go ahead and write your notes on the "haunted house" article. Who had a partner with some interesting observations about interview writing?*

You may choose to take volunteers or call on pairs at random. Students may mention items such as

- Interesting/unusual/vivid word choices ("fresh death")
- Each answer tells a story
- Specific details
- Some questions have two parts so the story gets continued
- Directly quotes other players in the story
- Subject of interview describes feelings
- Answers are in first person, as if the interview subject is talking to you
- Answers are short paragraphs, not just a few words or a single sentence

STEP 3 **Review Robeson information and brainstorm interview questions.** *Keeping good interview questions and answers in mind, look back at your identity web details about Paul Robeson. Imagine that you were going to share what you found out about Robeson with others but in the form of an interview. Look over your web and the articles as well; then brainstorm five questions that you could "ask" Robeson, questions that would get the information about him out in short, story-like examples, just like the "haunted house" interview.*

Monitor for question development and kids' use of *all* resources. Without guidance, students may attempt to rely on their identity webs alone versus skimming through the articles as well.

STEP 4 **Partners compare questions and choose the best ones.** *Now that everyone came up with his or her five questions, go ahead and compare them with your partner's. Then, each of you pick out two questions to use for your individual Paul Robeson interview. As you come up with your final questions, make sure that they are different from your partner's. Also, work with your partner to revise the wording of those final questions so that they will create the interesting answers that use the response elements we listed earlier.*

While you are working, I'll be checking in with you, so be ready to explain your question choices and how you will create some interesting stories in the answers.

This step will require some active monitoring on your part. Don't be afraid to butt in and ask partners to talk about the rationale for their question choices as well as what they imagine the answer might be. If you are feeling a little hesitant to talk to kids about their writing, just stick to these questions:

- What are your two final questions?
- What makes those questions interesting?
- How do you think Paul Robeson will answer them?
- What details will you be using from your web? From articles?

You don't have to ask all of these questions of every pair. (That would take forever!) Look over shoulders, read what they've jotted, notice how they're using their resources. If a pair is on track, give a quick thumbs up. A question or two will be necessary to redirect pairs who seem to be working off the cuff, versus studying their webs/articles.

STEP 5 **Individuals write interview answers.** *Looks like everyone has two really good interview questions. I bet you're curious about what other pairs chose. However, I'm going to keep you in suspense until later. Right now let's take some time to write up great answers to those questions. Remember that list we made earlier about interesting interview answers? Since we came up with so many great ideas for that list, it might seem a little overwhelming. So for now, as you write, think about just two things: First, make sure your answer tells a story that uses real details from your web and articles; and second, each answer should be a short paragraph versus just a couple of words or one sentence. Don't be afraid to go back and look at the "haunted house" interview. It's fine if you model your Robeson answers on the style of a couple of the answers you find in that article.*

As students work, monitor for writing, crossing out and rewriting, and looking back on webs and articles. If a student finishes hastily, zoom in to see what's going on. First, just glance at the answers for length. If you don't see a paragraph (the most likely problem), use one or more of these redirections:

- Rephrase your question so that greater detail can be put in the answer.
- Show me your favorite "haunted house" answer. Tell me how you could write Robeson's answer to your question like that.
- Which details did you use from your web and articles? What else could you use? (While we don't recommend telling kids what to put in their writing, it's perfectly okay to say, "Go back and read this part; I know you'll find some details there for expanding your interview answer.")

Second, if length isn't a problem, have the student read the answer aloud to you. It might be great. But sometimes a quickly written paragraph has insufficient detail. In that case, use that last bullet point question, which redirects the writer to her sources.

Finally, if a finished writer does have the detail, you can encourage him to return to the master list and see what else he can change/add/revise to make the answer even more engaging.

STEP 6 **Partners read aloud and revise.** *Get back with your partner and take turns reading your interview answers aloud. After reading, the listening partner should start by pointing out their favorite word, detail, sentence, or idea in the answer. Then together review our master list of interesting interview answer elements that we made earlier* (this is the list the class made in Step 2) *and talk about which ones the writer could use to make the interview even better.*

Writers, don't just let your partner tell you to use more exciting words or put in a direct quote. Demand that they actually help you figure out the exact revision! Eventually, you will be sharing your interviews with the class, so you want them to be as interesting as possible. As you work, I'll be listening in and answering questions.

Monitor pairs for following the directions and actively discussing revision using the master list. While the first draft writing was solo, the revision discussion should be 100 percent collaborative.

STEP 7 **Individuals incorporate revisions and rewrite their interview answers.** *Before we share our interviews with our class audience, I want you to work individually to make them great. Incorporate the revision ideas you discussed with your partner as you write a final draft. Start with your question and then write the answer. Put this new draft on a fresh sheet of paper—or on some digital space you can use to enhance the content. Make sure your writing is neat and can be easily read by others.*

This should take only a few minutes. Monitor for legibility since this is the draft that will be shared.

STEP 8 **Pairs share final drafts with the class.** Here, you have two choices for sharing drafts.

Option 1: Pairs read aloud. In turn, have each pair step to the front and perform their interview aloud. The partner should pose as the interviewer while the writer responds as Paul Robeson. After each performance, lead the class in a round of applause. If time is short, have each student pick one question and answer to present rather than reading both aloud.

OR:

Option 2: Gallery walk. Tape the interviews around the classroom walls. Give each student three sticky notes. Tell students to spread out and read other pairs' interviews. *After reading an interview, jot down something you found interesting or that you liked about the way it was written.* (Refer students to the master list of elements.) As students visit interviews, monitor so that they do not bunch up or get distracted from their task. Also, if you see kids finishing early, hand out more sticky notes and send them off to read and positively comment on interviews that seem to be getting less attention.

WHAT MIGHT THE WRITING LOOK LIKE?

Here's an example of one interview question and answer.

Question: How do you feel about your being called to testify before the House Un-American Affairs Committee?

Answer: At first I hoped that it would conclude quickly and, once I was sufficiently humiliated, my passport would be returned to me. However, as Mr. Arens pressed on with his questioning, it became clear that the goal of the committee was to label me a communist, a traitor out to destroy the United States. In fact, I am the one who deeply cares about the future of our country. My father and ancestors were slaves who helped build this nation. While I have been lucky to experience incredible success, most people with similar adverse backgrounds—white or black—struggle to support their families. Until workers unionize, until Negroes attain freedom, until all citizens enjoy equal rights, our nation will remain weak.

Paul Robeson, 1942, Leads Oakland, CA, Shipyard Workers in Singing the National Anthem: National Archives; Archive Identifier 535874. Office for Emergency Management. Office of War Information. Domestic Operations Branch. New Bureau.

Paul Robeson in Othello*:* Library of Congress Prints and Photographs Division; Call no. LC-USW33-054938-ZC. Farm Security administration. Office of War Information Collections.

Paul Robeson, 1943: Charles H. Alston/National Archives; Archive Identifier 535624. Office for Emergency Management. Office of War Information. Domestic Operations Branch. New Bureau.

Paul Robeson

Anne Leigh, WrapUp Media

Early Life

Paul Robeson was born in 1898 in Princeton, New Jersey, to Reverend William Drew Robeson and Maria Louisa Bustill. His father escaped slavery in 1860 at the age of fifteen, when he ran away from a plantation. In 1901, due to a racially tinged disagreement, William was compelled to resign from his congregation, which forced him into low-wage menial jobs. Three years later, Paul's mother died in a house fire. Despite this adversity, Paul excelled in high school, played four sports, and was awarded a scholarship to prestigious Rutgers University. Valedictorian for the graduating class of 1918, Paul, in his commencement speech, urged the audience to embrace equality for all Americans. Academically and athletically talented, Paul continued on to Columbia University Law School, supporting himself by playing professional football and teaching Latin.

Entertainer and Activist

Though Robeson worked briefly as a lawyer, racism deprived him of opportunity, so he followed his interest in theater. Cast in key roles on and off Broadway, Robeson was soon known for his superb acting and singing, eventually starring in fifteen films. Between 1924 and 1943, Robeson's popularity spread around the world. Even so, Robeson continued to speak up in the name of equality, condemning segregation and discrimination in the United States, while also speaking abroad on behalf of workers' rights and peace initiatives. Robeson's outspoken, uncensored nature created many fans but also made many enemies who resented his criticism of America.

Even though Robeson entertained troops during World War II, he was labeled a security threat and Communist during the subsequent Cold War period. When his words were twisted by the media and then picked up by the House Un-American Activities Committee (HUAC), the results were tragic. First, in 1950 the U.S. State Department canceled Robeson's passport because he refused to take a loyalty oath. Being unable to perform overseas struck a deathblow to Robeson's career. Then, thanks to his HUAC testimony, which displayed his determination to speak the truth, Robeson's stateside reputation was ruined as well. Though

Robeson was an immensely popular U.S. entertainer, his blacklisting curtailed any hope of performing in concert, on stage, or in film. Even worse, his previous successes were effectively erased: his films disappeared as well as all of his recordings. Robeson's persecution by the HUAC, State Department, and FBI (they kept up an ongoing investigation of him from 1949 until his death in 1976) crippled him financially; unable to work, his earnings plunged from hundreds of thousands of dollars per year to less than $3,000.

Robeson's Legacy

Pressure from the black community as well as international outcry eventually led to Robeson's passport being renewed in 1958. Sadly, the damage to his person and his career was insurmountable. After a triumphant Carnegie Hall concert, Robeson toured Europe one last time, retiring in 1961. The stress of his Cold War persecution manifested itself in depression and fragile health. While Robeson received many awards and honors over the remainder of his life, he remained largely reclusive, his extraordinary success as an African American largely forgotten. Robeson died from a stroke in 1976 at the age of seventy-seven. In 2007, a collection of his films was released on DVD. In vocal recordings, Robeson was prolific: close to fifty albums and one hundred songs are currently available on iTunes. Even so, few people really know of Paul Robeson's courage and accomplishment in an era of segregation, discrimination, and Jim Crow laws.

The Many Faces of Paul Robeson

How many people do you know who are athletes? How about an athlete who has won 15 varsity letters in four different sports? An athlete who has also played professional football while at the same time being valedictorian at his university? Does this athlete also hold a law degree? How many scholar-athlete performers can you name? Concert artists who have sold out shows around the world and who can perform in more than 25 different languages? Does this scholar-athlete-performer also act in Shakespearean and Broadway plays and in movies? Can you identify a scholar-athlete-performer who is also an activist for civil and human rights? Someone who petitioned the president of the United States of America for an anti-lynching law, promoted African self-rule, helped victims of the Spanish civil war, fought for India's independence, and championed equality for all human beings? Did this scholar-athlete-performer-activist also have to endure terrorism, banned performances, racism, and discrimination throughout his career?

Paul Robeson was all these things and more. He was the son of a former slave, born and raised during a period of segregation, lynching, and open racism. He earned a four-year scholarship to Rutgers University, making him the third African American to attend the school. There he was a member of the prestigious Cap and Skull Honor Society, played four varsity sports (baseball, football, basketball, and track), won speech and debate tournaments, and managed to graduate valedictorian of his class. After graduation, Robeson applied his athletic abilities to a short career in professional football. Aside from his prowess on the gridiron, he earned a law degree and changed the direction of his career. His legal career was cut short, however, after a secretary refused to take dictation from him solely because of the color of his skin. He left law and turned to his childhood love of acting and singing. Robeson starred in Shakespeare's *Othello*, the musical *Showboat*, and films such as *Jericho* and *Proud Valley*. He was one of the top performers of his time, earning more money than many white entertainers. His concert career spanned the globe: Vienna, Prague, Budapest, Berlin, Paris, Amsterdam, London, Moscow, New York, and Nairobi.

Robeson's travels opened his awareness to the universality of human suffering and oppression. He began to use his rich bass voice to speak out for independence, freedom, and equality for all people. He believed that artists should use their talents and exposure to aid causes around the world. "The artist must elect to fight for freedom or slavery. I have made my choice," he said. This philosophy drove Robeson to Spain during the civil war, to Africa to promote self-determination, to India to aid in the independence movement, to London to fight for labor rights, and to the Soviet Union to promote anti-fascism. It was in the Soviet Union where he felt that people were treated equally. He could eat in any restaurant and walk through the front doors of hotels, but in his own country he faced discrimination and racism everywhere he went.

While Robeson's activist role increased abroad, he met dissent and intimidation in the United States. Rioters at his concert at Peekskill, New York in 1949 smashed the stage, torched chairs, attacked concertgoers, and threatened Robeson's life. His outspokenness about human rights and his pro-Soviet stance made Robeson a prime target of militant anticommunists. In 1950 the State Department revoked his passport, thereby denying his right to travel and, ultimately, to earn income abroad. Robeson fought this injustice for years vigorously but with no success. He repeatedly applied for reinstatement of his passport but was turned down. He filed a lawsuit against the State Department and faced discouraging delays, adverse decisions, and rejected appeals. Yet Robeson stuck to his principles and refused to swear an affidavit that he was not a Communist. "Whether I am or not a Communist is irrelevant," he told the House Un-American Activities Committee in 1956. "The question is whether American citizens, regardless of their political beliefs or sympathies, may enjoy their constitutional rights." In 1958 the U.S. Supreme Court finally agreed, ruling that the State Department could not deny citizens the right to travel because of their political beliefs or affiliations.

To celebrate, Robeson gave his first New York concert in a decade at a sold-out Carnegie Hall. But the years of struggle had taken a personal and professional toll. Negative public response and the ban on his travel led to the demise of his career. Before the 1950s, Robeson was one of the world's most famous entertainers and beloved American heroes, once being named "Man of the Year" by the National Association for the Advancement of Colored People. Despite all his accomplishments, Paul Robeson remains virtually ignored in American textbooks and history.

May be photocopied for classroom use. *Texts and Lessons for Content-Area Writing* by Nancy Steineke and Harvey "Smokey" Daniels, © 2016 (Portsmouth, NH: Heinemann). Reprinted with permission.

Smithsonian.com

What Paul Robeson Said

Gilbert King, www.smithsonian.com

After the singer and activist spoke at a Soviet-sponsored peace conference, he was reviled in the United States. But was the most widely reported version of his remarks accurate?

In April 1949, just as the Cold War was beginning to intensify, actor, singer and civil rights activist Paul Robeson traveled to France to attend the Soviet Union-sponsored Paris Peace Conference. After singing "Joe Hill," the famous ballad about a Swedish-born union activist falsely accused and convicted of murder and executed in Utah in 1915, Robeson addressed the audience and began speaking extemporaneously, as he often did, about the lives of black people in the United States. Robeson's main point was that World War III was not inevitable, as many Americans did not want war with the Soviet Union.

Before he took the stage, however, his speech had somehow already been transcribed and dispatched back to the United States by the Associated Press. By the following day, editorialists and politicians had branded Robeson a communist traitor for insinuating that black Americans would not fight in a war against the Soviet Union. Historians would later discover that Robeson had been misquoted, but the damage had been almost instantly done. And because he was out of the country, the singer was unaware of the firestorm brewing back home over the speech. It was the beginning of the end for Robeson, who would soon be declared "the Kremlin's voice of America" by a witness at hearings by the House Un-American Activities Committee (HUAC).

Committee chair John Wood, a Georgia Democrat, summoned baseball great Jackie Robinson to Washington. Robinson, appearing reluctantly, denounced Robeson's views and assured the country that the singer did not speak on behalf of black Americans. Robeson's passport was soon revoked, and 85 of his planned concerts in the United States were canceled. Some in the press were calling for his execution. Later that summer, in civil rights-friendly Westchester County, New York, at the one concert that was not canceled, anti-communist groups and Ku Klux Klan types hurled racial epithets, attacked concertgoers with baseball bats and rocks and burned Robeson in effigy. A man who had exemplified American upward mobility had suddenly become public enemy number one. Not even Jackie Robinson, the leading black spokesmen of the day, felt safe enough to stand by the man dubbed as the "Black Stalin" during the Red Scare of the late 1940s and '50s.

Paul Leroy Robeson was born in 1898, the son of a runaway slave, William Drew Robeson. He grew up in Princeton, New Jersey, where he gained fame as one of the greatest football players ever, earning back-to-back first-team All-America honors in 1917 and 1918 at Rutgers University. But Robeson was a scholar as well. A member of the Rutgers honor society, Cap and Skull, he was chosen as valedictorian of his class, and after earning his bachelor's degree, he worked his way through Columbia Law

School while playing professional football. Although he had a brief stint at a New York law firm after graduating, Robeson's voice brought him public acclaim. Soon he was starring on Broadway, as well as on the greatest stages around the world, in plays such as Shakespeare's *Othello* and the Gershwin brothers' *Porgy and Bess*. His resonant bass-baritone voice made him a recording star as well, and by the 1930s, he became a box office sensation in the film *Show Boat* with his stirring rendition of "Ol Man River."

Yet Robeson, who traveled the world and was purported to speak more than a dozen languages, became increasingly active in the rights of exploited workers, particularly blacks in the South, and he associated himself with communist causes from Africa to the Soviet Union. After a visit to Eastern Europe in 1934, where he was nearly attacked by Nazis in Germany, Robeson experienced nothing but adulation and respect in the USSR—a nation he believed did not harbor any resentment or racial animosity toward blacks. "Here, I am not a Negro but a human being for the first time in my life," he said. "I walk in full human dignity."

When communists invited him to the stage at the Paris Peace Congress, Robeson was urged to say a few words after an enthusiastic crowd heard him sing. French transcripts of the speech obtained by Robeson's biographer Martin Duberman indicate that Robeson said, "We in America do not forget that it is on the backs of the poor whites of Europe . . . and on the backs of millions of black people the wealth of America has been acquired. And we are resolved that it shall be distributed in an equitable manner among all of our children and we don't want any hysterical stupidity about our participating in a war against anybody no matter whom. We are determined to fight for peace. We do not wish to fight the Soviet Union."

Lansing Warren, a correspondent covering the conference for the *New York Times,* reported a similar promise for peace in his dispatch for the newspaper, relegating Robeson's comments toward the end of his story. But the Associated Press's version of Robeson's remarks read: "It is unthinkable that American Negros would go to war on behalf of those who have oppressed us for generations against the Soviet Union which in one generation has lifted our people to full human dignity." (The source of that transcript remains unknown; the singer's son Paul Robeson Jr. has said that because it was filed before his father actually spoke, the anonymous AP correspondent might have cobbled it together from remarks his father had previously made in Europe.)

By the next day, the press was reporting that Robeson was a traitor. According to Robeson Jr., his father had "no idea really that this was going on till they called him from New York and said, hey, you'd better say something, that you're in immense trouble here in the United States." Instead, Robeson continued his tour, deciding to address the "out of context" quotes when he returned, unaware of how much damage the AP account was doing to his reputation.

Unbeknownst to Robeson, Roy Wilkins and Walter White of the National Association for the Advancement of Colored People (NAACP) were pressured by the U.S. State Department to issue a formal response to the singer's purported comments. The NAACP, always wary of being linked in any way to communists, dissociated itself from Robeson. Channing Tobias, a member of the NAACP board of directors, called him "an ingrate." Three months later, on July 18, 1949, Jackie Robinson was brought to Washington, D.C., to testify before HUAC for the purpose of obliterating Robeson's leadership role in the American black community. The Brooklyn Dodgers' second baseman assured Americans that Robeson did not speak for all blacks with his "silly" personal views. Everyone from conservatives to Eleanor Roosevelt criticized the singer. The former first lady and civil rights activist noted, "Mr. Robeson does his people great harm in trying to line them up on the Communist side of the political picture. Jackie Robinson helps them greatly by his forthright statements."

For Robeson, the criticism was piercing, especially coming from the baseball star. It was, after all, Robeson who was one of Jackie Robinson's strongest advocates, and the singer once urged a boycott of Yankee Stadium because baseball was not integrated. Newspapers across the country praised Robinson's testimony; one called it "four hits and no errors" for America. But lost in the reporting was the fact that Robinson did not pass up the chance to land a subtle dig at the communist hysteria that underlay the HUAC hearings. The committee chairs—including known Klan sympathizers Martin Dies Jr. of Texas and John Rankin of Mississippi—could not have been all smiles as Robinson finished speaking.

In a carefully worded statement, prepared with the help of Brooklyn Dodgers general manager Branch Rickey, Robinson said, "The fact that because it is a communist who denounces injustice in the courts, police brutality and lynching, when it happens, doesn't change the truth of his charges." Racial discrimination, Robinson said, is not "a creation of communist imagination."

For his part, Robeson refused to be drawn into a personal feud with Robinson because "to do that, would be exactly what the other group wants us to do." But the backlash against Robeson was immediate. His blacklisting and the revocation of his passport rendered him unable to work or travel, and he saw his yearly income drop from more than $150,000 to less than $3,000. In August 1949, he managed to book a concert in Peekskill, New York, but anti–civil rights factions within the American Legion and Veterans of Foreign Wars caused a riot, injuring hundreds, thirteen of them seriously. One famous photograph from the riot pictured a highly decorated black World War I aviator being beaten by police and a state trooper. The press largely blamed communist agitators for provoking anti-American fervor.

Robeson's name was stricken from the college All-America football teams. Newsreel footage of him was destroyed, recordings were erased, and there was a clear effort in the media to avoid any mention of his name. Years later, he was brought before HUAC and asked to identify members of the Communist Party and to admit to his own membership. Robeson reminded the committee that he was a lawyer and that the Communist Party was a legal party in the United States; then he invoked his Fifth Amendment rights. He closed his testimony by saying, "You gentlemen belong with the Alien and Sedition Acts, and you are the nonpatriots, and you are the un-Americans, and you ought to be ashamed of yourselves."

Toward the end of his life, Jackie Robinson had a chance to reflect on the incident and his invitation to testify before HUAC. He wrote in his autobiography, "I would reject such an invitation if offered now . . . . I have grown wiser and closer to the painful truths about America's destructiveness. And I do have increased respect for Paul Robeson who, over the span of twenty years, sacrificed himself, his career and the wealth and comfort he once enjoyed because, I believe, he was sincerely trying to help his people."

Testimony of Paul Robeson Before the House Committee on Un-American Activities

84th Congress, House, Committee on Un-American Activities, Investigation of the Unauthorized Use of U.S. Passports, *Part 3, June 12, 1956 (abridged)*

THE CHAIRMAN: The Committee will be in order. This morning the Committee resumes its series of hearings on the vital issue of the use of American passports as travel documents in furtherance of the objectives of the Communist conspiracy. . . .

Mr. ARENS: Now, during the course of the process in which you were applying for this passport, in July of 1954, were you requested to submit a non-Communist affidavit? Did you comply with the requests?

Mr. ROBESON: *I certainly did not and I will not.*

When I am abroad I speak out against the injustices against the Negro people of this land. That is why I am here. This is the basis, and I am not being tried for whether I am a Communist, I am being tried for fighting for the rights of my people, who are still second-class citizens in this United States of America. My mother was born in your state, [Chairman] Walter, and my mother was a Quaker, and my ancestors in the time of Washington baked bread for George Washington's troops when they crossed the Delaware, and my own father was a slave.

I stand here struggling for the rights of my people to be full citizens in this country. And they are not. They are not in Mississippi. And they are not in Montgomery, Alabama. And they are not in Washington. They are nowhere, and that is why I am here today. You want to shut up every Negro who has the courage to stand up and fight for the rights of his people, for the rights of workers. And that is why I am here today. . . .

Mr. ARENS: Did you make a trip to Europe in 1949 and to the Soviet Union? Did you go to Paris on that trip?

Mr. ROBESON: *I went to Paris.*

Mr. ARENS: And while you were in Paris, did you tell an audience there that the American Negro would never go to war against the Soviet government?

Mr. ROBESON: *May I say that is slightly out of context? No part of my speech made in Paris says fifteen million American Negroes would do anything. I said it was my feeling that the American people would struggle for peace, and that has since been underscored by the President of these United States.*

THE CHAIRMAN: Did you say what was attributed to you?

Mr. ROBESON: *I did not say it in that context.*

Mr. ARENS: At the Paris Conference you said it was unthinkable that the Negro people of America or elsewhere in the world could be drawn into war with the Soviet Union.

Mr. ROBESON: *I did not say that in Paris, I said that in America. And, gentlemen, they have not yet done so, and it is quite clear that no Americans, no people in the world probably, are going to war with the Soviet Union. So I was rather prophetic, was I not?*

Mr. ARENS: I lay before you a document containing an article, "I Am Looking for Full Freedom," by Paul Robeson, in a publication called the *Worker*, dated July 3, 1949.

Mr. ROBESON: *In Russia I felt for the first time like a full human being. No color prejudice like in Mississippi, no color prejudice like in Washington. It was the first time I felt like a human being. Where I did not feel the pressure of color as I feel [it] in this Committee today.*

Mr. SCHERER: Why do you not stay in Russia?

Mr. ROBESON: *Because my father was a slave, and my people died to build this country, and I am going to stay here, and have a part of it just like you.*

THE CHAIRMAN: Now, what prejudice are you talking about? You were graduated from Rutgers and you were graduated from the University of Pennsylvania. I remember seeing you play football at Lehigh.

Mr. ROBESON: *Just a moment. This is something that I challenge very deeply, and very sincerely: that the success of a few Negroes, including myself or Jackie Robinson can make up—and here is a study from Columbia University—for seven hundred dollars a year for thousands of Negro families in the South. My father was a slave, and I have cousins who are sharecroppers, and I do not see my success in terms of myself. That is the reason my own success has not meant what it should mean: I have sacrificed literally hundreds of thousands, if not millions, of dollars for what I believe in.*

In building America, sixty to a hundred million lives of my people, black people drawn from Africa on the plantations [were wasted]. You are responsible, and your forebears, for sixty million to one hundred million black people dying in the slave ships and on the plantations.

THE CHAIRMAN: Just a minute, the hearing is now adjourned.

Mr. ROBESON: *Can I read my statement?*

THE CHAIRMAN: No, you cannot read it. The meeting is adjourned.

CREATING A FACT SHEET ABOUT EDIBLE INSECTS

TEXT SET

Writing Focus: Nonfiction Informative

Texts Used ▶

TEXT	AUTHOR/SOURCE	TEXT TYPE	
"What Do Mealworms Taste Like?"	Mandy Oaklander, *Prevention Magazine*	Feature story	
"Edible Insects: Future Prospects for Food and Feed Security" (excerpts)	Arnold van Huis et al., Food and Agriculture Organization of the United Nations	Research report	
MENTOR TEXT	**AUTHOR/SOURCE**	**TEXT TYPE**	**WHERE TO FIND IT**
"Antibiotic Resistance: From the Farm to You"	Natural Resources Defense Council	Fact sheet	Lesson 9, page 67

TIME ▶

Reading/Discussion One class period

Writing Two class periods—one period for writing, one period for putting fact sheet together and conducting gallery walk

GROUPINGS ▶

Reading/Discussion Individuals, pairs, groups of four, whole class

Writing Individuals, pairs, whole class

STANDARDS MET ▶ See pages 306–307.

LESSONS USED ▶ The following lessons were used in the construction of this text set:

- Lesson 9: Quotable Quotes
- Lesson 15: Conceptual Annotation
- Lesson 28: Reread and Write with Questions in Mind

WHEN TO USE ▶ Another way to investigate a topic and convey the results is in the form of a fact sheet. The headings and short informative sections require concise, clear summarization of key details. Though explanatory in style, fact sheets typically have an underlying claim supported by the chosen data.

Why This Topic?

Ever see that old film *Soylent Green*? The mystery of the miracle food builds to an ironic end as Charlton Heston shouts to his fellow down-and-outers, "Soylent Green is people!"

Well, maybe that's one way to solve the food/environmental crisis, but here's another way: eating insects. *Entomophagy* (the scientific term for eating bugs) is a practice that people in Western culture definitely shrink away from—yet it is also intriguing. Insects trump other animal proteins due to their small environmental footprint. Maybe we won't be eating insects next week. But five or ten years from now, our menu may have changed, so we might as well be prepared.

Oh, and in case you haven't already guessed, we also chose this topic because of its attractive "yuck" factor. It's often the most repulsive topics that prove to be the most interesting reading!

READING/DISCUSSION PREPARATION

1. Download the cover of the report "Edible Insects: Future Prospects for Food and Feed Security," from the Food and Agriculture Organization of the United Nations. Be ready to project it at Step 1. It's a great montage of edible insects that will be a perfect conversation starter for your class!

2. If you'd like to include some videos, use the phrase "eating insects" to search YouTube, and all sorts of videos will pop up. It will take some reviewing on your part to find the perfect one for your students. There are long ones and short ones; videos from BBC, PBS, and National Geographic. There are also a lot of "I dare you" clips: "Eating a Scorpion—Bug War Challenge" is just one example that we recommend you *DO NOT* show to your students.

3. Determine how to form pairs at Step 1.

4. Download and make a copy of "What Do Mealworms Taste Like?" for each student. Download and be ready to project the annotation directions at Step 2.

5. Download an optional YouTube video to accompany the article: "Weird Stuff Mandy's Eating: Cricket & Mealworm Sushi." This short video features the author of the article dining at an insect sushi restaurant. You can also check out the same article online to see some great photos of those mealworm meatballs: www.prevention.com/food/healthy-eating-tips/entomophagy-eating-insects-and-mealworms.

6. Determine how to form groups of four at Step 5.

7. Duplicate the four-part "Eating Insects" text set, with each page on a different color of paper. You'll need one text set for each group of four. If you collate them in advance (one of each article per stack), you'll be able to simply hand these to the groups. Or, let kids walk up and grab their own materials at your Handout Bar. Students will be using this text set in Step 6.

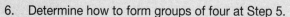

WRITING PREPARATION

1. Each student will need a hard copy of the mentor text: "Antibiotic Resistance: From the Farm to You," originally used in Lesson 9. If students still have their copies from the original lesson, there is no need to make copies again.

2. Determine how you will project the fact sheet in Step 2 when you conduct the heading analysis.

3. For Step 2, determine how you will reunite previous partners used during the previous day's reading/discussion lesson.

4. Determine how you will record notes when you analyze the headings. You could use a sheet of chart paper or, since the fact sheet will be projected, you might jot notes on the board around it. You may also assign a student scribe for note taking in Step 2.

5. For Step 4, determine how you will reunite the previous groups of four used during the previous day's reading/discussion lesson.

6. Gather the following materials:
   - Large sheets of white chart paper, one for each group
   - Transparent tape and scissors for chart paper work
   - Masking or painter's tape for displaying the finished charts
   - Fine-tip and thick markers in an assortment of colors
   - 3x5-inch sticky notes, three for each student

7. Decide how kids will create the final fact sheets. Our instructions are for paper and pen publishing, but digital options like PicCollage abound.

8. Make sure you have enough empty wall space to hang the finished charts for a cumulative gallery walk.

Reading/ ▶ Discussion Steps

STEP 1 **Introduce the topic of eating insects.** Project the cover of the FAO report "Eating Insects." *How many of you have tried or would try eating insects? Why or why not? Turn to your partner and talk about this for a minute.* Watch for conversation lull. *Who had a partner with some interesting ideas or experience related to this topic?* Listen to some responses. If you'd like to let this introductory conversation continue, show one of those YouTube videos you previewed.

STEP 2 **Introduce the article and explain the annotation.** Pass out the article "What Do Mealworms Taste Like?" *This is a pretty interesting article. The writer discusses why eating insects might be a good thing, but she also describes her attempt to make some mealworm meatballs. As you read this article, I want you to chart your reactions to the information. When you read something about eating insects that makes sense, underline it and put a smiley face in the margin. When you read something that grosses you out, underline it and put a frowny face in the margin.* As you explain those directions, project them on the board.

🙂 = Something about eating insects that makes sense

🙁 = Something about eating insects that grosses you out

STEP 3 **Individuals silently read and annotate.** Monitor student work and annotation. If any students finish early, encourage them to go back and jot some descriptive words next to the smiley and frowny faces that label their reactions to the underlined information.

STEP 4 **Pairs compare annotation.** *Get with your partner and compare your annotations. Does one of you have more smiley or frowny faces than the other? Take turns reading parts you underlined and then, instead of explaining, let your partner tell you what he's thinking first. Remember to take turns reading quotes aloud. Any questions? Okay, go ahead and talk about eating insects with your partner.* Monitor for on-task discussion and taking turns reading underlines aloud.

When you detect conversation dying down, you might choose to show that video of Mandy eating bug sushi or the photos of her mealworm meatball attempts. Or, just move on to the text set.

STEP 5 **Groups of four discuss and poll each other.** Direct pairs to combine into groups of four, and then give the new groups a few minutes to talk together about the article highlights—what was interesting, what grossed them out. *Before we do some more reading on entomophagy— that's the official name for eating insects—I want you to do a little poll in your group. On a scale of 1 to 10 (1 being never and 10 being a definite yes), how likely would you be to eat insects as part of your regular diet?* Give a minute for the poll and then continue. *How many rated your* *insect-eating likelihood a three or below? Raise your hands. Okay. Now let's see the hands of those who rated themselves 7 to 10.*

It looks like there are a lot of people in this room who need some more convincing that eating insects might be a good thing.

STEP 6 **Pass out the "Eating Insects" text set and explain the directions.** Distribute a collated text set to each group or send a materials monitor from each group to the Handout Bar for on-the-spot collating. Help direct the traffic; make sure each group has the correct number and color of sheets.

Everybody in your group have a different color? Good. All of the information on these sheets is taken from that United Nations report we looked at earlier. The report was also mentioned in the beginning of the mealworms article we just read.

Since each of your members has a different part of the report, you'll be pooling your information a little later. Right now, though, I want you to read your section and annotate with a question in mind: What information does this text use to convince others that eating insects is a good idea? When you find something, underline it and in the margin explain how the details are persuasive. Also, try to be creative with the information. Think about something that initially seems like a negative, but might be turned around and used as a positive reason for eating insects.

As mentioned in the "When to Use" section above, almost all text is persuasive in one way or another, and it might be useful to point out to students that organizations (both for-profit and nonprofit) frequently produce "explanatory" reports using extensive research and data in order to defend a claim. It is the reader's responsibility to recognize this and always ask the question, "Why did this company/organization release this report, and what is their reward if people subscribe to their claim?" In the case of the United Nations, we feel confident that the motivation behind this report is humanitarian: an attempt to alleviate global hunger as well as decrease pollutants and water use associated with food production.

STEP 7 **Individuals read and annotate excerpts.** Monitor reading and annotation. If you notice a student who isn't marking anything, stop and have a quick conversation on how to locate information that could be used advantageously for persuasion—to recruit people to insect cuisine.

STEP 8 **Groups reconvene and discuss persuasive information.** *Reconvene with your groups. Give each member a minute to tell about the information he or she found and how it could be used to persuade others. Then, before moving on, see if you can talk about that information a little more. Ask some questions. Make some connections with the excerpt and other things you now know about eating insects.*

Often students have a tendency to report briefly on their article, and then quickly move on to the next member. Monitor for on-task behavior, following directions, and spending some time talking about each excerpt.

STEP 9 Groups compile a list, then share with the class. *What are the most compelling reasons for eating insects? Turn back to your group and come up with a list that answers this question.* Monitor for completion. Students can just talk or you can have them all jot notes. As discussion quiets, call on a member of each group to share their group's conversation highlights.

Writing ▶ Steps: Creating a Fact Sheet

So far students have begun to think persuasively about entomophagy; the next step is to create an information sheet with the goal of educating and convincing others.

Day 1

STEP 1 Students review the previous fact sheet. Students will need to look at the "Antibiotic Resistance: From the Farm to You" fact sheet used in Lesson 9. Before starting the instructions, have students retrieve the lesson from their binders/folders or pass out a new copy.

A while ago we read the fact sheet "Antibiotic Resistance: From the Farm to You." Today we are going to use this piece of text as a model for our own writing. It's about a completely different topic from what we're writing about today, but it gives us a great model for how to write an informational text that really grabs readers. I want you to skim through the text now and take special note of how the headings create concern or alarm. Those headings are specifically designed to make it nearly impossible for the reader not to want to get the details.

Give students a chance to reread the fact sheet.

STEP 2 Students analyze headings. *Turn to your partner, look at the four headings in this fact sheet, and talk about how those headings grab a reader's interest.*

Give pairs a minute to talk and then discuss the projected fact sheet headings. If possible, enlarge the projection so students can focus their discussion on one heading at a time. *Let's take a look at each one of these headings and make a list of techniques they use to grab the audience's attention. As I jot down your ideas, make sure that you copy down the notes on your copy of the fact sheet.* If desired, enlist a student scribe to write notes on a whiteboard or chart paper so the fact sheet can remain projected.

Students may mention that the headings:

- Repeat focus words (*resistant bacteria*)
- Use action words (*threaten, spread, can pass*)
- Are short: word count is between seven and ten
- Lead to different information
- Make the reader ask how or why
- Invite the reader to connect the topic to self
- Imply a worsening situation if nothing is done

STEP 3 **Pairs brainstorm new eating insect headings.** *Using this list and our anchor text on antibiotic resistance, work with your partner to brainstorm possible persuasive/inviting headings you could use on a fact sheet for why people should try eating insects. Pool what you know with your text set resources* (hold up all of the handouts). *See how many different headings you can come up with. The more you brainstorm, the happier you will be later. Guaranteed! Be sure that each partner keeps his or her own written list of the potential headings. Do not assign a recorder.*

Monitor for brainstorming, recording ideas, and using all available resources.

STEP 4 **Groups of four choose headings.** *Walking around the room, I've seen lots of great headings. Get together with your group of four and read through all of your potential headings. Choose the four that you think best reflect all of the criteria we listed on the board. Also make sure that the four headings you choose are about four different subtopics. When you decide on your four best headings, make sure everyone in your group has them written down.*

Monitor for following directions, equal participation (maybe even some debate), and actively using the criteria list as they judge the merits of each heading.

STEP 5 **Explain writing directions.** *Now you'll each need to pick one of those four headings to work with, based on the text in your possession so that you will not have to do additional research. Each member of your group should be working with a different heading. Take a minute to negotiate and decide. When you know what heading you'll be using, draw a circle around it on your list.*

Monitor for choice completion and then continue.

Today we're going to create some fact sheets on eating insects, and each group member will create a quarter of that fact sheet. Grab your articles and a sheet of loose-leaf paper. At the top of your paper, write your heading.

But before we start writing, let's take a moment to examine the paragraphs under the headings on the antibiotic resistance fact sheet. Project the fact sheet. *Turn to your partner and see what you notice about how these paragraphs are written. As you notice something, jot it down on the fact sheet.*

Give pairs a chance to look and discuss. Then gather observations from the class. Students may mention that the paragraphs:

- Are short
- Use action words
- Give specific details and examples
- Promote concern and a need for action

STEP 6 **Individuals write a paragraph for their heading.** *Now go back through your articles and think about the details you can use to explain the topic of your heading as we get started on the writing.*

As you write, don't forget the list we just made, and use the antibiotics fact sheet as a writing model. Also, remember that these paragraphs are filled with important facts and details; you'll be able to find those in your articles on eating insects.

Monitor individuals for using the texts and getting words down. If you notice someone who is stuck, discuss what information their particular heading calls for and maybe give a hand locating it in the texts.

STEP 7 **Groups of four subdivide so that pairs can read their paragraphs aloud to each other.** *Before we put our paragraphs together for the fact sheet, I want you to read what you wrote aloud to your partner. Partners, listen carefully. If there is anything that is missing or sentences that need rewording, help each other so that your published piece shines.*

STEP 8 **Individuals write final drafts.** When pairs are satisfied their paragraphs are polished, pass out blank printer paper and dark-colored fine-tip markers. (Or set kids up to use the digital alternative you may have chosen. They can do both rough and final drafts digitally—or you can save the digital tool for finals only.)

These paragraphs are ready to publish. Turn your blank sheet of paper sideways, to landscape orientation. Using your marker, neatly print your heading. Then underneath, neatly print your paragraph. It's important that you do your best job on this because other people will be reading it.

When students finish this step, make sure they put their names on the reverse side of the sheet. Then collect them for safekeeping. You'll be returning the drafts to the groups the following day for project completion.

Day 2

STEP 9 **Groups create a fact sheet.** Return the final draft paragraphs. Give each group a piece of chart paper and access to tape, glue sticks, and scissors. Members will also need to get out the "Antibiotic Resistance" fact sheet. Project the fact sheet as well.

Today you're going to work with your group to create a giant fact sheet. When you affix your four paragraphs to the chart paper, be sure to leave some room at the top for your fact sheet title and some provocative statistics or facts. Point these out on the projected fact sheet. *Before you glue everything into place, let me take a quick look to make sure you've followed the instructions.*

As groups complete their assembly, remind them to let you review their work before gluing so they're sure to leave space for the fact sheet title and statistics. If a group gets stuck on its title or statistics, refer them to the "Antibiotic Resistance" fact sheet while asking a few probing questions to get members thinking. Don't be afraid to put a time limit on this activity so that you have time for the gallery walk.

As a group finishes up, give them the next instruction. *When your group is finished, grab some masking tape and hang your fact sheet up on the wall.* Indicate the location.

STEP 10 **Gallery walk.** Once all of the fact sheets are posted, give each student three 3×5 sticky notes. *Once you have your sticky notes, write your name on the front of each one in the upper left hand corner.* (Putting the names on the front improves accountability).

Okay, now it's time for a gallery walk. Go and check out the other groups' fact sheets. Read their paragraphs. See how they wrote about the same topic differently. After you've read another group's fact sheet, jot a note to them on the sticky. Make a comment about something you liked in the writing, a piece of information that was interesting, or a question that arose. Put your sticky on the wall next to that fact sheet and then move on to read another one. Continue reading and commenting until I call time. If you run out of stickies, come and get another one from me. Also, make sure that you don't get bunched up. Spread yourselves out and be sure to get to fact sheets that don't have any sticky notes around them yet. Any questions? Go!

Monitor the gallery walk for on-task behavior. When students try to sidestep the process for socializing, intervene and direct them in opposite directions to fact sheets that have fewer stickies. Call time when you notice an even distribution of sticky notes on the fact sheets.

STEP 11 **Large-group share.** *It's time for the gallery walk to end. I want each group to go back to their own fact sheet and read the comments your classmates posted. Then turn to your group and take a minute to discuss how your fact sheet compared with others you read. What were some different ways other groups used headings and details? What was something another group focused on that your group overlooked? In a moment we'll hear from each group.*

Give groups a couple of minutes to debrief and then use the final minutes to hear what each group noticed about the fact sheets.

WHAT MIGHT THE WRITING LOOK LIKE?

Here's an example of a heading and accompanying paragraph.

Eating Insects Is Painless

When we think of eating insects, we think of a bug that's prominently encased in a clear candy sucker or we imagine eating crispy fried beetles. Actually, you can eat bugs without even knowing it. Edible insects ground into a powder that is similar to flour can be added to any food in order to raise the protein level. Adding ground insects to a traditional meatball recipe will actually make it more nutritious, but thanks to the spices and other ingredients, no one will know they're eating bugs!

What Do Mealworms Taste Like?

The new sustainable supermeat? Bugs.

Mandy Oaklander

Staring down at the mealworms, a pile of curly, soil-colored corpses, I swore they were still alive. But these little guys were very much dead, and they were about to be my dinner.

I'd received them in an unmarked cardboard box from World Entomophagy, the only U.S. company selling food-grade insects to the public. I'd placed my order after reading an article online about a taste test engineered by an entomologist: He gave subjects meatballs made of half meat and half mealworm as well as a control meatball of 100% conventional meat. Surprisingly, most people preferred the buggy balls. That's good news for the environment, since insects are some of the most sustainable protein around. And it's also good news for me, since mealworms are high in healthy fats and vitamins A and B.

World Entomophagy's founder, Harman Johar, has catered to curious eaters like me since his sophomore year at the University of Georgia, when he started growing mealworms and scorpions in bins stacked in his dorm room closet. ("My roommate was surprisingly cool with it," Johar says.) Soon after, with the help of a handful of fraternity brothers, Johar took the bugs out of the closet and started a company. He now sells mealworms, crickets, cricket breadcrumbs, "Betty Cricket" pancake and cookie mixes, and sweet and spicy teriyaki cricket snacks online.

Ground crickets are about 64% pure protein. Mealworms are almost 50%—with as many omega-3s as fish.

His bugs have good breeding. They're all born and raised in Austin and fed a strict non-GMO (genetically modified organism) diet. Johar's team tests each new batch of insects for diseases and parasites by screening those that float during washing and heat-treating all of them. And they practice what Johar calls "good karma killing": slowly lowering the temperature until the bugs reach a kind of permanent hibernation. They're dried and processed without chemicals or preservatives.

With such cleanly raised bugs, it's little wonder why chefs and restaurants flock to World Entomophagy's stash. And even more so when you consider their nutritional profile: Ground crickets are about 64% pure protein. Mealworms are almost 50%—with as many omega-3s as fish. Insects are also incredibly sustainable. They use almost no land compared to conventional meat, and since you can grow them in stackable bins and tubs, insects are the rare kind of livestock that you can raise vertically. Further, growing bugs takes about 1/1,000th the amount of water that beef requires. And insects have a tiny carbon footprint, unlike industrial livestock, which as an industry is the single largest contributor to ozone-depleting greenhouse gases in the world. "You can grow crickets on just about anything," Johar said. "It's a very freeing form of food."

Governmental agencies are starting to see bugs the same way. Last year, the Food and

Agriculture Organization (FAO) of the United Nations issued a report hailing insects as the future of worldwide food security. And though the FDA doesn't currently have any regulations about insects as food, that's likely to change soon.

Ok, so bugs may be the future—but looking down at my jiggly package of worms, was I really ready to cook them? Johar assured me that bugs can be quite tasty when given to the right chef. I am not that chef.

My first mistake was bragging to my boyfriend about how brave I was. "I'm not scared! Insects will be delicious," I told him. I counted on him being grossed out and calling off the experiment. But he's a doctor, and was more than game to try an alternative healthy source of protein. So we talked about making those highly acclaimed mealworm meatballs together. He, unlike I, actually planned on following through. I suggested making plain turkey meatballs instead, but his mind was set. So on a Tuesday night after work, I tore open the package and plunked them into a bowl.

The first time you breathe in a sack of dead, room-temperature worms is one you'll never forget. It's an earthy, bitter perfume, like the excrement of 100 different species. Their texture surprised me, too. I thought they'd be soft and plump and squishy, but they were firm and slick. I slid the crawlers into a colander and gave them a good rinse. Then I gave them a good dicing. Tiny tubal exoskeletons flew across the counter as I chopped, but as much as I chopped, I couldn't make them look like anything but bugs. Next time, if there is a next time, I'll use the food processor.

The first time you breathe in a sack of dead, room-temperature worms is one you'll never forget. It's an earthy, bitter perfume, like the excrement of 100 different species.

We made the first meatball batch with half turkey, half mealworms. The mushroomy smell was masked by the garlic, egg, onion parsley, seasoning and breadcrumbs we added, and aside from those exoskeletons, the balls looked promising. (If you squint, they just look like mutant, oversized flaxseeds.)

Now it was taste test time. Ground meat really is ground meat, no matter what the source. The turkey-worm balls tasted like almost-normal turkey, with just a slight crunch. Delicious.

It's hard to mess up fried food, though, so we decided we would put them to a more honest test: roasting. I tossed the remaining worms with paprika, garlic powder, salt, and pepper, and after a couple minutes on a lined baking sheet, we took them out. During their first seconds cooling on the counter, they curled up like little wriggling synchronized swimmers. We both jumped.

Roasted alone, the insects smelled like the litter box at a pet store stocking only exotic species. Needless to say, the smell of dead worms sweating in an oven is one that sticks with you. Luckily, they tasted much milder, but I'd be lying if I told you they disappeared from the plate as fast as the wormballs did.

Will I eat insects again? Most definitely. But maybe I'd read up on flavor pairing for our little protein-packed friends before attempting my next experiment. I hear there's a food cart in San Francisco specializing in a salted cricket tostadita with mashed avocado, toasted sunflower seeds, and pickled red onion. Could I pull that off? Stay tuned. I have a frozen package of baby crickets in the freezer.

Edible Insects: Future Prospects for Food and Feed Security, Part 1

Arnold van Huis et al., Food and Agriculture Organization of the United Nations

Why Are Insects Not Eaten in Western Countries?

The Fertile Crescent, a region comprising fertile lands in western Asia and the Nile Valley and Nile Delta in northeast Africa is believed to be one of the regions in which agriculture originated. From there, food production (i.e., plant and animal domestication) spread swiftly throughout Europe. It is thought that it was because of the utility of domesticated animals that the use of insects—besides honeybees and silkworms—failed to gain much traction in the West. Insects simply could not offer the same benefits.

Food production in the Fertile Crescent and Europe led to incredible gains in productivity and efficiency. The importance of agriculture may have also resulted in the perception of insects as a nuisance and threat to food production. People in most Western countries view entomophagy (eating insects) with feelings of disgust, its origins rooted in culture that defines the rules on what is edible and what is not.

Negative Attitudes Towards Insects

It is safe to say that negative perceptions surrounding insects are fully entrenched in Western societies. Insect harvesting has been associated with the hunter-gatherer era and in turn with "primitive" forms of food acquisition. This is in stark contrast to many tropical regions of the world, where insects have decorative purposes, are used for entertainment and in medicine and sorcery, and are present in myth, legend, and dance.

In Western societies—where protein is still largely derived from domesticated animals—insects are virtually synonymous with nuisance: mosquitoes and flies invade homes; termites destroy wood possessions. Certain insects are also transmitters of disease. A housefly, for example, can pick up an infectious agent on the outside of its body, and transmit it to food prior to consumption. Mosquitoes, ticks, fleas, and lice harbor pathogens that are often responsible for serious blood-borne diseases such as malaria, viral encephalitis, and Lyme disease.

Edible Insects: Future Prospects for Food and Feed Security, Part 2

Arnold van Huis et al., Food and Agriculture Organization of the United Nations

Feed Conversion

As demand for meat rises, so too does the need for grain and animal proteins. This is because far more plant protein is needed for an equivalent amount of animal protein. For 1 kg (2.2 lb.) of high-quality animal protein, livestock are fed about 6 kg (13.2 lb.) of plant protein. Feed-to-meat conversion rates (how much feed is needed to produce a 1 kg increase in weight) vary widely depending on the class of animal and the production practices used. Typically, 1 kg (2.2 lb.) of live animal weight in the U.S. production system requires the following amounts of food: 2.5 kg (5.5 lb.) for chicken, 5 kg (11 lb.) for pork, and 10 kg (22 lb.) for beef.

Insects require far less feed. For example, the production of 1 kg live animal weight of crickets requires as little as 1.7 kg (3.7 lb.) of feed. When these figures are adjusted for edible weight (usually the entire animal cannot be eaten), the advantage of eating insects becomes even greater. Up to 80 percent of a cricket is edible and digestible compared with 55 percent for chicken and pigs and 40 percent for cattle. This means that crickets are twice as efficient in converting feed to meat as chicken, at least four times more efficient than pigs, and 12 times more efficient than cattle.

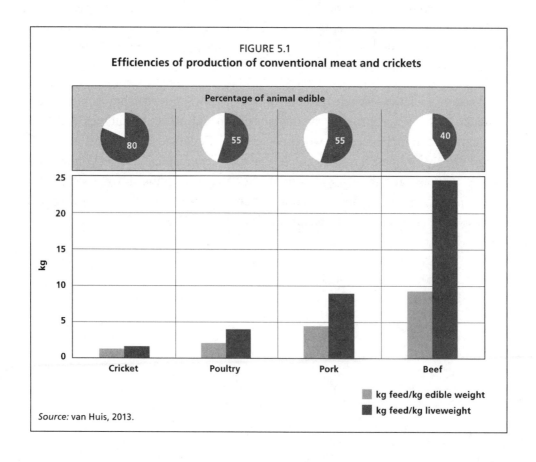

FIGURE 5.1
Efficiencies of production of conventional meat and crickets

Source: van Huis, 2013.

Edible Insects: Future Prospects for Food and Feed Security, Part 3

Arnold van Huis et al., Food and Agriculture Organization of the United Nations

Greenhouse Gas and Ammonia Emissions

Overall, livestock rearing is responsible for 18 percent of greenhouse gases (GHG), a higher share than the transport sector. However, livestock are responsible for almost 40 percent of methane pollution and 65 percent of nitrous oxide (ammonia) pollution, both of which have greater global warming potential (GWP) than carbon dioxide.

TABLE 5.1
The animal sector's contribution to GHG emissions

	Carbon dioxide (CO2)	Methane (CH4)	Nitrous oxide (N2O)
Percentage of global emissions	9	35–40	65
Caused by	Fertilizer production for feed crops, on-farm energy expenditures, feed transport, animal product processing, animal transport and land use changes	From enteric fermentation in ruminants and from farm animal manure.	From farm manure and urine

Note: This table shows how much the animal sector contributes to these emissions and why. According to Fiala (2008), 1 kg of beef causes emissions equivalent to 14.8 kg of CO_2, while emissions are lower for pigs and chickens 3.8 kg and 1.1 kg, respectively.

Source: Steinfeld *et al.*, 2006.

Among insect species, only cockroaches, termites, and scarab beetles produce methane. Yet insects deemed viable for human consumption in the Western World include species such as mealworm larvae, crickets and locusts, all of which produce far less greenhouse gases than pigs or beef cattle.

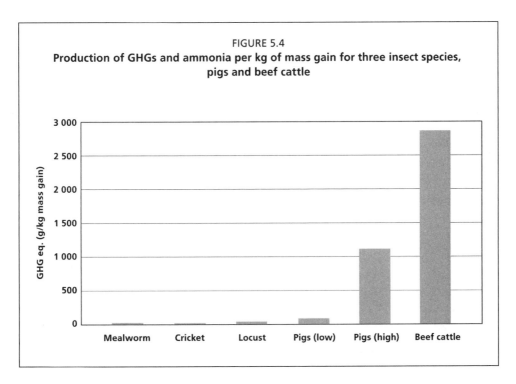

FIGURE 5.4
Production of GHGs and ammonia per kg of mass gain for three insect species, pigs and beef cattle

Edible Insects: Future Prospects for Food and Feed Security, Part 3 (continued)

Water Use

Water is a key determinant of land productivity. A growing body of evidence suggests that a lack of water is already constraining agricultural output in many parts of the world. It is estimated that, by 2025, 1.8 billion people will be living in countries or regions with absolute water scarcity, and two-thirds of the world population will likely be under stress. Increasing demands placed on the global water supply threaten biodiversity, food production, and other vital needs.

Agriculture consumes about 70 percent of freshwater worldwide. 1 kg (2.2 lb.) of animal protein requires 5-20 times more water than generating 1 kg of grain protein. This figure approaches 100 times if the water required for forage and feed grain production is included in the equation.

Estimates of the volume of water required to raise an equivalent weight of edible insects are unavailable but could be considerably lower. Mealworms, for example, are more drought-resistant than cattle.

Edible Insects: Future Prospects for Food and Feed Security, Part 4

Arnold van Huis et al., Food and Agriculture Organization of the United Nations

Processing Edible Insects for Food and Feed

After being wild-harvested or reared in a domesticated setting, insects are killed by freeze-drying, sun-drying, or boiling. They can be processed and consumed as whole insects or ground into a granular form. Insects can also be cooked live and consumed.

Whole Insects

In tropical countries, insects are often consumed whole, but some insects, such as grasshoppers and locusts, require removal of body parts (wings and legs). Depending on the dish, fresh insects can be further processed by roasting, frying, or boiling.

Granular Form

Grinding or milling is a common method for processing a variety of foods. Edible insects can be processed into more palatable form through grinding. Insect powder can be added to otherwise low-protein foods to increase their nutritional value, just as soy protein powder can be added to a fruit smoothie. In societies where consumers are not accustomed to eating whole insects, granular forms may be better accepted.

Overcoming the Disgust Factor

Common prejudice against eating insects is not justified from a nutritional point of view. Insects are not inferior to other protein sources such as fish, chicken and beef. Feelings of disgust in the West towards eating insects contributes to the common misconception that entomophagy in the developing world is prompted by starvation and is merely a survival mechanism. This is far from the truth. Although it will require considerable convincing to reverse this mentality, it is not an impossible feat. Arthropods like lobsters and shrimps, once considered poor-man's food in the West, are now expensive delicacies. It is hoped that arguments such as the high nutritional value of insects and their low environmental impact will contribute to a shift in perception.

Adapted from Arnold van Huis et al. *Edible Insects: Future Prospects for Food and Feed Security.* Food and Agriculture Organization of the United Nations. 2013.

CHAPTER 13

WRITING A LETTER TO THE EDITOR ABOUT MILITARY ANIMAL USE

TEXT SET

Writing Focus: Nonfiction Argument

Texts Used ▶

TIME ▶

Reading/Discussion Two periods

Writing One period

GROUPINGS ▶

Reading/Discussion

Day 1: Individuals, pairs, whole class, whole-class lineup

Day 2: Individuals, previous day's pairs, new standing pairs, whole class

Writing Individuals, pairs, groups of four, whole class

STANDARDS MET ▶ See pages 306–307.

LESSONS USED ▶ The following lessons were used in the construction of this text set:

- Lesson 24: Lineup for an Argument
- Lesson 25: Argument Notes
- Lesson 26: Supporting an Argument

WHEN TO USE ▶ Our content areas are rife with controversy. And kids do love to argue. But instead of letting students "spout off," let's teach them how to back up their opinions with accurate, significant support. Being able to write a good argument can be fun, challenging, and handy training for tackling high-stakes tests—as well as deconstructing a Sunday episode of *Meet the Press.*

TEXT	AUTHOR/SOURCE	TEXT TYPE	
"10 Ways Animals Have Served the Military"	Laura Moss, Mother Nature Network	Numbered list	
"Canines in Combat: Military Working Dogs"	Denise K. Sypesteyn, *San Antonio Magazine*	Feature story	
"Military Working Dogs Face Tough Re-entry into Civilian Life"	Anne Leigh, WrapUp Media	Feature story	
"U.S. Navy Marine Mammal Program (NMMP)"	www.public.navy.mil	Government website	
"Navy's Dolphin Use Raises Questions"	Anne Leigh, WrapUp Media	Feature story	
MENTOR TEXT	**AUTHOR/SOURCE**	**TEXT TYPE**	**WHERE TO FIND IT**
The Cure for Dreaming (excerpt—second letter)	Cat Winters, Harry Abrams Publishers	Letter to the editor	Lesson 25, page 174

Why This Topic?

The use of animals in the military is a topic that seems to rise and fall on the waves of public interest. In 1967, during the escalation of the Vietnam War, *The Day of the Dolphin* was released. The film, based on a French novel titled *A Sentient Animal,* featured George C. Scott as a scientist working to train a pair of dolphins for military purposes. Deemed science fiction at the time (1965–1975), real dolphins actually were patrolling Cam Ranh Bay, performing underwater surveillance and guarding military boats.

Military dolphins again swam into public consciousness more recently. In 2013 it was reported that three Russian "attack" dolphins had escaped from a Ukrainian naval training base. Although the story has since been labeled a hoax, this renewed dolphin interest led to sporadic coverage of U.S. military dolphins. Since then, the topic of military dolphins has again receded from headlines. While you can find bits of information on the navy's marine mammal training program website, it's not touted publicly or capitalized upon for navy recruiting like the Blue Angels, seen at air shows across the country. It seems that using marine animals (they also train seals!) for wartime work is controversial enough that the Pentagon keeps it on the down-low.

On the other hand, working dogs have far wider public acceptance. Due to their phenomenal sense of smell, dogs can be trained to sniff out drugs, bedbugs, cancer, catastrophe survivors, and bombs. This last use has been particularly critical in our most recent wars due to the frequent use of IEDs (improvised explosive devices). Military dogs can be directly credited for saving hundreds of lives. However, just like their human counterparts, dogs are leaving the service with physical and emotional injuries.

This text set introduces the controversy of using animals for military purposes. On the one hand, these animals have served in invaluable ways because of skills that augment and even surpass those of their human handlers. On the other hand, because they are not human, is it ethical to use animals for military purposes when they are unable to give informed consent?

READING/DISCUSSION PREPARATION

Day 1

1. Make a copy of "10 Ways Animals Have Served the Military" for each student.

2. Optional image search: You've probably noticed by now how valuable we think it is to introduce a topic visually. Just searching on the title of this introductory article will uncover a treasure trove of photos. And searching the title "Canines in Combat: Military Working Dogs" will reveal the photos that originally accompanied the article plus lots of other sites with great military dog images. Searching military dolphins is slightly trickier. The best search phrase we've found is "navy dolphin training." However, before you blithely download a prime dolphin shot, take a moment to check out the website where it resides. Mixed among legitimate military dolphin photos are many that have been photoshopped. No branch of the military is training any dolphins to operate automatic weapons!

3. Download the annotation directions for projection in Step 3.

4. Determine how you will form pairs in Step 5.

5. Be sure you have a stash of 3x5-inch index cards; you'll need one for each student in Step 6.

6. Using standard 8½-by-11-inch printer paper, prepare signs that say STRONGLY AGREE, AGREE, DISAGREE, STRONGLY DISAGREE. You'll need one sign for each position in Step 7.

7. Determine where students can stand for a lineup in Step 7.

Day 2

1. Determine how to reunite pairs from the previous day in Step 2.

2. Duplicate copies of each text set (one on dogs, one on dolphins) for use in Step 3. Half the class will read about dogs while the other half reads about dolphins. As we've mentioned earlier, topic balance and monitoring is much simpler if you use a different color of paper for each text set.

3. Determine where new standing partners will meet in Step 5.

1. Determine how to reunite the previous day's pairs at Step 1.

2. For Step 2, each student will need a hard copy of the anchor text: the excerpt from *The Cure for Dreaming*, which was originally used in Lesson 25. If students still have their copies from the original lesson, there is no need to reduplicate them.

3. Download *The Cure for Dreaming* excerpt and prepare to project it in Step 4. You may also use a document camera and hard copy.

4. Review the example of the annotated letter (Craft Annotation: Opening Sentences), located in Step 4 of the Writing section.

5. Download the Planning Your Argument questions and determine how you'll project the list at Step 5.

6. Download Steps for Giving Writing Feedback and determine how to project them at Step 8.

7. Determine how dog and dolphin text set pairs will combine into groups of four at Step 8 so that both animals are represented.

Day 1

Reading/ ▶ Discussion Steps

STEP 1 **Introduce the topic.** *How many of you have heard that animals assist U.S. soldiers in war? Raise your hands. Turn to your partner and take a minute to talk about the ways animals might help soldiers in times of war.* Give students a minute to talk and then ask for volunteers to share what they discussed.

STEP 2 **Show images of military animals (optional).** *Here are some photos of animals that have been used for military purposes. Some are still used, some have fallen out of favor, and some were unsuccessful experiments. As you view the images, notice what surprises you and how you respond.* Show the images.

I notice that some of you are already eager to talk about this topic, so let's get some more information about it.

STEP 3 **Pass out "10 Ways" and explain the annotation directions.** *Earlier, you thought of some of the ways that animals have been used for military purposes. This article lists some of those attempts—some successful, others not so much. As you read this article, I want you to do some annotation for discussion.* Project the annotation instructions as you explain.

Annotation Instructions

1. As you read each numbered section, underline something that you find interesting or surprising, or that raises a question.

2. After each numbered section, reread your underline and then code it:

- * Interesting
- ! Surprising
- ? Raises a question

3. Then, in the margin, jot down a sentence or two that explains your thinking or your question.

4. When you're done, you should have an underline, code symbol, and thought for each of the ten animals.

Any questions on how to annotate?

STEP 4 **Students read individually and annotate.** As students work, monitor their annotation. Intervene when you notice superficial comments. You might say: *I know you have some really interesting thinking about this, so jot some specific details that truly capture it.* Then go back to something already underlined and ask the student why she chose that. Listen, ask a question or two if necessary, and then help the student summarize that short transaction with some specific words.

STEP 5 **Partners discuss annotation.** *It's time to turn to your partner and share your thinking. As you talk about this article, don't be afraid to jump around; you don't need to discuss the items in their numerical order. Since time is limited, go ahead and start with the animal use that you found most interesting, surprising, or had the most questions about. Also, instead of just taking turns explaining your annotation, point out something you underlined to your partner and let him share his thoughts first while you listen. Then after he's done, it's your turn to add to the conversation or ask your partner a question. Remember to take turns pointing out things you've underlined. Any questions?*

Monitor for pairs taking turns, talking about article items of highest interest to them, and engaging in real conversation versus just marching through the annotation.

STEP 6 **Prepare for class lineup.** *As I was walking around the room just now, I saw a lot of animated conversation. It appears that some of you feel pretty strongly about whether or not animals should be used for military purposes. Now we are going to vote with our feet and demonstrate our personal opinions with a lineup.* Write this statement on the board as you read it aloud: *Animals should be used for military combat purposes.*

Grab those signs you made so that you can hold each one up as you announce the position choices. *You can choose one of four positions: strongly agree, agree, disagree, or strongly disagree. While you think about your choice and reasons, I'll pass out some index cards.*

On the index card, write your position and then jot down your reasons for thinking this way. Try to give specific evidence to back up your reasons. Look back at the article for this. And no, you can't choose a neutral "can't decide" position. You've got to take a stand. If you are conflicted, pick the side to which you lean a little bit more.

Give students a couple of minutes to work individually on their cards.

STEP 7 **Whole class creates a lineup.** *It's time for a lineup. We're going to start with those who strongly agree. Everyone who chose that position, grab your card and stand in a straight line right here.* Indicate where the line will begin. Give the first person in line the sign that says STRONGLY AGREE.

Next, we need the people who chose agree. *Grab your cards and continue the line.* Indicate where the line continues. Give the person who started this section the sign that says AGREE. Have both people hold up their signs. Now the rest of the class can see where the line divides between STRONGLY AGREE and AGREE.

Continue the same procedure until all students are lined up and the first person in each line is holding the sign declaring their position.

STEP 8 **Standing pairs compare their position reasoning.** *I'm going to start at one end and divide people into pairs. You should end up talking with someone who has a position similar to yours. Once you know who your partner is, go ahead and compare your reasons and support.*

Once pairs are designated, give them a minute to talk together. If you like, and time permits, call on one or two representatives from each position to explain their viewpoint. However, if time is short, move on to the next step.

STEP 9 **Class folds the line.** *Now you're going to have the chance to talk with a partner who will have a different viewpoint. I'm going to lead one end of the line over to the line's beginning. If the whole line keeps moving down, each of you will have a new partner facing you very soon. Follow me.*

Lead one end of the line to the other so that the line is folded. Then walk back down the line and make sure students are standing directly across from their new partners so that it is visibly clear who is working with whom. If you have the new pairs spread out more, it is less likely that they will morph into off-task clumps.

STEP 10 **Folded pairs compare opinions.** *Talk to your new partner across from you and find out the position they chose and why. Ask them some questions to test their thinking. See if you can persuade your partner to come over to your position. Remember, both partners get to argue their positions. Take turns. Discuss the issues but remain calm. Any questions? Go!*

Monitor for engaged, polite discussion and students focusing on their partners versus nearby friends. Call time as you see discussion winding down.

STEP 11 **Pairs share conversation highlights with class.** *Who had a partner with some interesting ideas about whether or not we should employ military animals?* Hear some ideas. *Anybody change her original opinion? Or lean a little more toward the other side? What was the reason that made a difference in your changing view?* Hear from students who switched.

We really did a lot of thinking today. Tomorrow we're going to read a bit more deeply about a couple of animals that are currently used by the U.S. military: dogs and dolphins. But right now we're just about out of time, so turn to your final partner and thank him for all of the interesting ideas and conversation he offered. Then, return to your seats. Be sure to hang on to today's index card; you'll need it tomorrow.

Day 2

STEP 1 **Reintroduce the topic.** *Yesterday we started discussing the topic of military animals. As promised, today we're going to look at the roles of two animals in more depth.* (Optional: Show photographs of military dogs and dolphins.)

STEP 2 **Previous day's partners meet and count off.** *Before we begin to research, I need our pairs to count off by twos.* Walk around the room and count off, giving each pair (not each individual) a number.

STEP 3 **Distribute text sets by number.** *Pairs, raise your hands if you are number ones.* Scan to see that you have an equal number of ones and twos. If pair number adjustment is needed, take care of that now. Then pass out the dog text set to the number one pairs and the dolphin text set to the number two pairs.

STEP 4 **Students read individually and annotate.** *Before we read, double check with your seat partner that you both have the same text set. Great. Looks good. I'm going to give you some time to individually read and annotate both of the articles on your text set. You'll see that one article focuses more on the positive contributions dogs and dolphins make to the military while the other article describes some of the problems these animals encounter in their military roles. Here's how we're going to mark the text.*

Underline and mark the passage with a plus if it is information that supports using the animal for military service.

Underline and mark the passage with a minus if it is information that describes a problem caused by using the animal for military service.

Any questions? I'll be cruising the room, so if something comes up, ask.

Monitor for the usual: correct annotation, individual work. If a student finishes in record time, direct her to reread and start categorizing the arguments for and against, thinking about which ones are strongest on each side. Since the dog and dolphin text sets each contain two articles to read and annotate, students may need fifteen or twenty minutes for completing the reading; it all depends on your class. Timing is something else you will be monitoring. When most students are finishing up, announce there are two minutes left. Then move on to the next step.

STEP 5 **Students find standing partners.** *Grab your dog or dolphin text set, stand up, and get ready to think on your feet. All of you who have "dogs," stand over there. All of you who have "dolphins," stand over there. Now find a partner on your half of the room that is different than your seated partner. Once you've got a new partner, stay standing but spread out. I should see distinct pairs with plenty of space in between. If I see you're having trouble setting up your pairs, I'll be over to help you.*

Monitor the pair formation, intervening when necessary. Insist that partners stand close together yet put significant space between themselves and other pairs. Otherwise, pairs will distract each other or evolve into larger, off-task groups. This is guaranteed human nature, no matter who the participants are.

STEP 6 **Standing partners neutrally discuss annotation.** *In your new pairs, work to compare the information in these articles. See if you can decide which arguments for or against using military dogs or dolphins are the strongest.*

Monitor for on-task discussion and active use of text and annotation.

STEP 7 **Standing partners discuss personal viewpoints.** *You probably noticed that there are some pretty good reasons on both sides of this controversy. Now I want you to talk with your standing partner about how you personally feel. Where do you stand on this issue? It's okay if you disagree with your partner, but do listen to his arguments. Also, try to find out more about why your partner holds this viewpoint by asking some questions. Remember to take turns hearing what each of you has to say.*

Monitor for on-task, calm discussion, taking turns talking, and asking questions. As conversation winds down, send students back to their seats and their original partners.

I just listened in on some great conversations. It's time to go back to your seats, but first take a moment to thank your standing partner for sharing ideas with you.

STEP 8 **Students return to their original seat partners and compare ideas.** *Now that you're seated, turn to your original partner and recap the conversations you just had with your standing partners. What were the most convincing reasons and support details for each side of this controversy? What side did you ultimately take and why?*

Give partners time to talk.

STEP 9 **Conclude with a whole-class opinion survey.** *After all this reading and discussion, let's take a quick survey. First, raise your hands if you think your animal should be used for military service. Interesting. Put your hands down. Those of you who believe your animal should not be used, it's your turn to vote.*

After the vote, ask students to describe how their opinions did or did not change after further reading on the topic of military animal use.

STEP 10 **Repeat the class lineup (optional).** If you choose not to complete the writing activity but would like a further examination of student opinion on this issue, repeat the lineup activities used in the previous day's lesson.

The readings from days one and two enabled students to develop an informed opinion on this issue. Now they will get to voice that opinion in the form of a letter to the editor.

◀ **Writing Steps: Letter to the Editor**

STEP 1 **Introduce the writing activity.** We have found that many classes get emotionally engaged in this topic. If you are seeing that response, you can open with: *By the time we finished reading and discussing those articles about the military's use of dogs and dolphins, it was pretty hard to ignore how this topic invigorates a variety of opinions. So, while it's still fresh in our minds, let's do a little writing about it in the form of a letter to the editor.*

STEP 2 **Students reread the mentor text from *The Cure for Dreaming* in Lesson 25.** Before beginning the instructions, have students retrieve the lesson from their binders/folders or pass out a fresh copy. They should also get out their dog/dolphin text set and the index card notes from the first day's lesson.

If you used Lesson 25 with the class, open the lesson by saying:

A while ago we analyzed a set of letters to the editor that argued opposing claims regarding women having the right to vote in the United States. Our argument analysis concluded that the second letter, in favor of the vote, had better argument support, so let's take another look at that one.

First, take a minute to reread the letter so that you can get reacquainted with the text. Give students a minute or two.

If you have not already used Lesson 25 with the class, open the lesson by saying:

This is a fictional letter to the editor from a novel set in the time of women's fight to gain the vote in our country. I'll give you a few minutes to read it.

No matter how you began the lesson, continue by saying: *Now go back through the text and underline the first sentence in each paragraph.*

STEP 3 **Partners discuss paragraph sentences.** *Turn to your partner and take a look at each of these sentences, one at a time, in the order they occur. Read each aloud and talk about the idea each opening sentence introduces. Jot your notes on the copy.*

STEP 4 **Whole-class discussion of paragraph sentences.** *Let's take a look at these sentences together and see if we can analyze how they're being used.*

Project the text. Move through this sample letter to the editor, one paragraph at a time, discussing each opening sentence in order. Call on pairs or take volunteers. As you talk about each sentence, be sure that paragraph is adequately projected. Underline the sentence and then jot student observations on how that sentence is working. Point out specific text details via the projection. If you are using a document camera, invite students to bring their text copies up and explain what techniques they noticed the author using.

A model of how this annotation might look appears on page 287. Rather than projecting this model or duplicating it for the class, guide the students to comments like the ones shown here.

STEP 5 **Plan the writing.** *Now we're going to use this letter to the editor as a loose model for our own writing. However, instead of writing about women's suffrage, you're going to write about whether or not you think dogs or dolphins, depending on your text set, should be used for military purposes. Before you begin writing, I want you to think about these questions.*

> ***Planning Your Argument***
> 1. Which details best support my viewpoint?
> 2. What arguments would the opposing viewpoint use?
> 3. How can I point out illogical elements and contradictions in those arguments?
> 4. What action do I want readers to take after they finish my letter?

Look over the articles you read on dogs or dolphins. It should be easy to find information for your letter because we used pluses and minuses to code it yesterday. The pluses stood for reasons to use animals and the minuses were reasons why we shouldn't. Also look back on the index

Craft Annotation: Opening Sentences

To Judge Acklen:

You state that women were made for domestic duties alone. Have you ever stopped to observe the responsibilities involved with domestic duties?

—Asks a question.

—Tries to turn the opposition's assumption around.

—Lists specific examples

What better person to understand the administration of a country than an individual who spends her days mediating quarrels, balancing household budgets, organizing and executing three complex meals, and ensuring all rooms, appliances, deliveries, clothing, guests, family members, and pets are tended to and functioning the way they ought to be? I do not know of any other job in the world that so closely resembles the presidency itself.

—Defines the argument focus (women) in positive terms

—Uses the first sentence to show a contrast in favor of her argument

Moreover, females are raised to become rational, industrious, fair, and compassionate human beings. Males are taught to sow their wild oats and run free while they're able. Which gender is truly the most prepared to make decisions about the management of a country? Do you want a responsible individual or a rambunctious one choosing the fate of our government?

—Shows an illogical contradiction in opposing argument

—Discusses subject (one's children) in order to play upon emotions

You insinuate that women's minds are easily muddled, yet you entrust us with the rearing of your children, America's future. Mothers are our first teachers. Mothers are the voices of reason who instill the nation's values in our youth. Mothers are the ones who raise the politicians for whom they are not allowed to vote. Why would you let an easily muddled creature take on such important duties? Why not hire men to bring up your sons and daughters?

I can already hear you arguing that women's bodies were designed for childbearing, but that is not true, sir. Our bodies may have been built for birthing children and nourishing them during their first meals, but it is our minds that are doing the largest share of the work. On a daily basis, we women prove that our brains are sharp and quick, yet you are too blind to see our intelligence.

—Predicts an opposition argument

—Openly states that assumption is inaccurate/untrue

Furthermore, you have no need to fear that we would forgo our domestic duties if we were to become voting citizens, for we have been trained all our lives to balance a multitude of tasks. We do not let our homes fall into ruin simply because we have been given one more item to accomplish. Worry more about the males who have only one job and no household chores. Their minds are more likely to stray than ours.

—Calms opposing viewpoint's fears

—Explains why he is wrong but should not worry

—Introduces a new worry related to opponent's viewpoint

Do you call your own mother "undereducated" and "ignorant," Judge Acklen? Was her mind in too much of a muddle to keep your childhood household intact? Was she so easily confused that she was unable to raise a boy who would one day become a judge? I think not. Your mother was undoubtedly a quick-witted, accountable individual who would probably make a far better president than the pampered male you gentlemen vote into office this Tuesday.

—Personalizes opponent's argument

—Mentions his mother

—Shows how his viewpoint insults those that he cares about

—Shows a contradiction

card notes you wrote after reading "10 Ways Animals Have Served the Military." Those cards might give you some argument ideas as well. Give students three to five minutes for quiet study. As they work, watch for engaged planning and rereading.

STEP 6 **Pairs discuss their writing plans.** *Turn to your partner and tell her about your position, support, and answers to the opposition. Be sure you answer all four of the posted questions in some detail. Partners, listen carefully. If you notice a question that doesn't have much of an answer, ask some questions that will help your partner's thinking. Also, writers, if you're stuck and need some suggestions, ask your partner what they think. Helping each other is totally okay.*

I'm going to give you about five minutes to talk about your writing plans. I will signal you when the time is half over and you'll need to switch roles. Any questions?

As usual, monitor for accountable talk, moving through the questions, and referring back to the texts. Don't be afraid to do quick check-ins with pairs to see if they have any questions.

STEP 7 **Individuals write their letters to the editor.** *While you are working, I'll be checking in with you, so be ready to explain your writing ideas and where you are in the piece. Also, if you have a question, don't be afraid to ask. Remember to use the letter to the editor piece as a guide for organizing your own letter. And don't forget to look back to your military animal articles for good details and information that you can include. What questions do you have?*

Finally, while writing, if you realize you don't like something, just cross out, rewrite, and move on. These are "sloppy copies" that will only be shared out loud. As long as you can read what you wrote, you'll be fine.

This step will require some active monitoring on your part. Look over shoulders, observe if the writing is flowing, and notice how kids are using their resources. Make a beeline toward the writers who look stuck or are not referring to the texts. Here are some quick mini-conference questions you might use.

- What's your position on using animals in the military?
- Which parts of the articles support your position?
- What would someone from the opposing viewpoint say?

You don't have to ask all of these questions if you see a stuck writer; probably one will suffice. The goal is to just get them talking and thinking.

Give kids at least ten minutes for the writing. As the speed writers finish up, encourage them to return to their pieces for revision and editing. If most students are still working ten minutes in, adding a few more minutes is fine. Offer writers a two-minute warning when they need to bring their pieces to a conclusion.

STEP 8 **Pairs form groups of four and read their letters aloud.** Direct partners to form groups of four so that you have dogs and dolphins represented. Project the Steps for Giving Writing Feedback.

Steps for Giving Writing Feedback

1. Writer reads piece while other group members listen silently.
2. Listeners remember the parts they really liked (word, phrase, sentence, detail).
3. After reading aloud, each member points out something in the piece they really liked. Ideally, each member points out something different.
4. After all listeners have "pointed out," the writer thanks his audience.
5. Be sure to *completely* finish listening and responding to one writer's piece before moving on to the next writer.
6. Next writer reads aloud and the process is repeated.

From what I read looking over your shoulders, your letters show some strong feelings and conviction. In your groups of four, I want each writer to take a turn reading his/her letter aloud. When it's your turn to share, be sure to read your piece authoritatively and enthusiastically. Show that you care about this topic. Group audience members, it is your job to listen carefully and be ready to point out a word, phrase, sentence, or detail that you really liked. Once the writer is finished reading, go around the group and listeners, tell the writer what you liked about the piece. Any questions? I'll keep the steps for reading, listening, and responding up on the board.

While groups read their letters aloud, move around, sit in on the groups, and enjoy being a listener. As groups finish up, direct them to go back and talk further about what made each letter interesting and persuasive.

STEP 9 **Groups elect a member to read his/her piece aloud to the class.** *It's time for the rest of the class to hear these letters. I wish we had time for us to hear every one of them, but we don't. So, each group will need to elect a member to read his or her piece aloud to the class.*

Give groups a minute to determine their readers. Monitor discussions and jot down who's going from each group so that there is no confusion or wasted time when a group is called upon to share.

When it is time for sharing, you may choose to have the writer stay with his group and stand up or you can have the entire group come to the front of the class with the writer.

When I call on each group, make sure your elected writer is ready to read aloud. Listeners, your first job is to be a great audience. Make sure that you are quiet and attentive while the writer is reading aloud. Then, when they've concluded, offer a big round of applause. Your second job is to consider how each piece affects your viewpoint and what techniques the writers used that made you either strongly agree or strongly disagree with them. How did each writer use facts and data? Appeal to your sense of right and wrong? Use humor? Tuck these moves away in the back of your mind for the next time you write an argument.

Variation ▶ We demonstrated the use of two simultaneous text sets; this lesson could be easily streamlined by having all members of a class read only one.

Extension ▶ If your students seem really invested/concerned about the use of animals in the military, you might want to spend some extra class time polishing up their letters and emailing them off to the local newspaper, where they may or may not be published. While some newspapers severely limit letters that appear in their print edition, publications often have a more generous online policy.

WHAT MIGHT THE WRITING LOOK LIKE?

Here's an example of what a student might produce for this assignment.

Dogs Are Needed in the Military

If you've ever had a dog, you already know how smart and devoted a canine can be. That's the exact reason why dogs are working as "four-legged" soldiers with our troops in the Middle East.

Unlike people, dogs have a keen sense of smell and can be trained to detect IEDs (improvised explosive devices). Working with their handlers, dogs prevent soldiers from unwittingly detonating bombs that could kill or maim them. Non-military people sometimes worry about a dog's safety in these situations, but they forget that a dog is always on leash, in close company with its soldier handler. No soldier is going to take chances with his dog since a careless risk will harm him as well.

When a dog has reached the end of his deployment and is retired, it is not discarded. Soldiers develop tight bonds with their brethren and it is no different between handlers and their dogs. 90 percent of retired military dogs are adopted by their handlers. The remaining dogs are adopted by civilians who have been on adoption waiting lists for more than a year.

Granted, some dogs return to "the world" with problems similar to human soldiers: physical injuries or post-traumatic stress disorder. But these dogs are loved by their adopted families who try their utmost to give them the very best of care.

Even though dogs on the frontlines face a risk, the risk soldiers would face without their help would be even greater.

mother nature network

10 Ways Animals Have Served the Military

Laura Moss

1. Leg-cuffing sea lions

Trained sea lions, part of the U.S. Navy's Marine Mammal Program, locate and tag mines just like dolphins, but that's not all these "Navy Seals" do—they also cuff underwater intruders. The sea lions carry a spring clamp in their mouths that can be attached to a swimmer or diver by simply pressing it against the person's leg. In fact, the sea lions are so fast that the clamp is on before the swimmer is even aware of it. Once a person is clamped, sailors aboard ships can pull the swimmer out of the water by the rope attached to the clamp. These specially trained sea lions, part of the Navy's Shallow Water Intruder Detection System, patrol Navy bases and were even deployed to protect ships from terrorists in the Persian Gulf.

2. Bat bombs

Toward the end of World War II, the Air Force was looking for a more effective way to attack Japanese cities when Dr. Lytle S. Adams, a dental surgeon, contacted the White House with an idea. Adams suggested strapping small incendiary devices to bats, loading them into cages shaped like bombshells and dropping them from a plane. Bats would then escape from the cages and find their way into factories and other buildings where they would rest until their miniature bombs exploded.

The U.S. military began developing these "bat bombs" in the early 1940s, but the first test went awry when the bats set fire to an Air Force base in Carlsbad, New Mexico. After that, the project was turned over to the Navy, which completed a successful experiment. More tests were scheduled for the summer of 1944, but the program was canceled because of its slow progress.

3. War pigeons

Homing pigeons were widely used by both American and British forces during World War II. In fact, the U.S. Army had an entire Pigeon Breeding and Training Center at Fort Monmouth, New Jersey, where the pigeons were trained to carry small capsules containing messages, maps, photographs and cameras. Military historians claim that more than 90 percent of all pigeon-carried messages sent by the U.S. Army during the war were received.

The birds even participated in the D-Day invasion because troops operated under radio silence. The pigeons sent information about German positions on Normandy beaches and reported back on the success of the mission. In fact, homing pigeons played such an important military role that 32 were awarded the Dickin Medal, Britain's highest award for animal valor.

4. Insect cyborgs

Insect cyborgs might sound like something out of a science-fiction movie, but the U.S. Department of Defense is developing such creatures as part of its Hybrid Insect Initiative. Scientists implant electronic controls into insects' bodies during the early stages of metamorphosis and allow tissue to grow around them. The insects can then be tracked, controlled and used to gather or transmit information. For example, a caterpillar could carry a microphone to record conversations or a gas sensor to detect a chemical attack.

5. Dolphin spies

Dolphins have been serving in the U.S. Navy for more than 40 years as part of the Navy's Marine Mammal Program, and they were used during the Vietnam War and Operation Iraqi Freedom. These highly intelligent animals are trained to detect, locate and mark mines—not to mention suspicious swimmers and divers.

For example, in 2009 a group of bottlenose dolphins began patrolling the area around Naval Base Kitsap-Bangor in Washington. The marine mammals are on the lookout 24 hours a day, seven days a week for swimmers or divers in the base's restricted waters.

What happens if a dolphin finds an intruder? The dolphin touches a sensor on a boat to alert its handler, and the handler then places a strobe light or noisemaker on the dolphin's nose. The dolphin is trained to swim to the intruder, bump him or her from behind to knock the device off its nose and swim away while military personnel take over.

6. Bomb-sniffing bees

Honeybees are natural-born sniffers with antennae able to sense pollen in the wind and track it down to specific flowers, so bees are now being trained to recognize the scents of bomb ingredients. When the bees pick up a suspicious odor with their antennae, they flick their proboscises—a tubular feeding organ that extends from their mouths.

In practice, a honeybee bomb-detection unit would look like a simple box stationed outside airport security or a train platform. Inside the box, bees would be strapped into tubes and exposed to puffs of air where they could constantly check for the faint scent of a bomb. A video camera linked to pattern-recognition software would alert authorities when the bees started waving their proboscises in unison.

7. Terrorist-fighting gerbils

MI5, the United Kingdom's counter-intelligence and security agency, considered using a team of trained gerbils to detect terrorists flying into Britain during the 1970s. According to Sir Stephen Lander, the organization's former director, the Israelis had put the idea into practice, placing gerbil cages at security checks at the Tel Aviv airport. A fan wafted the scent of suspects into the gerbils' cage, and the gerbils were trained to press a lever if they detected high levels of adrenalin.

The system was never implemented at UK airports because the Israelis were forced to abandon it after it was discovered that the gerbils couldn't discern between terrorists and passengers who were just scared of flying.

8. Anti-tank dogs

Anti-tank dogs were used by the Soviet Union during World War II to fight German tanks. Dogs with explosives harnessed to their backs were trained to seek food under tanks—when the dog was underneath the vehicle a detonator would go off, triggering an explosion. While some Soviet sources claim that about 300 German tanks were damaged by the dogs, many say this is simply propaganda trying to justify the program.

In fact, the Soviet anti-tank dog had several problems. Many dogs refused to dive under moving tanks during battle because they had been trained with stationary tanks, a fuel-saving measure. Gunfire also scared many of the dogs away, and they would run back to the soldiers' trenches, often detonating the charge upon jumping in. To prevent this, the returning dogs were shot—often by the people who had sent them—which made trainers unwilling to work with new dogs.

9. Spy cats

During the Cold War, the CIA attempted to transform an ordinary domestic cat into a sophisticated bugging device as part of Operation Acoustic Kitty. The idea was to surgically alter cats so they could eavesdrop on Soviet conversations from park benches and windowsills.

The project began in 1961 when the CIA implanted a battery and a microphone into a cat and turned its tail into an antenna. Finally, after five years, several surgeries, and intensive training, the cat was ready for its first field test.

The CIA drove the cat to a Soviet compound on Wisconsin Avenue in Washington, D.C. and let it out of a parked van across the street. The cat walked into the road and was immediately hit by a taxi. Operation Acoustic Kitty was declared a failure and completely abandoned in 1967.

10. Soldier bear

Voytek was just a baby brown bear when the Second Polish Transport Company found him wandering the hills of Iran in 1943. The soldiers took him in, feeding him condensed milk, and before long he became a part of the unit. As Voytek grew into a 6-foot, 250-pound bear, he was trained to carry mortar shells and boxes of ammunition during battle, and in 1944 he was officially enlisted in the Polish Army—complete with name, rank and number. The bear traveled with his unit and carried ammunition to soldiers under fire. After the war, the Edinburgh Zoo became Voytek's new home and he lived there until he died in 1963.

Canines in Combat: Military Working Dogs

The U.S. Armed Forces' 2,500 military working dogs detect mortars, find drugs and protect their fellow troops on bases around the world—and their training begins at Joint Base San Antonio-Lackland

DENISE K. SYPESTEYN

Air Force Tech Sgt. Aaron Lee remembers it well. His platoon was patrolling a village during a tour in Iraq in 2004. They cleared the area and were heading back to base when his partner, Dino, noticed something. "Dino was barking and pulling me toward a nearby ditch," Lee recalls. "We found three insurgents hiding there with mortars. They were planning to attack the base. Because of Dino's good work they were apprehended and their mission thwarted."

The first sentry dogs were trained at Lackland in 1958. It's now home to the Department of Defense Military Working Dog Program (MWD). The 341st Training Squadron, part of which is referred to as the "Dog School," procures and trains dogs to protect service members in various combat situations. The dogs must exhibit focused, aggressive behavior, with a heightened sense of smell and a strong desire to work for reward before they are assigned to military services worldwide. The squadron's trainers are experienced security forces airmen and previous handlers from each branch of the military. The facility now has 62 training areas with more than 1,000 dogs and a training staff of approximately 125 Army, Navy,

Marine Corps and Air Force personnel.

German shepherds and Labradors are commonly used, but the Belgian Malinois has proven to be one of the most outstanding working dogs used in military service. Around 85 percent of military working dogs are purchased in Germany or the Netherlands, where they have been breeding dogs for military purposes for hundreds of years. In addition, the Air Force Security Forces Center, Army Veterinary Corps and the 341st Training Squadron combine efforts to raise their own dogs; nearly 15 percent of all military working dogs are now bred here.

"It's a contingency plan," says Dr. Stewart Hilliard, chief of MWD evaluation and breeding at Lackland's 341st training facility. "These dogs are among our most effective counter measures against terrorists and explosives. We are uncomfortable being solely dependent on Europe for such a critical resource. The global market is becoming very competitive to purchase these working dogs, so since 1998 we have been scaling up our own breeding program."

The Malinois pups that are bred here are sent to foster homes in the area at the age of 6-8 weeks where they learn socialization skills in a home environment. When they are 7-9 months, they are taken into observation for consideration as a military working dog. Only puppies that exhibit a strong drive, are adaptable to different environments and respond to reward-for-work motivation move into the pre-training program. "We are looking for extraordinary dogs," says Hilliard. "Not all dogs have the natural characteristics to be fearless and brave. When the pups we keep for training turn 1 year old and pass advanced training, they will be

training they learn to apprehend someone if told to, attack on command, search a building and help in the detection of explosives or drugs.

About 500 dogs are deployed at any one time, but at some point every working dog's career ends. It can be due to age, injuries, or the loss of desire to do the tasks. Sometimes the dogs go on to work in another federal agency or law enforcement. If their health doesn't allow them to work, they are placed for adoption. Handlers adopt about 90 percent,

> "These dogs are among our most effective counter measures against terrorists and explosives. We are uncomfortable being solely dependent on Europe for such a critical resource. The global market is becoming very competitive to purchase these working dogs, so since 1998 we have been scaling up our own breeding program."

certified and deployed for dual purposes, as counter measures for explosives or narcotics detection and patrol for apprehension and search for the enemy."

Handlers work to build puppies' sense of drive, develop their biting grip and increase their environmental and social stability during training. Most important is their "play drive." Once that drive is heightened, they begin detection training by searching for a play object (often a rubber KONG toy) with an odor. "We evaluate the dog on how strong the bite is on the toy and how hard they will work to find the KONG when hidden," says Marine Sgt. Sam Corns, one of only nine master trainers in the 341st Training Squad.

To train the dogs to attack on command, handlers use a hard sleeve called a "bite wrap," covering their forearm. The dog must maintain a biting grip until commanded to let go. In advanced

but there is a long waiting list of civilians wanting to adopt retired military working dogs, too. "The average wait time for a K-9 to get its new home is about nine days, but the wait list to adopt is more than one year," says Collen McGee, chief of public affairs for the 37th Training Wing. "Never is a dog waiting for a home—it is always homes that are waiting for a retiring K-9."

There is a unique bond between a military working dog and his handler, which is why so many stay together in retirement. Although advised not to become emotionally attached to these dogs, it can be difficult for handlers not to. "You always remember your first dog," says Lee, whose first dog, Dino, had to be put down due to hip dysplasia. "But I'm looking forward to adopting another dog I worked with named Reggie, who is retiring soon."

Military Working Dogs face Tough Re-entry into Civilian Life

Anne Leigh, WrapUp Media

A Dog's Story

Sergeant 1st Class Matthew Bessler can pinpoint the event that triggered post-traumatic stress disorder (PTSD) in his military working dog (MWD), Mike, while both were stationed in Basra Province, Iraq. Bessler, an Iraqi Intelligence officer, and two other U.S. soldiers attempted a nighttime river crossing in a small inflatable boat in order to investigate a pocket of insurgent activity. Halfway across, the boat began sinking, so Bessler jumped to action, attempting to save those who could not swim: the Intelligence officer and his MWD, Mike. Gasping for air and struggling to free himself from thick kelp, Bessler did manage to save Mike, but the Intelligence officer drowned when his arm slipped from Bessler's grasp.

Soon after that horrific incident, Mike stopped sniffing for IEDs (improvised explosive devices); he was anxious and distracted. When Bessler took Mike to the 10th Group's lead dog trainer, he recognized that Mike needed to be retired; soldiers could no longer depend on Mike to keep them safe.

Luckily, Bessler and Mike were able to return together to Fort Carson, near Colorado Springs. The Department of Defense (DOD) is only required to retire MWDs to noncombat military bases, but not necessarily to the United States. While the DOD can allow individuals or groups to return retired military dogs to the U.S. (a task of complicated paperwork and expenses totaling up to $6,000), the DOD is under no obligation to shoulder any of that cost. Dogs that remain overseas are highly unlikely to be reunited with their handlers, a great disservice to the handlers and the dogs.

Back in Colorado, Bessler waited for Mike's adoption papers to be cleared so that he could bring K-9 Mike 5 #07-257 (Mike's official military name) home. In the meantime, Bessler visited Mike every day at his kennel at Fort Carson. It was Bessler's visits that kept Mike alive: the Belgian Malinois refused to eat unless Bessler was there with him. Those visits also forced Bessler, a highly decorated Army Ranger, to recognize his own PTSD, its severity necessitating his retirement as well.

After three weeks of visits, Mike's adoption was finalized and Bessler took him home to his farm. However, like Bessler, Mike's PTSD worsened. Mike engaged in self-destructive behaviors, was unable to focus, and was spooked by loud noises. The dog's symptoms did not decrease until six months after he was prescribed Prozac. Mike's medical care cost Bessler almost $12,000. Eventually, Bessler was able to retrain Mike as his service dog, helping Bessler function in "the world" when his PTSD anxiety and panic become overwhelming.

Military Working Dog PTSD

At the height of the wars in Afghanistan and Iraq, the U.S. military had roughly 3,000 dog-and-handler teams on active duty. According to Dr. Walter Burghardt Jr., retired chief of Behavior Medicine at the Daniel H. Holland Military Working Dogs Hospital at Lackland Airforce Base, about 5 to 10 percent of combat dogs will experience PTSD. It is only recently that PTSD in four-legged warriors has been recognized, and studying it is still difficult since dogs' health and deployment histories are not tracked like that of human soldiers.

The symptoms of canine PTSD vary. While still deployed, suffering dogs will no longer fulfill their wartime tasks. Some may completely refuse to work but others will attempt to continue in an unfocused manner. Either way, their behavior changes put themselves and the men they work with at risk. Once retired, former MWDs with PTSD may become clingy and timid, hypervigilant, or overly aggressive. Others avoid buildings or other physical settings that trigger memories of a distressing incident.

Treating combat dogs for PTSD is even more challenging than alleviating symptoms in humans because dog patients cannot describe their exact symptoms or the traumatizing events they continue to relive; veterinarians and handlers can only guess. Treatment, as mentioned earlier, often involves prescriptions for the same medications that treat panic attacks in humans. Really serious cases often require the dogs to go through "desensitization counterconditioning." This involves gradually exposing the dog, at a safe distance, to the stimulus that provokes panic. If the dog does not react, it is rewarded and the stimulus is moved a bit closer. If treatment is successful, eventually the dog does not react to the stimulus even when it is in close proximity. Sadly, when treatment fails, overly aggressive dogs are eventually euthanized.

The military attempts to treat dog PTSD in order to redeploy them. However, if a dog continues to show symptoms of PTSD after three months of treatment, it is transferred to different duties or retired. In the end, PTSD appears to be a condition that for humans and dogs is managed, not cured. According to Nicholas H. Dodman, director of the animal behavior clinic at the Cummings School of Veterinary Medicine at Tufts University, "Dogs never forget."

SSC PACIFIC | TEAM | PRESS | PRODUCTS AND SERVICES | CAREERS | CONTACT

U.S. Navy Marine Mammal Program (NMMP)

www.public.navy.mil

Everyone is familiar with security patrol dogs. You may even know that because of their exceptionally keen sense of smell, dogs are also used to detect drugs and bombs, or land mines. But a dog would not be effective in finding a sea mine. Sea mines are sophisticated, expensive weapons that are designed to work in the ocean where they can sink ships, destroy landing craft, and kill or injure personnel. Sea mines are made so that they cannot be set off easily by wave action or marine animals growing on or bumping into them. If undetected, sea mines can be deadly, destructive weapons.

But just as the dog's keen sense of smell makes it ideal for detecting land mines, the U.S. Navy has found that the biological sonar of dolphins, called echolocation, makes them uniquely effective at locating sea mines so they can be avoided or removed. Other marine mammals like the California sea lion also have demonstrated the ability to mark and retrieve objects for the Navy in the ocean. In fact, marine mammals are so important to the Navy that there is an entire program dedicated to studying, training, and deploying them.

In the Fleet's operational Marine Mammal Systems (MMS), the Navy uses dolphins and sea lions to find and mark the location of underwater objects. Dolphins, capable of repetitive deep diving, are essential because their exceptional biological sonar is unmatched by hardware sonars in detecting objects in the water column and on the sea floor.

Mine Hunting Systems

Enemy sea mines have been responsible for 14 of the 19 Navy ships destroyed or damaged since 1950. That is why the Navy created dolphin mine hunting systems. In the operation of these systems, a dolphin waits to receive a cue from its handler before it begins to search a specific area using its biological sonar called echolocation. When a dolphin echolocates, it emits a series of clicks that bounce off an object and return to the dolphin, allowing a dolphin to construct a mental image of the object. The dolphin reports back to its handler, giving one response if a target object is detected and a different response if no target object is detected. If a mine-like target is detected, the handler sends the dolphin to mark the location of the object so it can be avoided by Navy vessels or dealt with by Navy divers.

Frequently Asked Questions

Is the Navy exempt from following regulations for the keeping of marine mammals?

No. The Navy is subject to all federal laws regarding the protection and humane treatment of marine mammals. These include the Marine Mammal Protection Act (MMPA) and the Animal Welfare Act (AWA). The AWA is administered by the Department of Agriculture and ensures the humane care and treatment of marine mammals in aquariums, zoos, and research facilities. The Navy is responsible for meeting all requirements of these laws regarding acquisition, care and treatment of its marine mammals, and not only meets but exceeds them and leads the industry in many cases. Congress has provided the Navy with exemptions to a few specific requirements in support of national security, but none related to the care and well-being of the animals.

Does the Navy train its dolphins for offensive warfare, including attacks on ships and human swimmers or divers?

No. The Navy does not now train, nor has it ever trained, its marine mammals to harm or injure humans in any fashion or to carry weapons to destroy ships. A popular movie in 1973 ("The Day of the Dolphin") and a number of charges and claims by animal rights organizations have resulted in theories and sometimes actual beliefs that Navy dolphins are assigned attack missions. This is absolutely false. Since dolphins cannot discern the difference between enemy and friendly vessels, or enemy and friendly divers and swimmers, it would not be wise to give that kind of decision authority to an animal. The animals are trained to detect, locate, and mark all mines or all swimmers in an area of interest or concern, and are not trained to distinguish between what we would refer to as good or bad. That decision is always left to humans.

Who sets the care standards for the animals in the NMMP?

An instruction from the Secretary of the Navy requires that the Navy's "marine mammals will be provided the highest quality of humane care and treatment." The NMMP facilities in San Diego are state-of-the-art, including the food storage and preparation facilities, animal enclosures, and veterinary medical facilities. Regularly scheduled physical exams, balanced diets, an extensive database of health records, monthly briefs to all personnel on animal care topics, and a high level of professionalism mixed with genuine compassion all contribute to the health and welfare of the animals.

How are animals moved to and from remote deployment sites?

Over short distances, animals are trained to either swim alongside a small boat or to ride in the boat itself. For long distance trips, animals can be transported by sea in large naval vessels or by air in planes or helicopters. For these trips, dolphins are placed in fleece-lined stretchers that are suspended in fiberglass containers filled with enough water to comfortably support the weight of the animal. On these long transports, a veterinarian oversees the comfort and health care of all the animals while each animal is constantly monitored by an experienced trainer or handler. Upon arrival at their destinations, animals are housed in temporary facilities that are much like those in San Diego. In addition, a portable veterinary clinic accompanies the animals to provide veterinarians with everything they need to care for the health of the animals.

Navy's Dolphin Use Raises Questions

Anne Leigh, WrapUp Media

Military dolphins trained in mine detection made their first appearance in 1960. Charmed by this cetacean's abilities, which far exceeded human divers and other underwater apparatus, President John F. Kennedy expanded the program. Since then, dolphins have guarded ammunition piers during the Vietnam War as well as naval vessels off the coast of Bahrain in the Middle East. While former Navy SEAL Brandon Webb claims that dolphins have been trained to track enemies and kill them via gas needle injection, this rumor has never been substantiated. According to a Los Angeles Times article published in March of 2015, the Navy trains ninety dolphins in a program run by the Space and Naval Warfare System Pacific, located on San Diego Bay.

Curently, "war" dolphins are mostly used for mine detection in the Persian Gulf. Their keen echolocation, a sensory system that enables dolphins to transmit sound waves and "read" the returning echoes, allows them to distinguish natural and manmade objects underwater. It is this ability, along with their intelligence, that makes them so well suited for mine

> **The high intelligence and "sociability" of dolphins lends them to training and deployment, yet it is this same intelligence that raises ethical concern.**

detection. When a dolphin locates a mine, it returns for an acoustic transponder, which it deposits near the mine so that divers can find and remove it. Navy handlers assure the public that the dolphins' risks are minimal since they are trained to avoid getting too close to a detected mine. Also, modern-day sea mines are designed to detonate only when a large metallic surface—the hull of a ship—passes by.

Despite these assurances, animal rights activists question the U.S. Navy's use of marine animals in any wartime capacity. Stephanie Boyles, a wildlife biologist for PETA (People for the Ethical Treatment of Animals), argues that war is man's creation, no animal can volunteer to serve, and any animal "serving" cannot be fully aware of its endangerment. From the dolphin's perspective, it is playing a game, not risking its life detecting lethal weapons.

The high intelligence and "sociability" of dolphins lends them to training and deployment, yet it is this same intelligence that raises ethical concern. Dolphin scientist Thomas White points out that dolphins' acoustic skills enable them to maintain elaborate social and communicative structures; these strong emotional and empathic ties create personal identities. Dolphins are cognitively sophisticated; each has a signature whistle, its "name." Research by University of Chicago professor Dr. Jason Bruck shows that dolphins recognize the whistles of those they once knew for their entire lives.

Marine biologist Jeff Schweitzer believes humans choose to define and measure intelligence based on our greatest strengths and diminish the intelligence of other species in the process. In the case of dolphins, if self-generated sonar used to explore and communicate were included in a definition of intelligence, humans would not be considered particularly smart! Mark Xitco, supervisor of the navy program's scientific and veterinary support branch says, "They [dolphins] are large, smart, socially complex mammals with a mind of their own. We can't force them to do anything they don't want to do." Might this positive judgment be inaccurate due to a limited, human point of view?

Aside from being blown to bits by a sensitive mine, a military "career" jeopardizes dolphins in other ways. It disrupts their natural community, disconnecting tight social arrangements that result in lifetime bonds. For highly intelligent, creative, and social creatures, forced "enlistment" removes their sense of control. That loss of control includes a predictable environment. Though military dolphins are trained in San Diego, they can be deployed anywhere in the world. Deployed dolphins can face a long, disorienting trip. Arriving at their destination means being released into unfamiliar habitats that could possibly expose them to inclement weather, unsuitable temperatures, or life-threatening illnesses for which they have not built an immunity.

Finally, the use of military dolphins endangers the entire dolphin species, not just the warriors. In wartime, an enemy would be unable to tell which ones are "just dolphins" versus ones who pose a threat. The easiest way to solve the problem: mass slaughter.

The U.S. Navy Marine Mammal Program assures that it only deploys dolphins from their captive breeding program, and wild dolphins have not been used since 1999. The navy has also been promising to phase out this program as soon as equally sophisticated antimine robotics become feasible. However, in 2002 NBC reported that the Pentagon plans to back the program through 2020. While little is discussed openly about the U.S. military's use of dolphins, it seems the Pentagon has no intention of retiring its conscripts any time soon.

UNTIL WE MEET AGAIN

Thanks for stopping by and thinking with us. This is our sixth book written together, and we have ideas for at least a couple more before one of us cries *Uncle!* But it is all of you—our colleagues—who keep us fresh as we crisscross the country and talk with you about what is *really* working in your classrooms as you help kids find the rewards of reading and writing. Please continue to share your success stories with us (we'll also take requests, complaints, and well-worded rants).

In 2013, when *Texts and Lessons for Teaching Literature* was published, we declared, "This is a tough time to be a teacher." Here in 2016, our jobs haven't gotten measurably easier, though the newly passed Every Student Succeeds Act promises a bit more flexibility in our profession. Maybe we'll gradually recapture time for more real reading, writing, and discussion.

In the meantime, we will all soldier on, doing our best with whatever we've got, always keeping what's right for students front and center.

Also, if you stick with teaching long enough, you will eventually hear from former students who are now adults. And you know what? They will remember and thank you for those learning experiences that still shine brightly in their memories. We suggest that you savor those testimonies when you face tough times.

Until next time,

Smokey Daniels
Santa Fe, New Mexico
@smokeylit

Nancy Steineke
Brookfield, Illinois
@nsteineke

SKILLS ADDRESSED IN THE LESSONS

The list below shows skills addressed in each lesson and its research projects for extended writing.

Lesson Number	GETTING STARTED		REACHING AND ENGAGING STUDENTS			WRITING TO LEARN			
	Building Collaboration	Building Writing Fluency	Engaging Kids with Content	Supporting Struggling Readers/Writers	Supporting ELs as Readers and Writers	Note Taking and Capturing Thinking	Discussing Ideas	Short Writing	Coauthoring
1	●	●	●	●	●		●	●	
2	●	●	●	●	●		●	●	●
3	●	●	●	●	●	●	●	●	●
4	●	●	●	●			●	●	●
5	●	●	●				●	●	●
6	●	●	●		●	●	●	●	●
7	●	●	●	●	●	●	●	●	
8	●	●	●		●	●	●	●	
9	●	●				●	●	●	●
10	●	●	●	●	●	●	●	●	
11	●	●	●	●	●	●	●	●	
12	●	●	●	●	●	●	●	●	
13	●	●	●	●	●	●	●	●	
14	●	●	●			●	●	●	
15	●	●	●	●	●	●	●	●	
16	●	●	●	●	●	●	●	●	
17	●	●	●	●	●	●	●	●	
18	●	●	●			●	●	●	●
19	●	●	●	●	●	●	●	●	●
20	●	●	●	●			●	●	●
21	●	●	●			●	●	●	●
22	●	●	●	●	●	●	●	●	●
23	●	●	●		●	●	●	●	●
24	●	●	●		●	●	●	●	●
25	●	●				●	●	●	●
26	●	●				●	●	●	
27	●	●				●	●	●	●
28	●	●		●	●	●	●	●	●
29	●	●				●	●	●	
30	●	●	●		●	●	●	●	●
31	●	●				●	●	●	●
32	●	●	●	●	●	●	●	●	●
33	●	●	●	●	●	●	●	●	
34	●	●	●			●	●	●	
35	●	●	●			●	●	●	●
Chapter 11	●	●	●			●	●	●	●
Chapter 12	●	●	●			●	●	●	●
Chapter 13	●	●	●			●	●		

	CRAFTING WRITING			COMPREHENSION STRATEGIES THAT INFORM WRITING										
Lesson Number	Narrative Writing	Explanatory/Expository Writing	Persuasive/Argumentative Writing	Close Reading/Critical Viewing	Making Inferences	Determining Importance	Promoting Metacognition	Self-Monitoring Reading	Recognizing Claims and Support	Using Background Knowledge	Reading Complex Text	Reading/Rereading with a Purpose	Summarizing	Identifying Author's Purposes
1	●	●	●	●	●	●	●			●	●			●
2	●	●	●	●							●			
3	●	●	●	●	●	●		●			●	●		
4	●	●	●	●						●				
5	●	●	●	●	●	●				●	●			
6	●	●	●							●	●			
7	●	●	●		●	●				●	●			
8	●	●	●		●	●				●	●			
9	●	●	●	●		●			●	●	●	●	●	●
10	●	●	●	●							●	●		
11	●	●	●	●	●	●	●	●		●	●	●		
12	●	●	●		●	●			●	●	●	●	●	●
13	●	●	●		●	●	●			●	●	●		
14	●	●	●	●	●	●		●			●	●		
15	●	●	●	●	●	●	●	●	●		●	●	●	●
16	●	●	●	●	●	●				●	●	●	●	●
17	●	●	●	●	●	●				●	●	●		
18	●	●	●	●	●	●		●		●	●	●		
19	●	●	●	●	●	●	●	●		●	●	●		
20	●	●	●							●	●	●		
21	●	●	●	●	●	●				●	●		●	●
22	●	●	●		●	●		●	●	●	●	●		●
23	●	●	●		●	●	●	●	●	●	●	●	●	
24	●	●	●		●	●	●	●	●		●	●	●	
25	●	●	●		●	●		●		●	●	●		●
26	●	●	●	●	●	●		●		●	●	●		●
27	X	X	●							●	●			
28	●	●	●		●	●	●	●			●	●		
29	●	●	●	●	●	●					●	●	●	
30	●	●	●	●	●	●	●	●	●		●	●	●	●
31	●	●	●	●	●	●	●	●			●	●	●	
32	●	●	●	●	●	●		●			●	●	●	
33	●	●	●							●	●			
34	●	●	●	●	●	●	●	●			●	●		●
35	●	●	●	●	●	●		●		●	●	●	●	●
Chapter 11	●			●	●	●				●	●	●	●	
Chapter 12		●		●	●	●			●	●	●	●	●	●
Chapter 13			●	●	●	●				●	●	●	●	●

APPENDIX 2

COMMON CORE WRITING STANDARDS ADDRESSED IN THE LESSONS

The list below shows which standards are addressed in each lesson and its research projects for extended writing

Lesson	Writing Anchor 1	Writing Anchor 2	Writing Anchor 3	Writing Anchor 4	Writing Anchor 5
	Write arguments to support claims in an analysis of substantive topics or texts using valid reasoning and relevant and sufficient evidence.	Write informative/explanatory texts to examine and convey complex ideas and information clearly and accurately through the effective selection, organization, and analysis of content.	Write narratives to develop real or imagined experiences or events using effective technique, well-chosen details, and well-structured event sequences.	Produce clear and coherent writing in which the development, organization, and style are appropriate to task, purpose, and audience.	Develop and strengthen writing as needed by planning, revising, editing, rewriting, or trying a new approach.
1	●	●	●		●
2	●	●	●	●	●
3	●	●	●		●
4	●	●	●		●
5	●	●	●		●
6	●	●	●	●	●
7	●	●	●	●	●
8	●	●	●		●
9	●	●	●	●	●
10	●	●	●		●
11	●	●	●		●
12	●	●	●	●	●
13	●	●	●		●
14	●	●	●	●	●
15	●	●	●	●	●
16	●	●	●	●	●
17	●	●	●		●
18	●	●	●	●	●
19	●	●	●	●	●
20	●	●	●	●	●
21	●	●	●		●
22	●	●	●		●
23	●	●	●	●	●
24	●	●	●	●	●
25	●	●	●		●
26	●	●	●		●
27	●	●	●		●
28	●	●	●	●	●
29	●	●	●		●
30	●	●	●	●	●
31	●	●	●		●
32	●	●	●	●	●
33	●	●	●		●
34	●	●	●	●	●
35	●	●	●	●	●
Ch 11			●	●	●
Ch 12		●		●	●
Ch 13	●			●	●

Lesson	Writing Anchor 6	Writing Anchor 7	Writing Anchor 8	Writing Anchor 9	Writing Anchor 10
	Use technology, including the Internet, to produce and publish writing and to interact and collaborate with others.	Conduct short as well as more sustained research projects based on focused questions, demonstrating understanding of the subject under investigation.	Gather relevant information from multiple print and digital sources, assess the credibility and accuracy of each source, and integrate the information while avoiding plagiarism.	Draw evidence from literary or informational texts to support analysis, reflection, and research.	Write routinely over extended time frames (time for research, reflection, and revision) and shorter time frames (a single sitting or a day or two) for a range of tasks, purposes, and audiences.
1	●	●	●	●	●
2	●	●	●	●	●
3	●	●	●	●	●
4	●	●	●	●	●
5	●	●	●	●	●
6	●	●	●	●	●
7	●	●	●	●	●
8	●	●	●	●	●
9	●	●	●	●	●
10	●	●	●	●	●
11	●	●	●	●	●
12	●	●	●	●	●
13	●	●	●	●	●
14	●	●	●	●	●
15	●	●	●	●	●
16	●	●	●	●	●
17	●	●	●	●	●
18	●	●	●	●	●
19	●	●	●	●	●
20	●	●	●	●	●
21	●	●	●	●	●
22	●	●	●	●	●
23	●	●	●	●	●
24	●	●	●	●	●
25	●	●	●	●	●
26	●	●	●	●	●
27	●	●	●	●	●
28	●	●	●	●	●
29	●	●	●	●	●
30	●	●	●	●	●
31	●	●	●	●	●
32	●	●	●	●	●
33	●	●	●	●	●
34	●	●	●	●	●
35	●	●	●	●	●
Ch 11		●	●	●	●
Ch 12		●	●	●	●
Ch 13		●	●	●	●

Lesson 4: "Five Ways to Get Fired from Your After-School Job"

Ashworth, Holly. "10 Ways to Get Yourself Fired from a Job." About.com, Dating & Relationships. Accessed November 05, 2015. http://teenadvice.about.com/od /jobsmoney/tp/how_to_keep_a_job.htm.

Soergel, Andrew. 2015. "Why Teens Are Getting Shut Out of the Workforce." *U.S. News & World Report*, March 26. www.usnews.com/news/blogs/data -mine/2015/03/26/studies-suggest-teens-getting-shut-out-of-workforce.

Tuggle, Kathryn. 2011. "The 12 Quickest Ways to Get Fired." Fox Business, September 1. www.foxbusiness.com/personal-finance/2011/09/01/12 -quickest-ways-to-get-fired/.

West, Beverly. "Top 10 Ways to Get Fired." Monster Career Advice. Accessed November 05, 2015. http://career-advice.monster.com/in-the-office /workplace-issues/10-ways-to-get-fired/article.aspx.

Lesson 12: "How Much Water Do You Waste?"

"Fix a Leak Week." *WaterSense*. U.S. Environmental Protection Agency, Office of Wastewater Management. www3.epa.gov/watersense/our_water/fix_a_leak .html.

Mooney, Chris. 2015. "The Incredibly Stupid Way That Americans Waste 1 Trillion Gallons of Water Each Year." *Washington Post*, March 17.

Richter, Amanda. 2008. "Harvesting Rainwater." *Irrigation and Green Industry*, March 1.

Tardif, Rachel. 2013. "Greywater: What Is It and How Can It Make a Difference in Your Home?" Greenhome.com/blog, April 1.

USA Today. 2014. "So How Much Rain Is Falling?" *Usatoday.tumblr.com*, April 30.

Village of Brookfield. 2013. "How Is My Utility Bill Determined?" October 22. http://brookfieldil.gov/group/utilities/page/2/.

Lesson 19: "My Atom Bomb Is in the Shop"

"Fact Sheets & Briefs." U.S. Nuclear Modernization Programs. Accessed November 05, 2015. www.armscontrol.org/factsheets/USNuclearModernization.

Los Alamos National Laboratory. Our History. www.lanl.gov/about/history -innovation/index.php.

"Modernized B61-12 Nuclear Bomb Boasts Two New Features." 2015. Sputnik News, November 18. http://sputniknews.com/military/20151118/1030339603 /new-us-nuclear-bomb.html.

U.S. Department of Energy. Nuclear Security and Nonproliferation. http:// energy.gov/public-services/national-security-safety/nuclear-security -nonproliferation.

Lesson 20: "Bye-Bye Bake Sales"

Armour, Stephanie. 2014. "Put Down the Cupcake: New Ban Hits School Bake Sales." *Wall Street Journal*, August 1. www.wsj.com/articles/schools-plan-to -lighten-up-on-bake-sales-1406923280.

Chumley, Cheryl K. 2014. "Michelle Must Be Thrilled! USDA Bans All Junk Food Sales at Schools." *Washington Times*, April 14. www.washingtontimes.com /news/2014/apr/14/usda-bans-all-junk-food-sales-schools-around-nation/.

"Let's Move." Healthy Schools. Accessed November 05, 2015. www.letsmove.gov /healthy-schools.

"Study: Many Students Throwing Out Fruits, Vegetables from School Lunches." 2015. CBS Connecticut, August 26. http://connecticut.cbslocal. com/2015/08/26/study-many-students-throwing-out-fruits-vegetables-from -school-lunches/.

United States Department of Agriculture. "Smart Snacks in School." www.fns.usda .gov/sites/default/files/allfoods_infographic.pdf.

Lesson 24: "Benefits and Risks of Searching for Extraterrestrial Intelligence"

Boyle, Alan. 2015. "To Be or Not to Be Signaling the Aliens: That Is the Question for SETI." NBC News, February 13. www.nbcnews.com/science/space/be-or-not -be-signaling-aliens-question-seti-n305546.

Choi, Charles Q. 2015. "In Alien Solar Systems, Twin Planets Could Share Life." Space.com, December 7. www.space.com/31297-alien-planets-could-share-life .html.

Falk, Dan. 2015. "Is This Thing On? The Fierce Debate Over Whether We Should Try to Contact Extraterrestrial Life or Wait for Aliens to Contact Us." Future Tense, March 29. www.slate.com/articles/technology/future_tense/2015/03/active _seti_should_we_reach_out_to_extraterrestrial_life_or_are_aliens_dangerous.html.

Ghosh, Pallab. 2015. "Scientists in US Are Urged to Seek Contact with Aliens." BBC News, February 12. www.bbc.com/news/science-environment-31442952.

Zolfagharifard, Ellie. 2015. "ET Will 'Conquer and Colonise' Humanity, Warns Stephen Hawking: Physicist Claims Nomadic Aliens Could Destroy the World." *DailyMail.com*, October 1. www.dailymail.co.uk/sciencetech/article-3256753 /ET-conquer-colonise-humanity-warns-Stephen-Hawking-Physicist-claims -nomadic-aliens-destroy-world.html#ixzz3vFOHbvwM.

Lesson 28: "Time Off: Fact Sheet on Vacation Days"

"Annual Leave." Wikipedia. Accessed November 05, 2015. https://en.wikipedia .org/wiki/Annual_leave.

"I'm Going on Vacation—What Are YOU Going to Do?." 2015. Career Movers and Shapers, May 20. Accessed November 05, 2015. http://careersfl. com/2015/05/20/im-going-on-vacation-what-are-you-going-to-do/.

"Public Holiday Entitlement Varies Greatly Around the World." 2014. Mercer, September 10. www.mercer.us/newsroom/public-holiday-entitlement-varies -greatly-around-the-world.html.

Ray, Rebecca, Milla Sanes, and John Schmitt. 2013. "No-Vacation Nation Revisited." Center for Economic and Policy Research, May. www.cepr.net /publications/reports/no-vacation-nation-2013.

"Table 5. Average Paid Holidays and Days of Vacation and Sick Leave for Full-time Employees." U.S. Bureau of Labor Statistics. Accessed November 05, 2015. www .bls.gov/news.release/ebs.t05.htm.

U.S. Travel Association. "Project: Time Off." Accessed November 05, 2015. www .ustravel.org/programs/project-time.

Lesson 11: "Paul Robeson"

"August 16, 1955: Paul Robeson Loses Appeal Over His Passport." *This Day in History.* www.history.com.

"Paul Robeson—About the Actor." www.pbs.org/americanmasters.

"Paul Robeson Biography." www.biography.com.

"Paul Robeson Collection 1925–1956." New York Public Library Archive and Manuscripts. http://archives.nypl.org/scm/20649.

"Paul Robeson." www.wikipedia.org.

Chapter 13: "Military Working Dogs Face Tough Re-entry into Civilian Life"

Dao, James. 2011. "After Duty, Dogs Suffer Like Soldiers." *New York Times,* December 1.

Kershaw, Sarah. 2015. "A Soldier and His Combat Dog Both Returned from Iraq with PTSD—and Found Support in Each Other." *Washington Post,* July 2.

Loyd, Ryan. 2013. "Four-Legged Warriors Show Signs of PTSD." NPR, Texas Public Radio, March 11.

Schulberg, Jessica. 2015. "New Bill Would Bring Retired War Dogs Home." *Huffingtonpost.com,* June 5.

Strum, Lora. 2015. "Soldier, Combat Dog Share PTSD Diagnosis, Road to Recovery." Army.mil, July 20. www.army.mil/article/152522/Soldier__combat _dog_share_PTSD_diagnosis__road_to_recovery.

White, Kimberly. 2012. "The Dogs of War: Training, Deployment and the Golden Years." *Santa Cruz Sentinel,* February 4.

Chapter 13: "Navy's Dolphin Use Raises Questions"

Biernaime, Pierre. 2015. "The U.S. Navy's Combat Dolphins Are Serious Military Assets." *Businessinsider.com*, March 12.

"Elephants? It's Dolphins That Never Forget: Mammal Found to Recognize Long-Lost Friends After 20 Years Apart." 2013. *The Daily Mail*, August 6.

Gasperini, William. 2003. "Uncle Sam's Dolphins: In the Iraq War, Highly Trained Cetaceans Helped U.S. Forces Clear Mines in Umm Qasr's Harbor." *Smithsonian Magazine*, September.

Grant, Steve. 2003. "Animals at War: Ethical Questions." *SunSentinel*, April 8.

Milloy, Steven. 2003. "PETA: No Porpoise in War." FoxNews.com, April 3.

Morano, Marc. 2003. "Dolphins Did Not Volunteer for War Animal Rights Activists Say." Crosswalk.com, March 26.

Neiwert, David. 2015. "Are Killer Whales Persons?" *Salon.com*, June 27.

Perry, Tony. 2015. "Dolphins, Sea Lions Train for Navy Deployment to Overseas Trouble Spots." *Los Angeles Times*, March 29.

Rucke, Katie. 2014. "U.S. Military's Dolphin Use Prompts Animal Rights Debate." Mintpress.news.com, April 29.

REFERENCES

Allington, Richard. 2011. *What Really Matters for Struggling Readers.* 3rd ed. New York: Allyn and Bacon.

Atwell, Nancie. 2014. *In the Middle: A Lifetime of Learning About Writing, Reading, and Adolescents.* 3rd ed. Portsmouth, NH: Heinemann.

Bangert-Drowns, R. L., M. M. Hurley, and B. Wilkinson. 2004. "The Effects of School-Based Writing-to-Learn Interventions on Academic Achievement: A Meta-analysis." *Review of Educational Research* 74: 29–58.

Common Core State Standards. 2010. Washington, DC: National Governor's Association and the Council of State School Officers.

Countryman, Joan. 1992. *Writing to Learn Mathematics.* Portsmouth, NH: Heinemann.

Daniels, Harvey, ed. 2011. *Comprehension Going Forward: Where We Are, What's Next.* Portsmouth, NH: Heinemann.

Daniels, Harvey, and Marilyn Bizar. 2005. *Teaching the Best Practice Way: Methods That Matter.* Portland, ME: Stenhouse.

Daniels, Harvey, and Elaine Daniels. 2013. *The Best-Kept Teaching Secret: How Written Conversations Engage Students, Activate Learning, and Grow Fluent Writers.* Thousand Oaks, CA: Corwin Literacy.

Daniels, Harvey, and Nancy Steineke. 2004. *Mini-Lessons for Literature Circles.* Portsmouth, NH: Heinemann.

———. 2011. *Text and Lessons for Content-Area Reading.* Portsmouth, NH: Heinemann.

———. 2013. *Texts and Lessons for Teaching Literature.* Portsmouth, NH: Heinemann.

———. 2014. *Teaching the Social Skills of Academic Interaction.* Thousand Oaks, CA: Corwin Literacy.

Daniels, Harvey, and Steven Zemelman. 1988. *A Community of Writers.* Portsmouth, NH: Heinemann.

———. 2014. *Subjects Matter: Exceeding Standards Through Powerful Content-Area Reading.* Portsmouth, NH: Heinemann.

Daniels, Harvey, Steven Zemelman, and Nancy Steineke. 2005. *Content-Area Writing: Every Teacher's Guide.* Portsmouth, NH: Heinemann.

Danielson, Charlotte. 2013. The Framework for Teaching. https://danielsongroup.org/framework.

Fulwiler, Toby. 1986. *Teaching with Writing.* Portsmouth, NH: Heinemann.

———. 1987. *The Journal Book.* Portsmouth, NH: Boynton-Cook.

Graham, Steve, and Michael Hebert. 2010. *Writing to Read: Evidence for How Writing Can Improve Reading.* New York: The Carnegie Corporation.

Graham, Steve, and Dolores Perin. 2007. *Writing Next: Effective Strategies to Improve Writing of Adolescents in Middle and High Schools.* New York: The Carnegie Corporation.

Harvard College Library. 2011. "Interrogating Texts: 6 Reading Habits to Develop in Your First Year at Harvard." http://hcl.harvard.edu/research/guides/lamont _handouts/interrogatingtexts.html.

Harvey, Stephanie. 1998. *Nonfiction Matters: Reading, Writing, and Research in Grades 3–8.* York, ME: Stenhouse Publishers.

Harvey, Stephanie, and Anne Goudvis. 2004, 2008. *The Comprehension Toolkit* (Intermediate and Primary). Portsmouth, NH: Heinemann.

———. 2007. *Strategies That Work: Teaching Comprehension to Enhance Understanding.* York, ME: Stenhouse Publishers.

Harvey, Stephanie, and Harvey Daniels. 2015. *Comprehension and Collaboration: Inquiry Circles for Curiosity, Engagement, and Understanding, Revised Edition.* Portsmouth, NH: Heinemann.

Hoyt, Linda. *Revisit, Reflect, Retell: Time-Tested Strategies for Teaching Reading Comprehension.* Portsmouth, NH: Heinemann, 2009.

Ivey, Gay, and Joan Broaddus. 2007. "A Formative Experiment Investigating Literacy Engagement Among Adolescent Latina/o Students Just Beginning to Read, Write, and Speak English." *Reading Research Quarterly* 42, no. 4 (October): 512–545.

Johnson, David W., and Roger T. Johnson. 1995. *Creative Controversy: Intellectual Challenge in the Classroom.* Edina, MN: Interaction Book Company.

Lacina, Jan and Cathy Collins Block. 2012. "Progressive Writing Instruction: Empowering School Leaders and Teachers." *Voices from the Middle.* March. Urbana, IL: National Council of Teachers of English.

Laminack, Lester L., and Reba M. Wadsworth. 2015. *Writers Are Readers: Flipping Reading Instruction into Writing Opportunities.* Portsmouth, NH: Heinemann.

Lenhart, Amanda. 2008. "Writing, Technology & Teens: The Findings of the Pew Internet Project and the National Commission on Writing." Washington, DC: Pew Charitable Trust.

Lenhart, Amanda, Sousan Arafeh, Aaron Smith, and Alexandra Macgill. 2008. *Writing, Technology, and Teens.* Washington, DC: Pew Charitable Trust and the National Commission on Writing.

Marzano, Robert. 2013. Marzano Teacher Evaluation Model. www.marzanocenter .com.

National Council of Teachers of English. 2012. *Writing Now: A Policy Research Brief.* Urbana, IL: NCTE.

Olson, Carol Booth. 2003. *The Reading/Writing Connection: Strategies for Teaching and Learning in the Secondary Classroom.* Boston: Pearson Education.

Paul, Anne Murphy. 2013. "How the Power of Interest Drives Learning." NPR/KQED. http://ww2.kqed.org/mindshift/2013/11/04/how-the-power-of-interest-drives-learning/.

Pearson, P. David, Gina Cervetti, and Jennifer Tilson. 2008. "Reading for Understanding and Successful Literacy Development." In *Powerful Learning: What We Know About Teaching for Understanding,* edited by Linda Darling-Hammond, 71–112. San Francisco: Jossey-Bass.

Pearson, P. David, Laura Roehler, Janice Dole, and Gerald Duffy. 1992. "Developing Expertise in Reading Comprehension." In *What Research Has to Say About Reading Instruction.* 2d ed. Edited by S. J. Samuels and A. E. Farstrup, 145–199. Newark, DE: International Reading Association.

Robb, Laura. 2003. *Teaching Reading in Social Studies, Science, and Math.* New York: Scholastic.

Steineke, Nancy. 2003. *Reading and Writing Together.* Portsmouth, NH: Heinemann.

———. 2009. *Assessment Live! 10 Real-Time Ways for Kids to Show What They Know—and Meet the Standards.* Portsmouth, NH: Heinemann.

Tovani, Cris. 2007. *I Read It But I Don't Get It.* Portland, ME: Stenhouse.

Vopat, James. 2009. *Writing Circles: Kids Revolutionize Writing Workshop.* Portsmouth, NH: Heinemann.

Zemelman, Steven, Harvey Daniels, and Arthur Hyde. *Best Practice: Bringing Standards to Life in America's Classrooms.* 4th ed. Portsmouth, NH: Heinemann, 2012.